THE GORDIAN KNOT

THE CAUCASIAN KNOT

The History & Geopolitics of Nagorno-Karabagh

LEVON CHORBAJIAN
PATRICK DONABEDIAN
CLAUDE MUTAFIAN

ZED BOOKS
LONDON & NEW JERSEY

The Caucasian Knot was first published by
Zed Books Ltd, 7 Cynthia Street, London N1 9JF, UK, and
165 First Avenue, Atlantic Highlands, New Jersey 07716, USA,
in 1994.

Cover design by Andrew Corbett.
Laserset by Opus 43, Cumbria, UK.
Printed and Bound in the United Kingdom
by Biddles Ltd, Guildford and King's Lynn

A catalogue record for this book
is available from the British Library.

US CIP data is available from
the Library of Congress.

ISBN 1 85649 287 7 Hb
ISBN 1 85649 288 5 Pb

CONTENTS

4   KARABAGH IN THE TWENTIETH CENTURY   109
Claude Mutafian

5   CONCLUSION   171
Patrick Donabedian and Claude Mutafian

LIST OF MAPS

ABOUT THE AUTHORS

Levon Chorbajian is Professor of Sociology at the University of Massachusetts-Lowell. He specializes in racial and ethnic minorities and has edited two sociology texts. In 1986–1987 he lived and taught in Soviet Armenia as a Fulbright Senior Lecturer. He has translated Pierre Verluise's *Arménie: La Fracture*, published in English as *Armenia in Crisis: The 1988 Earthquake* (Detroit: Wayne State University Press, 1994).

Patrick Donabedian is cultural attaché at the French Embassy in Yerevan. Trained as an art historian, he is a graduate of the University of Paris X–Nanterre and holds a PhD from the Academy of Fine Arts in Leningrad. His work on the medieval art of Transcaucasia, in particular Karabagh, has taken him to the USSR, where he lived for several years. He is the author of numerous studies published in specialized journals, and the co-author of *Les Arts Arméniens* (Paris: Mazenod, 1987), published in English as *Armenian Art* (New York: Abrams, 1989).

Claude Mutafian is a former student at the Ecole Normale Supérieure and a graduate of the University. He is a Senior Lecturer in mathematics at the University of Paris XIII–Villetaneuse. He is particularly interested in regions of the Near East whose history is linked with that of Armenia. He has published a series of algebra texts with Editions Vuibert and, more recently, *La Cilicie au carrefour des empires* (Paris: Les Belles Lettres, 1988).

TRANSLITERATION NOTE

Patrick Donabedian and Claude Mutafian published the original version of this work as *Le Karabagh: Une terre arménienne en Azerbaïdjan* (Paris: Le Groupement pour les Droits des Minorities, 1989). An expanded and updated volume appeared as *Artsakh: Histoire du Karabagh* (Paris: Sevig Press 1991). *The Caucasian Knot* is the complete English language translation of the expanded Sevig Press edition with a preface by Gerard Chaliand and an introduction by Levon Chorbajian.

On the matter of transliteration we have relied mainly on Randall K. Barry's American Library Association and Library of Congress system for the transliteration of non-Roman scripts. But exceptions have been made, most commonly for individuals who spell their names in ways which do not conform to this system and in the case of place names where alternative orthographies have become commonplace in the Western print media. Thus Etchmiadzin is preferred over Ejmiatsin, Yerevan over Erevan, and Nakhichevan over Nakhijevan.

PREFACE

Gerard Chaliand

The question of whether it is the Armenians or the Azerbaijanis who have an historic right to the territory of Mountainous Karabagh has been amply debated during the last half-dozen years.

Historians on both sides have laboured to find evidence for their case. What matters today, in the context of twentieth-century conceptions, is who is actually in physical possession of the disputed ground. Ever since Mountainous Karabagh came into existence as an administrative unit – since the beginning of the 1920s – the territory, attached to Azerbaijan as an autonomous entity *(oblast)*, has been populated largely by Armenians. The Armenian population accounted for 94 per cent of the total in 1921 and 75 per cent in 1988. The decline is due to Baku policies promoting Azerbaijani settlement. The principle which holds sway today is self-determination. In this respect the feelings of the majority of the population of Mountainous Karabagh have been evident since 1988. They have expressed a clear desire not to remain dependent on Baku. As for the successive governments of Azerbaijan, they have all rejected any change in frontiers. This impasse, ending up in violence and armed conflict, is one more reminder that the two principles underlying international law in the contemporary world, namely the inviolability of frontiers and the right to self-determination, are often in contradiction. In practice, following the Second World War, the right to self-determination has amounted to the right of those peoples once colonized by Europeans to determine their own destiny. The exceptions are few and far between: Bangladesh only gained its independence thanks to the intervention of Indian troops, Mrs Gandhi being only too happy thereby to weaken Pakistan. The people of Eritrea, the ex-Italian colony attached to Ethiopia as an autonomous entity in 1952 and then incorporated as the fourteenth province of the Empire in 1962, had to struggle for thirty years before finally winning their independence following the fall of the Mengistu regime.

The conflict in the former Yugoslavia is a case in point. Originally, the Western states backed the principle of the inviolability of frontiers and therefore Belgrade's pro-Serbian policies. This solution seemed, to the

Europeans of the EC at any rate, to present the least risk of instability. Later on, stability seemed best served by taking account of the aspirations of Slovenia and Croatia. However, it would be a mistake to believe that the example of the former Yugoslavia has set a precedent. There seems little doubt that in the future the principle of the inviolability of frontiers will, in the last analysis, prevail over the principle of self-determination, in the name of stability.

What Has Actually Been Going on in Mountainous Karabagh?

On one hand there was a population the majority of whom rejected the *status quo*, which they believed to be only a pseudo-autonomy. On the other, there was a state which had no intention of giving up its prerogatives. The result: Baku's attempt to solve the problem by an initially successful attempt, in 1990–1992, to force the Armenian population of Mountainous Karabagh to flee. The counter-offensive then mounted by the Armenians of Mountainous Karabagh, backed by Armenia, which was itself blockaded by the Azerbaijanis, enabled Mountainous Karabagh's troops to gain control not only of almost all of the once autonomous territory (this status having been removed by Baku in 1991) but also of 5,500 square kilometres outside Mountainous Karabagh from which the Azerbaijani population had fled. How had all this come to pass?

The Origin of the Conflict

Leaving aside the Armeno–Azerbaijani antagonisms of 1905 or 1920, one can say that relations between the two communities during the Soviet period were not openly hostile, although there were many tensions. The state was Azerbaijani, there had been Armenian minorities in Azerbaijan ever since the formation of the Soviet Caucasus in 1920, and in 1923 the Armenians accounted for 95 per cent of the population of Mountainous Karabagh.

The imperial divide and rule policy had laid down that Mountainous Karabagh, populated by Armenians and lying only 15 kilometres from Armenia, was placed under Azerbaijani rule, whilst Nakhichevan, populated mainly by Azerbaijanis, was separated from Azerbaijan by an Armenian province. During the 70 years of Soviet rule, the Armenian population of Nakhichevan fell from some 25 per cent to nil, and that of Mountainous Karabagh from 95 per cent to 75 per cent.

Mikhail Gorbachev's main concern was not to resolve those national contradictions of the empire masked by the Soviet gag. An explanation of history based on class struggle served as a way of containing national antagonisms, as it did under Tito in Yugoslavia. The ideology, which offered as its model Soviet man or the Yugoslav citizen, had made possible marriages between Azerbaijanis and Armenians or between Croats and Serbs, in the towns at least. The children were brought up in their father's religion. However, as the Soviet and Communist system entered its death throes in Europe, the national question, sometimes reinforced by religious considerations, came back to the fore, especially along the fault lines where the old empires had clashed: Austro-Hungarians and Turks, Russians and Muslims, Ottomans and Iranians.

Although he might have been in a position to bring a solution to the conflicting demands of the Armenians of Mountainous Karabagh and the Azerbaijani state, Gorbachev chose, at first, to do nothing. Then he opted in favour of Azerbaijan, whose leadership was at the time a Communist one, as against the elected and non-Communist President of Armenia, Levon Ter Petrosian.

The peaceful demands of the Armenians for Mountainous Karabagh to be reunited with Armenia were met, in February 1988, by pogroms; dozens of Armenians died in Sumgait, one of Azerbaijan's main towns. Further atrocities followed, in Kirovabad and in Baku, over the next two years. The 400,000 Armenians who lived in Azerbaijan, mainly in the larger towns, fled. A similar exodus saw the 170,000 Azerbaijanis living in Armenia pushed into Azerbaijan. Nationalist tension grew. In August 1990, the Soviet army, which had consistently backed Communist-led Azerbaijan, participated in military operations with armed Azerbaijanis and forced 150,000 to 200,000 Armenian villagers living in the north of Mountainous Karabagh to flee.

In the meantime, within what was still the Soviet Union, Armenia and Mountainous Karabagh invoked Soviet law and called for an administrative change, but not for any change in the frontiers between the two nations. In Spring 1991, matters came to a head. The conflict became militarized as Azerbaijani forces occupied the north of Mountainous Karabagh, in the Shahumian region, forcing Armenians to flee towards Armenia.

Following the abortive August 1991 *putsch* in Moscow, the entire Soviet system began to unravel. The political situation in the USSR became increasingly chaotic, especially in the Caucasus. In August 1991, Azerbaijan proclaimed its independence. In early September, Mountainous Karabagh indicated its desire not to be part of Azerbaijan and proclaimed its own independence. In December 1991, a referendum in Mountainous Karabagh confirmed the Armenian population's desire for independence. Later that month, the USSR ceased to exist.

The Phases of the Conflict

All the elements of the confrontation were now in place. The Armenians of Mountainous Karabagh demonstrated a desire for independence as manifest as the refusal of the Azerbaijanis to give up an inch of territory that was legally theirs – especially as Mountainous Karabagh's proclamation of independence had led Baku to cancel the autonomous status of the province. Armenia gave diplomatic support, backed by logistical support and volunteers, to the Mountainous Karabagh Armenians, who were insisting on self-determination. Both sides complained about the exodus of their own people and accused the other side of atrocities: in many cases, sadly, these accusations were correct. From that point on, the war went through four phases.

First came an Azerbaijani offensive from the South, pushing up to Chute, from where Stepanakert was bombarded from December 1991 to May 1992. The Armenians counter-attacked in February, taking Khojaly, from where the country's sole airport was being bombarded, and again, in May, with the audacious seizure of Shushi and the Lachin Strip, establishing a road link with Armenia.

The second phase took place during the summer of 1992. A major Azerbaijani offensive backed, according to some sources, by Afghan Mujaheddin and by a few Ukranian and Russian mercenaries, occupied in a few months about half of Mountainous Karabagh's 4,300 square kilometres. Despite difficult conditions, the Armenian population did not flee. Those who wanted to go had already gone. Mountainous Karabagh prides itself on a heroic streak, and visitors will often be reminded that this small region produced over twenty 'Heroes of the Soviet Union' during the Second World War, along with more generals than the whole of Azerbaijan. With the help of logistical support from the Armenian Republic, which had no intention of allowing a second massacre of Armenians after the 1915 genocide, trained and organized Karabagh troops launched a counter-attack under the aegis of their Supreme Defence Council.

The Armenian counter-attack represents the third phase, the war of October 1992 to September 1993, in the course of which the Armenian forces not only liberated most of Mountainous Karabagh, but also occupied some 5,500 of Azerbaijan's 86,500 square kilometres, forcing the Azerbaijani population to flee.

This aggressive policy was necessary, according to the authorities in Mountainous Karabagh, to achieve a purely defensive aim, namely to narrow the military front down to some 120 kilometres instead of twice that. The demographic balance, Karabagh's 100,000 inhabitants against Azerbaijan's 7.5 million, made this essential, despite the modest aid supplied by Armenia. Azerbaijan complained, quite rightly, about the number of refugees created by the extension of the conflict: 250,000 to 300,000 on top of those who had already fled Armenia, bringing the total up to at least 500,000. As for the Armenians of Mountainous Karabagh, they still see the conflict in terms of survival and their right to stay in a land where they have formed the majority since time immemorial.

The fourth stage of the struggle is still taking place. Following the demise of President Elchibey in July 1993, in which Moscow played an indirect part (the former President having evinced too pro-Turkish a position for Russian tastes), the situation was taken in hand by Gaidar Aliev, Azerbaijan's fifth president in six years. The Azerbaijani counter-offensive started in September 1993 and cost the Armenian forces dear during the winter, but did not achieve any marked success. These attempts to break through are still continuing, especially on the eastern front, while the main preoccupation of the Armenian forces is to counter-attack in the north-east, in a part of Mountainous Karabagh still held by Azerbaijani troops. Reinforcements are pouring in on both sides. Moscow, meanwhile, remains the ultimate arbiter of the situation, even though its mediation continues through the Minsk group incorporating Sweden, Russia, the US, Turkey, France, Germany, Belarus, Hungary, Italy, Armenia, Azerbaijan and Mountainous Karabagh.

For Moscow, the aim is to achieve in Azerbaijan what Russia has just pulled off in Georgia. Having worked towards the destabilization of a state that did not, at first, wish to be part of the Confederation of Independent States, the Russians are now able to maintain their military bases in Georgia. Azerbaijan is the only country of the CIS where Russian troops are not currently stationed. The Azerbaijanis had hoped, and still hope, that their oil, their proximity to Turkey, perhaps even the encouragement of certain Western countries or business circles would be enough to stave off a Russian military presence. The Russians will have none of it, however. Everything will be done to ensure that Azerbaijan remains within the Russian orbit. In this respect the conflict in Mountainous Karabagh is useful to Moscow. Perhaps circumstances will lead Russia to send in troops to separate the warring parties. If so, who will pay the political price, Mountainous Karabagh or Azerbaijan? No one can yet be sure, but it seems likely that the independence that the Armenians of Mountainous Karabagh are fighting for is a realistic objective. In today's world, generally speaking, the inviolability of frontiers takes precedence over the right to self-determination, despite the counter-example of the former Yugoslavia. However, a variety of other outcomes are possible, so long as the military balance of forces remains in favour of the Armenians of Mountainous Karabagh.

One other factor is of concern to Moscow: the course of the pipeline that will eventually carry Baku's oil. Of the two probable options, the route straight to Turkey via Armenia or that initially heading northwards towards the Black Sea, Moscow favours the latter and will push for its adoption.

The regional powers, Turkey and Iran, have differing positions concerning the conflict in Mountainous Karabagh. The Western media are no longer preoccupied with the idea that these two ancient rivals are going to compete to fill the void in central Asia and the Caucasus created by the collapse of the Soviet Union. Russian geopolitical interests are not so easily disposed of. -

Turkey is limiting its present ambitions to the provision of some support to Azerbaijan, although it entertains hopes of a growing influence around the Black Sea and in Central Asia. As for Iran, a multi-ethnic state in which Persians account for a little less than half of the total population, the government there is suspicious of the dynamic of Azerbaijani nationalism, and the fact that the Azerbaijanis are Shi'ite matters less than the fears of an eventual destabilization of Iran, 25 per cent of whose population is Azerbaijani. Furthermore, any reinforcement of Turkey's position which would turn the latter into a major regional power is a source of anxiety in Teheran.

Armenia, under the remarkably wise diplomatic policy conducted by its President, Levon Ter Petrosian, has accepted unconditionally both the Russian and the CIS propositions for a negotiated end to the conflict. President Aliev, on the other hand, has initially rejected such propositions, perhaps in the hope of seizing some interim military advantage, or perhaps because the situation at home makes it difficult for him to negotiate. Time is on Azerbaijan's side, but perhaps not on Aliev's, who as yet can point to no successes. Moscow now seems decidedly chilly towards him, but it remains to be seen if his hand will be forced. The war can still spread. An attack could be launched on Armenia from Nakhichevan. The Karabagh forces may broaden the front towards the north-east.

Only Moscow is sure to achieve its ends in the long run, providing the political situation there remains stable. In the meantime, it is the guns that are doing the talking.

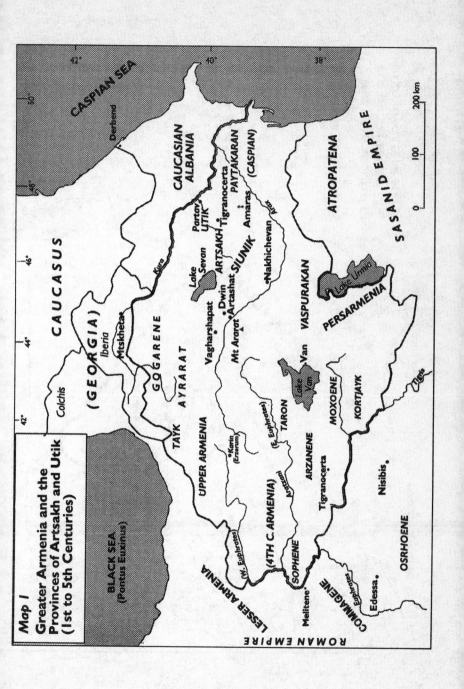

Map I

Greater Armenia and the Provinces of Artsakh and Utik (1st to 5th Centuries)

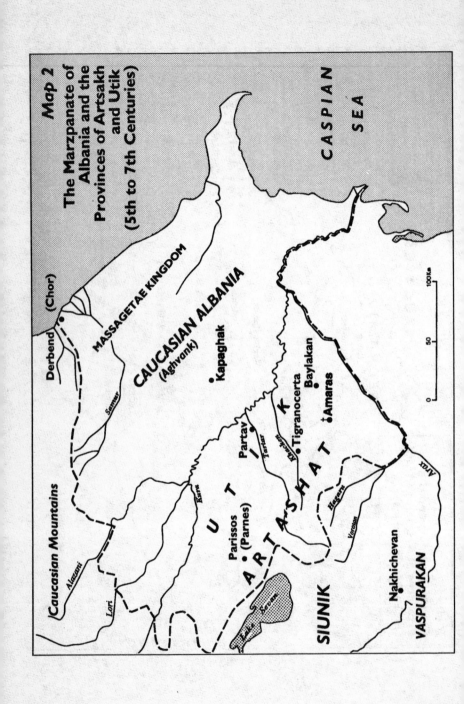

Map 2
The Marzpanate of
Albania and the
Provinces of Artsakh
and Utik
(5th to 7th Centuries)

CASPIAN

SEA

Caucasian Mountains

Derbend

(Chor)

MASSAGETAE KINGDOM

CAUCASIAN ALBANIA

(Aghvank)

Kapaghak

Alazani

Lori

Semur

Kura

U T I K

Partav

Tartar

Tigranocerta

Baylakan

Amaras

Khachen

A R T S A S H A T

Hagari

Varotan

Parissos
(Parnes)

Lake Krum

Nakhichevan

SIUNIK

VASPURAKAN

Arax

100 km

50

0

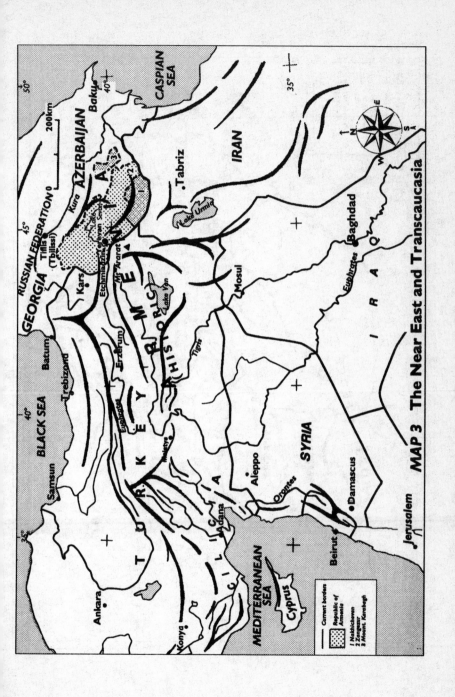

MAP 3   The Near East and Transcaucasia

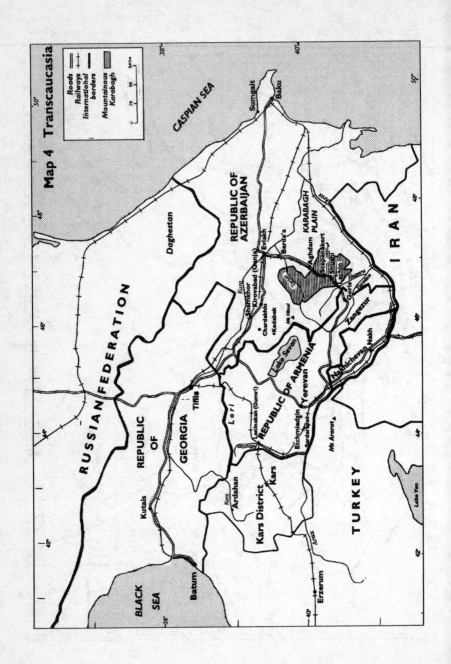

Map 4 Transcaucasia

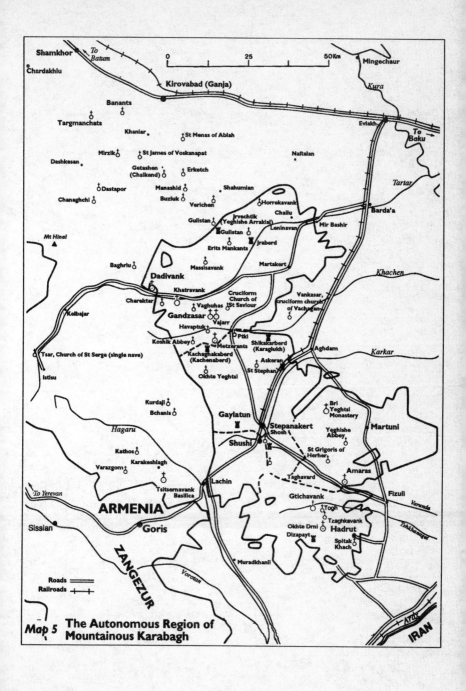

Map 5 **The Autonomous Region of Mountainous Karabagh**

1

INTRODUCTION TO THE ENGLISH LANGUAGE EDITION

Levon Chorbajian

> For Azerbaijan the issue of Karabagh is a matter of ambition, for the Armenians of Karabagh it is a matter of life and death.
>
> *Andrei Sakharov (1921–1989)*
> *Physicist, Human Rights Activist, Nobel Peace Laureate*

In his history of modern Armenia, Ronald Suny wrote that 'the single most volatile issue among Armenians is without doubt the question of Karabagh, the autonomous region heavily populated by Armenians but lying within the Azerbaijani Soviet Republic'.[1] These words were published in 1983. Two years later, Mikhail Gorbachev assumed power and initiated a series of modest reforms which opened the way to a surge of popular protest throughout the Soviet Union.

Professor Suny's implicit prediction concerning Nagorno-Karabagh found expression in February 1988, when the region emerged at the cutting edge of social change in the Soviet Union. Under the banner of Gorbachev's reform agenda, Armenian protesters defined the 1921 assignment of Nagorno-Karabagh to Soviet Azerbaijan as a Stalinist injustice and called for its redress. Demonstrations in Nagorno-Karabagh and massive popular rallies in the Armenian capital city of Yerevan rocked the Soviet Union, providing a model for peaceful mass protests by other national groups at the same time that they exposed the falsehood of the Soviet claim to have resolved the age-old national question.[2]

By the end of 1991 the scale of change had exceeded even the boldest predictions made half a dozen years before. In what was certainly one of the very few defining historical moments since the Second World War, the Soviet Union was dissolved in December 1991. The Communist parties were out of power nearly everywhere, and the former minority republics had claimed independence, gained diplomatic recognition, and become part of the international community as members of the United Nations and the International Monetary Fund (IMF).

In the rush of excitement about the end of the Cold War and the heady possibilities for activating long-frustrated plans for market penetration by Western investors, the collapse of the Soviet Union was hailed in the West. Yet for the peoples of Russia and the former minority republics, the transition to the post-Soviet era has brought with it pogroms, civil wars, the rise of authoritarian states, and economic hardships caused by disruptions in trade and the erosion of the Communist safety net which had heavily subsidized basic necessities. These broad patterns of conflict and disruption have been played out in the contexts of particular national histories and geo-political frameworks, and neither Armenia, the Karabagh Armenians, nor Azerbaijan has escaped them.

On 21 September 1991 the Armenians cast their ballots on independence. Over 95 per cent of the eligible voters went to the polls and 99.3 per cent of those voted for independence. It was an overwhelming mandate. Yet despite the enormous scale of change in Armenia and the former Soviet Union, the matter of Nagorno-Karabagh was not resolved. The territory stands as a devastated war zone subjected to air and ground attack and an economic blockade which has resulted in acute shortages of food and medicines. The war has spread to large areas of south-western and western Azerbaijan which were overrun by Karabagh Armenian forces in 1992 and 1993. By the spring of 1994 over 20,000 people had lost their lives, including 4,000 civilians. Many more have been seriously wounded, and hundreds of thousands are without shelter. Nearly all of the 40,000 Azerbaijani inhabitants of Karabagh have fled, and 90,000 Armenians from the region have been displaced, most to the Republic of Armenia. Many of those refugees have returned to Nagorno-Karabagh and live behind Karabagh Armenian lines, joining those who refused to leave under any circumstances.[3] Estimates of the number of Azerbaijani refugees created in the wake of Karabagh Armenian advances run as high as one million, and many of them live in miserable conditions in refugee camps and on the outskirts of Baku and Sumgait.

The Republic of Armenia has waived any territorial claim to Karabagh, and the Armenian government professes a policy of non-engagement in the conflict between Azerbaijan and the Armenians of Nagorno-Karabagh. Meanwhile, the Karabagh Armenians held their own referendum on 10 December 1991 in which they voted overwhelmingly in favour of national independence. Azerbaijan responded on 2 January 1992 by dissolving Nagorno-Karabagh as a separate territorial entity, thereby officially absorbing it into the Republic of Azerbaijan. In fact, this formal structure of move and counter-move bears little resemblance to the actual situation which is quite different, a good deal less neat, and far more complex.

The issue of Armenia's involvement in the Karabagh struggle is a sensitive one since Turkey and Azerbaijan view Armenia as a combatant and use that as their rationale for their economic blockade of Armenia and for Azerbaijan's continual shelling of Armenian border areas and violations of Armenia's air space. The Republic of Armenia is non-engaged in that it does not have military forces fighting in Nagorno-Karabagh or in the other areas of fighting which now include Kelbajar and the Lachin Strip linking Nagorno-Karabagh to the Republic of Armenia, Aghdam and occupied areas of Azerbaijan east of Nagorno-Karabagh, and south of the enclave to the Azerbaijani–Iranian border. The Republic of Armenia has been, however, a source of food, fuel, medical personnel and supplies, and volunteer fighters. Many of these volunteers are from native Karabagh families who had fled the fighting in recent years or who had been pushed out of the territory in the years, and sometimes decades, before the outbreak of armed conflict. Other sources of fighters are Armenians returning from the Soviet diaspora – Russia or Central Asia, for example – and volunteers without Karabagh roots from Armenia itself. On the issue of ammunition and weapons, the Karabagh Armenians have secured large caches of both from retreating Azerbaijani troops, and there have been black market purchases by both sides. The Russians have also served as a source by sometimes funnelling weapons to the Karabagh Armenians from their bases in Armenia.

The government of the Republic of Nagorno-Karabagh, as independent Karabagh is called, has not secured diplomatic recognition from any other state, including the Republic of Armenia, which fears that by extending recognition, it will be drawn even deeper into the conflict. Meanwhile Azerbaijan's dissolution of Nagorno-Karabagh as a separate entity under Azerbaijan's authority and its absorption into Azerbaijan proper is utterly belied by the fact that at the end of 1993 all but a small portion of Nagorno-Karabagh was under the control of the Karabagh Armenians along with a fifth of the territory of Azerbaijan itself. And Armenia, officially a non-combatant, has had its towns and villages bombed and pillaged by Azerbaijani forces along the entire length of its border with Azerbaijan. Azerbaijan has also subjected landlocked Armenia to an economic blockade so severe that human rights activist Elena Bonner Sakharov has compared conditions in Armenia to those of Leningrad (St Petersburg) under the Nazi siege during the Second World War.[4]

Yet despite the scale of the conflict, the hardship and suffering it has engendered, and its continued lack of resolution, little is known about Nagorno-Karabagh in the West. Occasional newspaper articles inspired by a new offensive or a ceasefire initiative provide the usual fleeting snippets: 'the enclave inhabited largely by Armenians', 'ceded to Azerbaijan in 192'. Patrick Donabedian and Claude Mutafian's sections of *The Caucasian Knot* fill this gap by examining the history of Nagorno-Karabagh from the period of the earliest records up to 1990. In this introduction I address two complementary objectives which are (1) to situate the issue of Nagorno-Karabagh in the larger context of Soviet nationalities policy and the Cold War, and (2) to examine developments which have occurred since the publication of the enlarged French edition of the Donabedian and Mutafian text in 1991.[5]

Armenia and Karabagh: An Overview

The origin of the Armenian people remains the subject of debate. Herodotus wrote that the Armenians originated in Thrace and migrated from there to north-east Asia Minor. They eventually emerged there as the dominant people in what had been the Kingdom of the Urartians. Others argue that the Armenians were indigenous to the region and that they supplanted the Urartians and established their own kingdoms by the sixth century BC. At the height of their power, during the reign of Tigran the Great (95–55 BC), the Armenians forged a short-lived empire which stretched from the Caspian to the Mediterranean. Since that time, periods of independence have been interrupted by periods, often long periods, of conquest and subjugation by more powerful peoples.

In the early fourth century, Armenia converted to Christianity; the Armenian alphabet, which is still in use, was invented a century later. Located at the crossroads of Asia and Europe, Armenia was subject to successive invasions and conquests, by the Arabs in the seventh and eighth centuries, the Seljuk Turks in the eleventh and twelfth centuries, the Mongols in the thirteenth and fourteenth centuries, and the Persians in the sixteenth and eighteenth centuries. The last major eastern Armenian kingdom at Ani fell to the Byzantines in 1045 and was razed by the Seljuks in 1064. A later Cilician (southern Asia Minor) Armenian kingdom survived until 1375, when it fell to the Egyptian Mamluks. From that time until a brief interlude of independence beginning in 1918, Armenians were a stateless people whose national identity was expressed through language, church, and literature.

By virtue of its inaccessible terrain and its remoteness, the mountainous portion of Karabagh represented a partial exception to this loss of national independence. Even when all else was lost to conquest, Armenian princes there managed to assert a degree of authority in the region.[6] These princely families in Karabagh survived until the Russian conquest in the early nineteenth century.

Beginning in the mid-nineteenth century, Armenians underwent a national revival which incorporated literary/cultural and political dimensions.[7] Members of the Armenian intelligentsia grappled with the problem of a nation divided between the Russian and Ottoman Turkish empires. This period of growing Armenian national consciousness on both sides of the Russian–

Turkish border was contemporaneous with the decline of the Ottoman Empire, its earlier loss of Greece and its defeats in the Balkans. At the same time, Armenians in the eastern provinces of Anatolia found their position eroded by the more rapidly increasing Turkish and Kurdish populations, and by the settlement of Moslems from the Balkans and others from the North Caucasus whose resistance to the southward Russian advance had been broken during this period.

During the years 1894–6, Anatolian Armenians were massacred on the order of Ottoman Sultan Abdul Hamid II and up to 200,000 Armenians perished. Some Armenians later allied themselves with the Young Turk movement in the belief that the overthrow of the sultanate and its replacement by a constitutional form of government offered the best hope for Ottoman minorities. In 1908 the Sultan was forced to sign a modern constitution. A year later Abdul Hamid was forced to abdicate his office, and the sultanate was stripped of much of its power. These events were welcomed by Turks and Armenians alike, but Armenian hopes were dashed with the coming to power of the most virulently nationalistic elements of the Young Turk movement. This new leadership took the Ottoman Empire into the First World War as an ally of Germany and Austro-Hungary. In 1915, under cover of the world war, the Ottoman Turkish leadership ordered and implemented a policy of genocide against the Armenian people. Three hundred thousand Armenians fled across the Turkish–Russian border to the safety of Russian Armenia. Adult males who could not escape were killed, while the women, children, and elderly males were driven on forced death marches to the deserts of northern Syria. The precise number of Armenian deaths will never be known, but the most reliable estimates are between 1 and 1.5 million for the period 1915 to 1922.[8]

In the post-war peace settlements, two successive treaties were negotiated by the Allied powers, the first with the Ottoman Empire and the second with its successor state the Republic of Turkey. The Treaty of Sèvres called for the establishment of an independent Armenian state in parts of the Transcaucasus and eastern Anatolia. Because of the rise of the nationalist movement, led by Mustafa Kemal (Atatürk), the treaty could not be enforced and was, in effect, a dead letter. In the subsequent Treaty of Lausanne signed by Turkey, not only was there no provision for an Armenian state, but no mention of Armenia by name. The only territorial Armenia was the independent Transcaucasian republic the Armenians had reluctantly proclaimed in 1918. That first Republic of Armenia came under attack by Kemalist forces and the Bolsheviks, and it surrendered its independence to the latter in late 1920.

The independence of the Transcaucasian states was made possible by the turmoil created by the world war and the Bolshevik Revolution. The future of the fledgling Bolshevik state was itself thrown in doubt by three factors, including invasions by Western imperialist armies and armed struggles by indigenous counter-revolutionary forces. Both were attempting to overthrow the Bolsheviks. The third threat came from the large number of national minorities in the old Russian Empire who took advantage of war and revolution to declare national independence. The Finns and the Baltic peoples were the most successful in defending their declarations of independence. The other nationalities, including the Transcaucasian states, were subdued by the Bolsheviks and brought into the new Soviet empire over the course of a few months to several years. Armenian and Azerbaijani independence lasted from 1918 to 1920 and the Georgian from 1918 to 1921.

That the Republic of Armenia was able to defend its independence for two and a half years should be attributed largely to the disarray in which the Turks and Bolsheviks found themselves after the war. Armenia was landlocked and the home of a large and destitute refugee population. Edmund M. Herzig has written that 'Armenia in 1920 was a devastated and desperate land – the post-First World War equivalent of today's Ethiopia or Sudan....'[9] Compared to neighbouring Azerbaijan and Georgia, Armenia was the weakest and least viable of the three independent Transcaucasian states, and when it became possible for Turkey and the Bolsheviks to assert their interests in the region, they did so, to a large degree, at Armenian expense.

The Bolsheviks sought to secure their borders to prevent them from serving as invasion corridors and supply routes for their enemies. Lenin's policy of establishing reliable and defensible borders for the Soviet Union began in negotiations with Turkey. Atatürk was viewed by the Bolsheviks as a bourgeois but anti-imperialist figure, and he was also favoured because the vast Moslem world was seen as a fertile area for the expansion of Communism. Lenin and Atatürk agreed that the Soviets were to have secure borders with Turkey in return for certain Bolshevik concessions. With the exception of Zangezur the fate of contested territories between Armenia and Azerbaijan, and between Armenia and Georgia, went against Armenia. In the cases of Nagorno-Karabagh and the Akhalkalak region of Georgia, where the Armenians based their claims on the principle of self-determination, they lost contests to Azerbaijan and Georgia respectively. In the case of Nakhichevan, where the Armenians put forth economic and strategic arguments, their loss was the gain of Azerbaijan. Furthermore, when Armenia was Sovietized in 1920, Armenia lost to Turkey both its western regions of Kars and Ardahan, which had been part of the Russian Empire since 1878, and the Surmalu District south-east of Yerevan, which had been won by the Russians from Persia in 1828. What Shireen Hunter writes about Nagorno-Karabagh reflects the overall pattern of territorial realignments:

> In the case of NKAO (Nagorno-Karabagh Autonomous Oblast), the fate of the region was not decided on the basis of its ethnic composition nor on the principle of self-determination.[10]

Thus were sown the seeds of the current conflict. Decades later, in February 1988, when the Armenian protests calling for the reunification of Nagorno-Karabagh with the Armenian SSR became international news, the region was described in the Western press as 'obscure'. Indeed, it was scarcely known in the West, and few in other regions of the Soviet Union could identify it. Nevertheless, the impact of the protests for Armenia, Azerbaijan and the Soviet Union are difficult to overestimate.

In the summer of 1987, Armenia saw the beginnings of protests which would gain some momentum in the autumn. The issues were pollution, a nuclear power plant not far from Yerevan which activists charged had been sited on an earthquake fault, widespread corruption, and the slow pace of reform. None of these protests drew more than a few thousand people.

This dramatically changed a few months later when hundreds of thousands of people took to Yerevan's streets to protest over a broad range of issues, with Karabagh unmistakably the centrepiece.[11] Nora Dudwick, an anthropologist from the University of Pennsylvania, was an eyewitness to the events. One of Dudwick's informants spoke to her about the shared feelings of exhilaration and transcendence among participants in an all-night solidarity march through Yerevan.

It was an unforgettable night, very moving. The mood was radiant, lofty, calm. People marched without feeling tired ... we forgot about our injuries and impotence.[12]

Another observer noted that 'In these days, as if in one leap, we came to a new level of humanity.'[13]

One of the most striking features of these protests was that the Yerevan demonstrations in support of the Karabagh Armenians began with a demonstration by 5,000 people on a Saturday and escalated into a protest involving half a million people by Monday – in effect, a general strike within a few days. Dudwick argues persuasively that the issue of Nagorno-Karabagh struck a responsive chord in Armenians and galvanized them in a way that other issues could not. She quotes a schoolteacher who explained:

Pollution touches people physically but is more difficult to internalize. Karabagh, on the other hand, strikes at the core of our collective essence.[14]

At the core of the 'collective essence' stands the 1915 genocide, the death of over a million people, and the loss of national independence, Kars, Ardahan, Nakhichevan, and Nagorno-Karabagh. Dudwick found that genocide was, in fact, a commonplace metaphor among Armenians for expressing concern over a range of issues. Assimilation was seen as 'cultural genocide', air pollution as 'ecological genocide', and the de-Armenianization of Nakhichevan as 'white genocide'. Of the territorial issues, only Nagorno-Karabagh, with its Armenian majority still intact, offered realistic hope for redress.

Nagorno-Karabagh touched every Armenian regardless of age, sex, occupation, or social standing. Dudwick captures the collective meaning of the protests:

> Armenians had the experience of feeling themselves united as a people, of feeling the barriers of structure temporarily dissolved, of remembering their common humanity, history, and destiny. Perhaps we can consider the Karabagh Movement as a national *rite de passage*, which is transforming Karabagh from a symbol of past glories and past losses into a symbol of the Armenians' ability to wage a sustained struggle for the reappropriation of their own past, present, and future.[15]

For the Soviet Union, the Karabagh protests brought the issue of national minorities to the fore. There had been protests by Crimean Tatars and others as well as large demonstrations and state repression in Kazakhstan's capital of Alma-Ata in December 1986, but nothing had the electrifying effect of Nagorno-Karabagh. Gorbachev was indecisive and visibly shaken by the scale of the demonstrations at the same time that other nationalities were emboldened by them. The Baltic republics, for example, had largely employed low-key consciousness-raising methods and pursued legalistic, constitutional means to press for the redress of their grievances. In the wake of Nagorno-Karabagh, they began organizing more visible, larger-scale mass protests which contributed to their declaration of independence after the failed August 1991 coup.

In Armenia, the Karabagh Organizing Committee was assembled to give direction to the protests. The members were largely made up of scholars who were recognized by the people for their independence from the Communist Party apparatus and for their national commitment. In December 1988 the Committee took over direction of relief efforts in the aftermath of the earthquake which devastated the cities of Leninakan and Spitak, and other areas of north-west Armenia.[16] Gorbachev and his wife Raisa cut short their visit to the United States, and they toured the stricken areas. Gorbachev cynically used the distraction of the earthquake to order the arrest of the Committee as a means of reasserting central government authority. The Committee members spent six months in Russian jails and were released without trial in May of 1989. The arrests backfired on Gorbachev. The Committee members' national hero status among the Armenian people was strengthened, while the status of the national and republican Communist parties weakened further. Eventually, the Committee disbanded and regrouped as a political party, the Armenian National Movement (*Hayots Hamazgayin Sharzhum*), and Levon Ter-Petrosian, one of the original Committee members, was elected president of a non-Communist Armenia as it cautiously moved to full independence.

Is Islam a Factor in the Struggle for Nagorno-Karabagh?

In 1988 and 1989 I did a content analysis of major US daily newspapers to see how the developing Armenian–Azerbaijani conflict was being presented to readers.[17] The newspaper coverage was characterized by sparse background information, numerous factual errors, and a consistent reliance on an inappropriate Christian versus Moslem framework. From the point of view of informing its readership, the media's reliance on a Christian–Moslem paradigm served as a poor substitute for historical background material and analysis, offering in their stead a simplistic and inaccurate reductionist framework for reader 'understanding'.[18]

The media's dependence on a religious framework is clearly seen in its repeated references to Christian and Orthodox Christian Armenians, Moslem and Shiite Moslem Azerbaijanis, and long-standing, perennial religious conflict.[19] For this kind of religious paradigm to have validity, two conditions would have to be met. First, proponents of the religious model would have to demonstrate that Azerbaijani relations with other Christian peoples have been as contentious and violent as their relations with Armenians and, secondly, they would have to show that the same kind of deep and prolonged hostility has characterized Armenian relations with Moslem peoples other than Turks and Azerbaijanis. In fact, neither of these logical requirements can be met.

The Georgians, like the Armenians, are Christians and share contiguous borders with Azerbaijan. When we examine Azerbaijani relations with the Armenians and compare them to Azerbaijani relations with the Georgians, we discover rather striking contrasts. To be sure, there are contentious issues which separate the Georgians and the Azerbaijanis, including the treatment of their respective minorities and even territorial matters.[20] Absent in Azerbaijani–Georgian relations, however, is a history of war comparable to that between the Armenians and Azerbaijanis (1905, post-First World War, and the present conflict over Nagorno-Karabagh) and anything like the deep enmity which many, though not all, Armenians and Azerbaijanis feel toward one another.

When we examine the Christian–Moslem dimension from the Armenian side of the equation, the model becomes further attenuated. There are sizeable Armenian communities in the Arab world, particularly in Lebanon and Syria and to a lesser degree in Egypt, Jordan, and Iraq. Smaller numbers live in Jerusalem, Saudi Arabia, and the rest of the Arabian Gulf. Some of these communities, such as the dwindling one in Jerusalem, are long-standing. Others were created or greatly expanded by the arrival of survivors of the 1915 genocide and their offspring. Armenians and Arabs shared the common experience of persecution by the Ottoman Turkish state, and Armenian refugees in Syria and elsewhere during and after the First World War received a generally sympathetic reception as well as assistance from Arab residents. Armenian settlers were able to establish their churches and schools and to participate in the economy. Armenian communities were generally residentially separate and endogamous since neither the Armenians nor the Arabs aspired to assimilation as a model for ethnic relations. Inter-ethnic relations, however, have generally been harmonious, mutually respectful, and certainly devoid of the persecution experienced by Armenians in Ottoman Turkey and, to a lesser degree, the Republic of Turkey. The same can be said for the large and centuries-old Armenian community in Iran.

The Kurds present a more ambiguous case, since some Ottoman Kurds were recruited by the state to aid in carrying out the 1915 genocide.[21] Yet since that time there have been countervailing factors which have placed Armenian–Kurdish relations on a less hostile and mutually distrustful footing, particularly among Armenian and Kurdish intellectuals. First, both the Armenians and Kurds (and Palestinians) were to achieve national statehood according to the Treaty of Sèvres, the First World War peace settlement between the Allies and Ottoman Turkey which was unenforced. As a result, both peoples have suffered from a frustrated nationalism. Second, the Kurds and Armenians have shared animosities toward Turkey. The Kurds were themselves massacred in their hundreds of thousands by the Turkish state in the late 1920s, and they have been denied basic human rights in Turkey to this very day. Third, although the number of Kurds in Armenia is small, the community there has fared better than have Kurds in Azerbaijan as well as in Iran, Iraq, and Turkey, and this has played a role in generating solidarity between the Christian Armenians and the Moslem Kurds.

The large number of Armenians who have left the Middle East over the last four decades have left as a result of various push and pull factors including family reunification, perceived greater economic opportunity in the West, the rise of Arab nationalism in the cases of Egypt and Iraq, the continuing Arab–Israeli conflict, and the civil war in Lebanon. In none of these instances of Armenians residing in the Arab world have Armenians suffered persecution as a national minority. This remains the case even in the Islamic fundamentalist case of Iran (non-Arab), where Armenians have had to accept the regulation of their churches and schools as well as strict public dress codes for their women.

Religious differences do play a role in the Karabagh conflict because they are imbedded in the consciousness of both peoples as distinguishing national characteristics, and these differences can be fairly easily stirred up by demagogues. Even so, religion is a secondary factor. It is the case that Armenians frequently refer to Azerbaijanis as Moslems. However, when Armenians are questioned about this usage, it soon becomes apparent that they are not using the term Moslem in a generic religious sense but as a synonym for Turk. And that brings us to the heart of the matter, for, as we have seen, the real line of

cleavage in the struggle for Nagorno-Karabagh is not a religious Christian–
Moslem one but an ethnic Armenian–Turkish one with a lengthy history
behind it.[22]

The Azerbaijani Claim to Nagorno-Karabagh

Patrick Donabedian and Claude Mutafian present the Armenian case for
Nagorno-Karabagh, a case they base on history and demography backed by
prevailing standards of human rights and the right to self-determination. The
Azerbaijanis make their own case for the territory and employ it to reject the
legitimacy of the Armenian claim. These counter-arguments are used to justify
Azerbaijan's insistence on maintaining Nagorno-Karabagh and its unwilling-
ness to concede any more than cultural autonomy to Karabagh's Armenians.

Most historians in the West agree that the term Azerbaijani as a national
nomenclature, as opposed to Azerbaijan as a geographical term, is of recent,
twentieth-century origin. Azerbaijani historians, in contrast, attempt to
portray Azerbaijanis as the heirs to earlier civilizations or, in a more extreme
version, to trace a continuous Azerbaijani presence far back into history, prior
to any records of a Turkic or even Moslem presence.[23]

Of particular importance in the debate over territorial claims are the
Caucasian Albanians, an ancient and no longer extant people who pre-date the
time of Christ. These Caucasian Albanians – unrelated to the better-known
Adriatic Albanians – ruled over much of central and eastern Transcaucasia,
including what is now Nagorno-Karabagh. They were converted to
Christianity in the fourth century by the Armenians and later conquered by
the Arabs, Islamicized, and eventually assimilated. Armenian historians
acknowledge that Caucasian Albanians in the eastern Transcaucasian lowlands
were Islamicized and later Turkified, but they argue that those in the western
Albanian regions, including what later became Nagorno-Karabagh, were
largely absorbed by the Armenians and to a lesser degree by the Georgians.
Azerbaijani historians, in stark contrast to this position, view Caucasian
Albania, *in toto*, as the precursor of modern Azerbaijan, and, on this basis, they
lay claim to all erstwhile Caucasian Albanian territories, including Nagorno-
Karabagh.[24]

Azerbaijani interpretations of more recent history also point to Nagorno-
Karabagh as an Azerbaijani territory. The significance of the Armenian
majority in Nagorno-Karabagh is discounted by claiming that it dates only
from Armenian migrations from Iran under the Treaty of Turkmanchai in
1828.[25] The Azerbaijanis also employ formalistic arguments to by-pass
historical and demographic factors. For example, the claim is made that

Nagorno-Karabagh rightfully belongs to Azerbaijan because it was part of the tsarist Elisavetpol *guberniia* which was consolidated with the Baku *guberniia* to form Azerbaijan. It is further argued that the Armenians and the Azerbaijanis agreed to what was essentially a pact in which the contested territory of Zangezur went to Armenia and Nagorno-Karabagh to Azerbaijan. The Armenians are now seen as opportunistically seeking to break this implicit agreement without making any concessions to Azerbaijan.[26]

The Azerbaijani perception of themselves as victims of a colonial experience at the hands of the Russians, an experience in which it is argued that they were exploited in typical imperial fashion, also feeds their claim to the territory. Azerbaijanis point to the low prices they received for their cotton, fruits, wool, sheep, steel, carpets, and oil and oil drilling equipment during the Soviet period. While Soviet leaders pointed with pride to the industrialization of Azerbaijan under Soviet tutelage, the Azerbaijanis came to resent that tutelage and its attendant consequences in pollution and mounting health problems.[27] According to Tamara Dragadze, growing Azerbaijani awareness of their economic backwardness and exploitation is a key variable in explaining their intransigence over the Karabagh question in the late Soviet period and after:

> ... the Azerbaijanis have learned to think of their nationhood in territorial terms. It would have been seen by the Azerbaijanis as the ultimate insult if the Soviet authorities had ordered them to hand over territory which they had thought was their only inalienable resource at a time when they had been increasingly aware of the way they had been economically exploited by the centre.[28]

The Azerbaijanis, in addition, reject the position of Karabagh Armenians that Nagorno-Karabagh was economically exploited by Soviet Azerbaijan. The Azerbaijanis argue that pollution and shortages in material goods, including housing, are worse in Azerbaijan proper, outside of Nagorno-Karabagh. The territory is also said to have received a larger share of the republic's budget and greater subsidies than the larger and more populous Nakhichevan Autonomous Soviet Republic.[29]

Historian Audrey Altstadt develops the argument that the very circumstances of the formation of the Nagorno-Karabagh Autonomous Oblast fuel Azerbaijani resentment and de-legitimize Armenian claims in Azerbaijani eyes. Although Armenia lost a territory Armenians regarded as unequivocally theirs, Altstadt argues that the loss was only nominal since the Armenians lost formal control but gained many guarantees and concessions at the same time that Armenia was in no way held responsible for the Azerbaijani community within its own borders. The four points of Altstadt's argument are as follows: (1) Azerbaijan was forced, against its wishes, to accept Nagorno-Karabagh as an autonomous oblast (district) rather than have it incorporated directly into

Azerbaijan; (2) to the degree possible, Armenian villages were included within the territory's borders and Azerbaijani ones excluded to ensure an Armenian majority; (3) Armenian was designated the official language of instruction and daily transaction; and (4) the territory's legislature, party organs, and heads and staff of educational and cultural institutions have been overwhelmingly Armenian from the inception. Altstadt's claims allow her to argue that the cultural and administrative character of the region encouraged Azerbaijani emigration and that to the degree that problems and abuses existed, they ought to be laid at the doorstep of the local Armenians who effectively ran Nagorno-Karabagh, and not Baku.[30]

Finally, the Azerbaijanis support their own historical claim by arguing that Karabagh is the cradle of Azerbaijani civilization since it has produced numerous Azerbaijani artists, composers, poets, and other literary figures.[31]

These Azerbaijani perspectives, so diametrically opposed to the Armenian ones, clarify why the struggle for Nagorno-Karabagh has been so bitter, intractable, and, so far, immune to settlement.

Military and Related Issues

Assessing military capability is always difficult because so many factors come into play. Simple tallies of numbers of military personnel and weapons systems exclude consideration of such significant factors as the training, morale, and motivation of troops; the maintenance of weapons; the quality of military and political leadership; the suitability of weapons systems for weather and terrain conditions; logistical support; and political stability and will.

In the case of Nagorno-Karabagh, there is also the question of whether Armenia should be included in the calculations, since the Armenian government has relinquished territorial claims and plays a moderating role in the search for a settlement. Armenian President Levon Ter Petrosian went so far as to dismiss his Defence Minister Vazgen Manukian in the summer of 1993 when Manukian was lobbying for increased military aid and diplomatic recognition for Karabagh.[32]

Despite the Armenian government's disclaimers, however, there remain compelling reasons for including Armenia in these calculations. First, it was in response to the protests of Karabagh Armenians in January and February 1988 that the unprecedented support rallies began in Yerevan, and the Ter Petrosian government traces its roots to that early struggle. Second, Armenia has been a source of military aid to Karabagh and of volunteer fighters, and Armenia has served as a conduit for Russian arms going to Karabagh. Third, Armenia is a participant in negotiations seeking a resolution to the crisis. Fourth, there is a portion of the Armenian population which rejects the moderate policies of the

Ter Petrosian government and calls for a more active and direct involvement in the struggle for Karabagh. Fifth, Armenians see the history of Nagorno-Karabagh as part of their larger twentieth-century history of human and land loss and identify closely with the struggle. Sixth, Armenians fear that the loss of Nagorno-Karabagh will embolden Azerbaijan and Turkey to seek Armenia's southern provinces. Seventh, by bombing and raiding Armenian border areas and subjecting Armenia to a withering economic blockade, Azerbaijan treats Armenia as a combatant. And finally, the possibility of open warfare between Armenia and Azerbaijan, or even a larger regional war involving other neighbouring nations, cannot be discounted. Taking these factors into consideration, it seems reasonable to consider Armenian and Azerbaijani military forces and then to proceed to examine more specific aspects of the conflict.

In any direct confrontation between Armenia and Azerbaijan, Armenia would appear to be at a distinct disadvantage. Armenia's population is half that of Azerbaijan. This and Azerbaijan's higher birth rate are reflected in the numbers of people eligible for military service. Armenia has 550,000 men in the 17 to 32 years old age group, compared with 1,300,000 for Azerbaijan.[33] In terms of weapons, both Armenia and Azerbaijan began with relatively low levels of mobilization and light armaments for the most part, but this has changed. Both sides were able to purchase weapons from rogue Russian officers in the Transcaucasus when the central military command had loose control over its personnel and equipment. When Russian forces withdrew from the region – they pulled out of Azerbaijan in May of 1993, a year ahead of schedule – they left weapons behind. The Azerbaijanis have also relied on oil revenues to purchase weapons from abroad, notably from Turkey, China, the Ukraine, and Israel, while the Karabagh Armenians have captured weapons from retreating Azerbaijani troops. The following chart summarizes the best available information on comparative military forces.

COMPARATIVE MILITARY FORCES

Political unit	Military personnel	Artillery	Tanks	Armoured personnel carriers	Armoured fighting vehicles	Fighter aircraft
Republic of Nagorno-Karabagh	20,000[a]	16	13	120		
Republic of Armenia	20,000[b]	170	160	240	200	
Republic of Azerbaijan	42,000[c]	330	280	360	480	170

[a] Includes 8,000 volunteers from Armenia. [b] All in the army. [c] 38,000 in the army, 1,600 in the air force.
Source: The Military Balance, 1993–1994 (The International Institute for Strategic Studies, London, 1993), pp. 68–69, 71–73.

There is also the Turkish factor to consider. Turkey borders on Armenia and the Azerbaijani province of Nakhichevan. In any intervention, Turkey would be a potent player with over half a million military personnel, nearly 8,000 tanks and armoured personnel carriers, and nineteen air attack squadrons.[34] In its worst nightmare, Armenia would face a joint Azerbaijani and Turkish invasion which would subdue Nagorno-Karabagh and prove catastrophic to Armenia, since she would lose her southern provinces, thus allowing for the fulfilment of the long-sought pan-Turkic desire for territorial linkage between Turkey and Azerbaijan and from there to the Turkic regions of Central Asia. This worst-case scenario for Armenia is tempered, however, by Turkey's fear of a response by superior Russian forces, and the chance of an Iranian one, to head off the possibility of Turkey obtaining a greatly enhanced strategic position in the region. The Ter Petrosian government has been ever mindful of its vulnerability, and Armenia therefore immediately joined the Russian-sponsored Commonwealth of Independent States (CIS) and is protected under the CIS collective security umbrella.

The actual struggle for Nagorno-Karabagh has been a seesaw battle with escalating levels of firepower and casualties. The Armenian forces, estimated at 15,000 to 20,000 Karabagh Armenians and volunteers from Armenia and elsewhere in the former Soviet Union, were able to take advantage of political disarray in Azerbaijan to launch a successful offensive in early 1992 and to bring all of Nagorno-Karabagh under Armenian control for the first time since 1920. This contributed heavily to the fall of two Azerbaijani governments within a period of months in early 1992. The Azerbaijani political crisis was temporarily resolved by the June 1992 elections which brought Abulfaz Elchibey and the Azerbaijani Popular Front to power. Elchibey pursued an anti-Russian, anti-Iranian policy, vowing to bring Azerbaijan closer to Turkey, a state he defined as an historical ally with an appropriate model for democratic secular development. He also committed himself to re-taking Nagorno-Karabagh within two months of assuming office. The Azerbaijani offensive easily took the Armenian-populated Shahumian District north of Nagorno-Karabagh and then half of Nagorno-Karabagh itself.

Beginning in early 1993, Karabagh Armenian forces reversed these Azerbaijani gains. The local Armenian forces re-took nearly all of Nagorno-Karabagh, and they successfully defended the Lachin Strip, the thin territorial link which joins Nagorno-Karabagh and Armenia at the narrowest point of their separation. The Lachin corridor was part of the original Nagorno-Karabagh ceded by the Soviets to Azerbaijan in the early 1920s, and it was its obvious strategic importance which led Azerbaijan to separate it out from Nagorno-Karabagh and incorporate it directly into Azerbaijan. Karabagh Armenian forces also took another portion of western Azerbaijan, Kelbajar – longer and broader than the Lachin Strip – which gave them a second territorial link with Armenia at the same time that it denied the Azerbaijanis a military staging area for raids and rocket attacks on the Republic of Armenia to the west, the Lachin Strip to the south, and Nagorno-Karabagh to the east. Spectacular Karabagh Armenian offensives continued through the summer and autumn of 1993. In July, the Karabagh Armenians took Azerbaijan's major military staging area, the city of Aghdam. This city, to the east of Nagorno-Karabagh, had a pre-offensive population of 100,000. The city of Fizuli to the south and the town of Goradiz, on the Iranian border, fell in late August. By the end of November, the entire south-western portion of Azerbaijan to the Iranian border was under the control of the Karabagh Armenians.

The unresolved struggle for Nagorno-Karabagh has been costly to both sides. Much of Nagorno-Karabagh has been reduced to rubble, a process beginning with the Azerbaijani GRAD missile assaults on the capital city of Stepanakert and continuing with the various offensives and counter-offensives since that time.[35] The Armenian economy stands devastated as a result of the Azerbaijani rail blockade. The winter of 1993–1994 has been another Armenian winter with virtually no heat, hot water, or industrial fuel. There have been severe food and medical supply shortages, only partly allayed by US and other foreign assistance. Hundreds of thousands of Armenians have been unwilling or unable to stand the hardship and have left Armenia to settle in Russia or the West. Yet although the level of hardship has been severe, the Ter Petrosian government has survived, even in the face of open challenges to its authority in the form of anti-government demonstrations and several attempted votes of no confidence in parliament.

While Armenia has been strengthened by political stability, Azerbaijan has been plagued by failed policies and political instability. The blockades imposed on Armenia and Nagorno-Karabagh have caused great suffering, but they have failed to bring either the Republic of Armenia or Nagorno-Karabagh to the negotiating table on Azerbaijani terms. Furthermore, Elchibey not only failed to make good his promise to re-take Nagorno-Karabagh, but his forces suffered major reversals at the hands of the Karabagh Armenians. Elchibey's most serious miscalculation, however, was in allying himself with Turkey while cutting his ties with Russia. Elchibey's Turcophile policies alienated Russia, the major power in the region, while Turkey proved unable to provide Azerbaijan with the level of economic and military assistance it needed.

In 1993, Russia was able to exploit the failures of the Elchibey government to reassert its authority. The medium for doing so was the old Russian stand-by – ethnic minorities, in this case the Lezghi and Talish minorities in Azerbaijan. With Russian assistance, Azerbaijani military setbacks paved the way for large-scale public dissent in Azerbaijan. Demonstrations were reported in early March 1993 in the northern Azerbaijani city of Kusary. There, 70,000 Lezghis, a non-Azerbaijani Moslem people who are split between northern

Azerbaijan and the Russian Federation, took to the streets to protest against the conscription of 1,500 Lezghi youth to fight in Nagorno-Karabagh. The Lezghis, who number in the hundreds of thousands, had been seeking regional autonomy and even union with their co-ethnics to the north in Russia. The demonstrations were held under the banner 'We will not go to war for Karabagh, we will fight for our freedom.' The Associated Press reported that six were killed when police fired on the crowd.[36]

In June, dissident Azerbaijani forces made their move against a weakened Elchibey. Rebel Azerbaijani military forces took the country's second-largest city, Ganja, the former Kirovabad (Elisavetpol), in fighting that claimed sixty lives. When Elchibey dispatched troops to quell the rebellion, many defected to the rebels and joined the march on Baku. The rebel forces were led by Colonel Surat Huseinov, a former military commander on the Karabagh front who had been dismissed for battlefield failures. Huseinov's march on Baku created a serious political crisis for Elchibey and posed the threat of civil war. With Huseinov's forces at the gates of Baku, Elchibey fled and left seventy-year-old Gaidar Aliev as the *de facto* president.

Immediately prior to returning to Baku, at Elchibey's request Aliev had headed the legislature in Azerbaijan's western province of Nakhichevan. However, his history as a party operative dates back to the early 1940s. Aliev joined the KGB in 1945 and was named to head the Azerbaijani KGB in 1967. He assumed the post of First Secretary of the Azerbaijani Communist Party in 1969. He was a member of Leonid Brezhnev's inner circle, and was named a full member of the Soviet Politburo by Yuri Andropov in 1982. Five years later he was dismissed by Gorbachev and branded a corrupt, anti-*glasnost* hardliner.[37] In his latest persona as the head of Azerbaijan, Aliev presents himself as an anti-Communist Azerbaijani nationalist committed to democracy and a free market economy. He ran a successful campaign for president in October 1993, winning 90 per cent of the vote.

Aliev retained Elchibey's commitment to defeating the Karabagh Armenians and reasserting Azerbaijani control, but he argued that the most effective route to doing so was to broaden Azerbaijan's alliances. In a series of moves designed to renew relations with Russia, Aliev dismissed Elchibey's cabinet and virtually neutralized pro-Turkish forces in the government. He admitted Russian officers and some troops into Azerbaijan, brought Azerbaijan into the CIS, and authorized the shipment of Azerbaijani oil from Georgian and Russian ports. Aliev also sought foreign military assistance from all possible sources, including Russia, Iran, Turkey, the US, France and Britain. There are also confirmed reports of over 1,000 Afghan veterans being brought in to fight on the Karabagh front. Aliev has spurned ceasefire plans initiated by Russia and the Conference on Security and Cooperation in Europe (CSCE), saying it is not the correct time for a settlement. In the meantime he has tried to build up his military capability, and in mid-December 1993 he launched a well-coordinated winter offensive in yet another pursuit of a military solution.

The December 1993 Azerbaijani offensive raged into the spring of 1994. The most determined fighters are without question the Karabagh Armenians who know that their fate is death or permanent exile if they lose, but they cannot bring the struggle to a close because they face a stronger opponent in Azerbaijan. Thus far, the dozens of attempts at ceasefires and negotiations have failed because the Karabagh Armenians feel they cannot let go and the Azerbajianis will not let go. In such a situation the short-term prognosis for peace is not good.

Strengths and Weaknesses of the Armenian and Azerbaijani Economies

Both Armenia and Azerbaijan have undergone radical reorganizations of their economies. Land, housing, and industry are being privatized, foreign investment capital is being courted, and modern banking and budgetary procedures are being implemented. In both countries, this process has encountered the general run of problems found in all the former Soviet republics: mounting inflation, declining job security, growing unemployment, factory shutdowns, and disruptions in production due to the unreliable supply of raw material, energy and component parts as well as to corruption.

While Armenia and Azerbaijan face these difficulties in common, they do so with dramatically different resource bases and in quite contrasting geopolitical contexts. An examination of these issues is important because the struggle for Nagorno-Karabagh has had significant effects on both economies, particularly on Armenia's, and those effects bear upon both the ability of the parties to sustain their struggles and, ultimately, their willingness to consider compromise solutions in return for peace.[38]

ARMENIA

To a great degree Armenia is the prisoner of its geography. Much of the country consists of rocky and arid mountains and high plains. There are few forest resources and little in the way of easily exploitable mineral resources. Agriculture, even on the fertile plain of Ararat, depends on irrigation. To add to these problems, Armenia is landlocked and separated from Russia by Georgia, embroiled in civil war, and Azerbaijan. Lacking a common frontier with Russia, Armenia has no reliable means to export agricultural products and manufactured goods, or to receive fuel, raw materials, and component parts for industry. The absence of such a frontier has enabled the Azerbaijanis to impose an economic blockade, cutting off shipments to and from Armenia.

During the Soviet period, Armenia's economy, which had been devastated during and after the First World War, experienced high rates of growth in the agricultural and industrial sectors. Armenia has some heavy industry, the major examples being the controversial aluminium and chemical complexes in Yerevan. Most of the industrialized sector consists of secondary heavy industry, – for example, motor vehicle assembly – and such light industry as the manufacture of timers, light bulbs, computer components, cognac, shoes, and watches. The agricultural sector accounts for about 20 per cent of net material product (NMP) and employs about 10 per cent of the labour force. The industrial sector accounts for 50 per cent of NMP and employs a third of the labour force.[39]

Copper and molybdenum are Armenia's only proven and easily exploitable mineral resources, but what makes the economy particularly vulnerable is its high level of energy dependence. Armenia produces no oil or natural gas and possesses no easily accessible coal deposits.[40] The Medzamor nuclear power plant has been closed due to environmental and safety concerns including vulnerability to earthquakes. In 1985 Armenia produced only 5 per cent of its energy needs, and its contribution to its total energy usage had declined to 1 per cent by 1990 due to the shutdown of the nuclear plant.[41]

During the Soviet period Armenia obtained most of its oil and natural gas from Russia and Azerbaijan, and the bulk of its inter-republic trade (about 85 per cent) went via Azerbaijan and the rest through Georgia. When Armenia began its mass demonstrations demanding Nagorno-Karabagh, the Azerbaijani Popular Front, not yet in power, organized to exploit Armenia's economic vulnerability. The economic blockade of Armenia became critical in November 1991. In December of that year, Armenia was able to import only 2.5 million cubic metres of the 9.7 million cubic metres of natural gas it had planned to import. During that winter of 1991–1992, Armenian industry operated at only 15 per cent of capacity; Yerevan had only six hours of electricity a day; ten of the city's 39 hospitals operated without heat; and schools, universities, and cultural centres were closed.[42] An assessment of the Armenian economy by the International Monetary Fund (IMF) predicted that

> If the transportation and energy situations do not improve significantly, most of the economy is likely to remain at the virtual standstill it reached in 1991, implying a further precipitous fall in real GDP in 1992 and an intolerable drop in living standards.[43]

The IMF's grim prediction has proved accurate for the period 1992–1994. There has continued to be no heat or hot water, and industry has been at a standstill. Food rationing and a limited airlift of food and other necessities by Western nations and international humanitarian agencies has helped to avert a catastrophe. Still, the human suffering has been great, as one witness, a physician in Gumri, formerly Leninakan, attests:

How we lived through this winter is hard to imagine. Of course it is better to see it once than to hear about it many times, but I would not wish those inhumane conditions on my friends or any other human being. The wards of the intensive care unit were like silent and cold caves where the temperature in the night went down to 0 degrees centigrade. There was no way to heat the intravenous solutions. Even if we could heat them, they would turn cold again in a few minutes. It makes no sense to speak about monitoring the patients because in the night, under candlelight, it was difficult to see the natural color of a patient's face. People were waiting with hope and faith for the morning to come. We had many cases of frostbite and many deaths.[44]

Armenia has survived the winters of 1992–1993 and 1993–1994, but questions remain. Can Armenia survive another winter of economic blockade, and, if so, how many after that? There is also the question of the political fallout from the economic crisis. Armenia has not been plagued by the same degree of political instability which has hurtled Azerbaijan from crisis to crisis, but Ter Petrosian does not have the mandate he had at the time of independence. He insists that the economic hardships are the result of the blockade, while the opposition argues that the administration is incompetent. Discontent among the people has been sufficient to enable opposition groups to mount anti-Ter Petrosian demonstrations of 25,000 to 50,000 people from 1992 onwards.[45] So far the government has been able to contain and withstand those protests, in part because the opposition forces are disunited and unable to put forth any convincing and viable political and economic alternatives to the policies of the current government.[46]

AZERBAIJAN

Azerbaijan, like Georgia, possesses hot, humid lowlands absent in Armenia and is, therefore, capable of a more diversified and productive agriculture. During the 1980s Azerbaijan produced nearly 700,000 metric tons of cotton and over 30,000 metric tons of tea annually, as well as a considerable harvest of citrus fruit, whereas Armenia's production of these crops was negligible.[47]

Azerbaijan also possesses 'ample mineral resources', according to the IMF, and is best known for its oil and natural gas reserves.[48] Azerbaijan was the oldest oil-producing area of the old Russian Empire and the centre of world oil production at the turn of the century, prior to the widespread use of internal combustion engines. Much of Azerbaijan's industrial sector has developed as a logical extension of its oil extraction industry in the form of refineries, petro-chemical complexes, and manufactures of refinery and oil drilling equipment. The light industrial sector produces processed foods, beverages, clothing, electrical equipment, and appliances.

It was thought for many years that Azerbaijan's oil fields had peaked and were in decline, but recently the territory's oil and natural gas potential has been boosted by large new discoveries. Proven oil reserves stand at 3.3 billion barrels while actual reserves may be as high as 7 billion barrels. Proven natural gas reserves stand at 6 trillion cubic feet.[49] With the development of new fields, reclamation of older wells, and other investments, it is conservatively estimated that Azerbaijan could export 700,000 bpd (barrels per day) and possibly as much as 1.1 million bpd by the late 1990s. This would produce an annual yield of 5 to 8 billion dollars in foreign currency.[50] In 1992, despite a 26 per cent drop in net material product, Azerbaijan generated a $500 million economic surplus, largely due to the sale of petroleum products abroad at world market prices.[51]

Despite these recent successes, however, Azerbaijan's entry into the international market is problematic. Whether we speak of crude oil, its refined products, or industry-related equipment, Azerbaijani industry suffers from inadequate investment, poor design, and outmoded technologies. This was not a problem in a controlled Soviet and Eastern European market, but it is a serious liability if Azerbaijan is to receive the maximum return on its resources and seriously compete in the international market. As an example of the sorts of problems confronting Azerbaijan, consider that drilling at depths of 100 to 300 metres is not uncommon in the Gulf of Mexico and the North Sea. Many of Azerbaijan's undeveloped Caspian fields are at these depths, but work cannot proceed because Azerbaijan does not possess the ability to extract oil and natural gas from these depths.

This is a situation which calls for foreign expertise and investment, and the government has been seeking it aggressively. Saudi Arabia, Oman, and South Korea have been in negotiations, and the number of foreign firms anxious to participate in the development of Azerbaijan's Caspian fields is large and growing.[52]

The struggle over Nagorno-Karabagh makes it difficult for Azerbaijan to attract the foreign investment it needs because it denies the political stability foreign investors seek. This is significant in narrow economic terms but also carries with it deeper political implications. Despite its status as a major oil producer throughout the twentieth century, Azerbaijan lagged behind most other Soviet republics on a variety of social indicators. Even compared to Armenia, which ought to be poorer when resources are compared, Azerbaijan had a lower *per capita* GDP (3,100 roubles compared to Armenia's 4,800), lower life expectancy, higher infant mortality, and fewer doctors and hospital beds *per capita*.[53] Tamara Dragadze cites *per capita* income figures to further substantiate this argument on the depressed standard of living of Azerbaijanis. In 1988, 16 per cent of Georgians earned less than 75 roubles per month and 18 per cent of Armenians, but fully one-third of Azerbaijanis had such low incomes. At the upper income levels, 18 per cent of Georgians earned between 150 and 200 roubles and 17 per cent earned over 200 roubles. The figures for Armenia were 16 per cent and 10 per cent respectively while the Azerbaijanis lagged behind at 11 per cent and 6 per cent.[54] This would be of purely economic interest were it not for the fact that many Azerbaijanis are now aware of their relative lack of economic development and interpret it as economic exploitation, seeing a connection between their standard of living and the forced low prices at which they had to sell their goods during the Soviet years.[55]

Dragadze points to a younger generation of rural migrants coming into the cities seeking education, housing, and employment, only to discover the realities of unemployment and irregular work and housing in the form of hostels and virtual shacks on the outskirts of cities.[56] This is a generation more demanding and less patient than its predecessors. While the hundreds of thousands of Azerbaijani refugees created by the war can be expected to be militant in their support of continued conflict in the hope of returning to their homes, an undetermined number in the rest of the population will see the war as a threat to the promise of a better life held out by the country's petroleum wealth.

The war contributes to this growing economic frustration in several ways. Supplies of meat, dairy products, and fruit from Nagorno-Karabagh to Azerbaijan were disrupted and are now non-existent. Supply routes for raw materials and other inputs have also been disrupted. Furthermore, the Azerbaijani government has decided to create its own military force, and it has invested several billion roubles to do so.[57] The state may make normative appeals to people's sense of patriotism and duty, but there are limits in Azerbaijan to how long people will sacrifice the diversion of resources from social needs to military expenditures. The importance of this factor can be expected to increase with time.

The Politics of the Armenian Question and the Karabagh Question

We saw earlier that when the issue of Nagorno-Karabagh hit the world head-lines in early 1988, the media described the region as 'obscure'. Here we will argue that 'obscurity' is only in small part a function of geography and to a much greater degree a socially constructed category. Three factors with roots in the period after the First World War and the more recent past have combined to marginalize the issue of the Armenian genocide and the question of Nagorno-Karabagh. The factors we need to consider in this regard are Soviet nationality policy, the academic discipline of Sovietology, and the Armenian question as it related to the evolution of US–Turkish relations, particularly during the Cold War.

SOVIET NATIONALITY POLICY

By the mid-1920s the Bolsheviks had expelled the invading imperialist armies and defeated the indigenous counter-revolutionary forces. Yet they still found themselves face to face, as the czars had been, with the problem of the non-Russian nationalities, an issue which was never brought to a successful resolution and which represented such a severe source of underlying tension that it eventually played a major role in the fall of the Soviet Union.

Lenin and the early Bolsheviks understood the dangers which confronted them, and they acted boldly to cut their losses to secure the safety of the revolution itself. An early and separate peace was negotiated with Germany in 1918, and the Soviets made major territorial concessions as the price for withdrawal from the war. This was followed by initiatives to secure Soviet borders, beginning with agreements, as we have seen, with Turkey. The government, likewise, made other concessions to reduce sources of resistance at a time when it could not easily neutralize them. A case in point was the New Economic Policy (NEP), which incorporated market incentives into the Soviet economy of the 1920s. This policy should be seen, in part, as an attempt by a relatively weak state to win over the peasantry at a time when the state was dependent on rural support and incapable of imposing collectivization in the face of peasant resistance.

In their relations with the national minorities, the Bolsheviks similarly adjusted the logic of theory to bring it into line with the political reality. For the Bolsheviks, ethnic identification and its collective expression, nationalism, were forms of false allegiance promoted and encouraged by bourgeois leaders. Lenin and the other early Bolsheviks initially opposed any type of federative system based on ethnic geographic units. Instead, they proposed non-ethnic geographic units which would serve as the basis for an ethnically neutral, universalistic identity rooted in class consciousness. The intent of this assimilationist policy was to replace the false consciousness of nationalism, which had led to so much hostility and bloodshed in the past, with a scientific foundation for social and cultural development.

Breakaway nationalism by the national minorities of the former Russian Empire forced the Bolshevik leadership to alter its policies on the national question. Although most of the national minorities which had declared independence were brought back into the Soviet Union by force, Lenin understood that coercion alone could not serve as the foundation for a multinational Communist state, and he therefore promoted the position that national minorities should have political and cultural autonomy within a Soviet system dominated by the Communist Party. The largest of these minorities, including the Armenians and Azerbaijanis, were organized into republics; in return for the loss of political independence, they were guaranteed territorial status as well as cultural and linguistic rights. The smaller minorities were organized into sub-republican units, such as autonomous republics and regions, within the Russian Federation and, in some cases including the Nagorno-Karabagh Autonomous Oblast, within other Union republics.

Grants of territorial status were not made solely on the basis of the size of a particular national group or the strength of historic claims by that group to a particular territory as its homeland. Looming large in Bolshevik considerations were the requirements of empire itself. In this the Soviet state differed little from the Russian Empire which preceded it. Thus territorial allocations were made in ways which would embitter certain groups and allow for ethnicities to be pitted against one another. While there was always the possibility that frustrated ethnic conflicts rooted in past territorial injustices could be directed against the centre, the centre, nonetheless, succeeded in creating what amounted to a reserve of possibilities to be drawn upon for playing out a classic 'divide and conquer' strategy. As examples, we find certain groups split between Russia and the minority republics.[58]

In the case of Nagorno-Karabagh, the criterion of self-determination which would have resulted in the territory being allocated to Soviet Armenia was ignored in favour of promoting a Bolshevik agenda *vis-à-vis* Turkey. At the same time that Armenia was denied what was hers, the wishes of the people of Nagorno-Karabagh were rejected, and Azerbaijan, the seeming winner, had an angry, disillusioned population planted in its midst. Nearly seventy years later these ingredients would be publicly played out in the streets of Stepanakert when the Armenians of Nagorno-Karabagh asserted their right to self-determination.

The overall impact of Moscow's policies on the constituent republics was complex and textured. Soviet leaders did make significant concessions to minority peoples. Each of the minority republics possessed the symbols, if not the full substance, of independent states, including flags, anthems, national political parties, parliaments, and even foreign ministries. Republics had their film studios, television stations, newspapers, and printing facilities, dance troupes, national museums, and opera houses. Schools were built, and students instructed in them in local languages. Alphabets were developed for peoples who lacked them, and national cultures were encouraged within politically defined limits. At the same time, the Soviet Union underwent a process of modernization and secularization which further undermined traditional centres of power and allowed new national centres of power to emerge. Whatever might be said of the motivations of the Soviet leadership, the impact of concessions to the minority republics and the successes of the Soviet educational system and its cultural policies was to strengthen national identity and consciousness among the titular peoples of the minority republics.[59]

The real successes of Soviet policies with regard to minority peoples, especially in the growth of national identity, coupled with repression in the political sphere, allowed Soviet propagandists during the Cold War to favourably contrast racial exploitation and oppression in the US with an idealized vision of Soviet racial and ethnic harmony.[60] In situations where people had real and substantial grievances, Nagorno-Karabagh being one among others, there was little possibility of making those grievances known within Soviet society or in the outside world.

While it is not correct to say that the possibilities for dissent within the Soviet Union were non-existent, it is correct to say that there were heavily circumscribed limits. The price one had to pay for violating officially defined and enforced limits was more than most people were willing to pay. It was only when the sanctions against speaking out on national issues were relaxed under Gorbachev that people like the Armenians of Nagorno-Karabagh felt safe enough to air their grievances and make mass public demands for fundamental social changes. Prior to that fateful moment, Nagorno-Karabagh had been relegated to obscurity by the dual, interlocking pattern of Soviet ideology, which proclaimed that there were no nationality problems, and a system of repression which levied heavy sanctions on those who, by speaking out, showed that they disagreed.

SOVIETOLOGY

While it is understandable that conditions in the Soviet Union would work to conceal ethnic conflicts, the second factor is both closer to home and less obvious. Sovietology, the discipline devoted to the detailed study of the Soviet Union, made its own unique contribution to clouding the issue of ethnic persecution in the Soviet Union. There had always been Western scholars who had been interested in Russia and later in the Soviet Union, but Sovietology, the discipline, owes to the Cold War its regular funding, academic bases, training and research centres, publishing outlets and access to the media.

For the West, the Soviet Union was no ordinary state, but, from 1947 to its collapse in 1991, the official enemy state of the US, the other global superpower in what fairly quickly became a bi-polar post-war world. Just as the Soviet Union was no ordinary country, Sovietology, with its mission of monitoring trends and collecting data on the Soviet Union, and analysing and interpreting them, was no ordinary academic discipline. It was, rather, and to an inordinate degree, a discipline in the service of national power.

The impact of this linkage between the academic discipline of Sovietology and the highest echelons of national power was the tendency for the study of Soviet minorities to be downplayed in favour of glamour topics such as Soviet political ideology, the economy, and the military.[61] This emphasis allowed the Soviet Union to be portrayed in the US as a monolithic enemy state – exactly the threat to national security required to win public consent for the permanent war economy which developed after the Second World War.

Sovietology was heavily Russocentric. Beginning with the Russian Empire and moving on to the Russian Revolution, Russia was the ubiquitous prism through which Soviet events were filtered. Within this framework, Soviet minorities met one of three fates – (1) they were most often ignored or, at best, treated as an afterthought, (2) ethnic grievances were sometimes highlighted to 'prove' the failure of the Soviet system, or (3) if ethnic minorities were subjects of serious study, the emphasis was on the centre and not the periphery: the dynamics of their own histories and patterns of development were subordinated to their roles in and impact upon the larger Soviet system. The case of Nagorno-Karabagh illustrates this process. When the Armenian protests broke out in 1988, Western Sovietologists and the media were much more interested in the possible impact of the protests on Gorbachev and the Soviet reform movement than they were in the history of Nagorno-Karabagh and the grievances of the majority of its residents.

The unspoken assumptions of Sovietology blinded nearly all of its practitioners to the powerful ethnic contradictions which were tearing the Soviet Union apart. In 1989, a time when nearly one-third of the Armenian population had taken to the streets in protest over Karabagh, when Armenia and Azerbaijan were in open conflict, when Georgia and the Baltic republics were beginning to speak openly about independence, and when a host of grievances in the Central Asian republics were taking on an increasingly ethnic–national cast, prominent Sovietologists were debating whether Eastern Europe or the Soviet economy presented a greater obstacle to Gorbachev's reform movement. National minorities as a possible flashpoint ranked a distant third in these calculations. The unfolding drama missed by nearly all Sovietologists was that economic and ethnic grievances and their interplay were bringing about the collapse of the Soviet Union, whereas Eastern Europe, excepting Romania, passed into the Western sphere with relative ease.[62]

The combination of political forces in the Soviet Union and in the West meant that Nagorno-Karabagh received almost no serious academic attention in the West during the entire Soviet period. As is often the case with issues which lack the imprimatur of official 'experts', it was only in the light of protest and resistance by Karabagh Armenians and other Soviet minorities that the national question came to be appreciated as a powerful dynamic in Soviet history and a force in defining the future.

THE ARMENIAN QUESTION, US–TURKISH RELATIONS, AND THE COLD WAR

Nagorno-Karabagh's long struggle for self-determination, first expressed in the struggle for unification with Armenia and now for independence, must be understood within the larger framework of Armenia's relations with the West and the West's relations with Turkey, particularly during the Cold War period.

At the time of the Armenian genocide, then known as the 'Armenian massacres', the events were a *cause célèbre* in the West. They received wide coverage in the press and were documented by US Ambassador to the Ottoman Empire Henry Morgenthau, British historian Arnold Toynbee, and others.[63] After the war and into the 1920s, Western interest in Armenia and Armenians waned, and with it the opportunity for Nagorno-Karabagh and its Armenian majority, now within an authoritarian and quintessentially enemy state, the Soviet Union, to publicize their fate.

Meanwhile, Atatürk's military and political successes transformed Turkey from the status of successor state to a defeated First World War combatant into a newly independent regional force. The military cost to the West of insisting on the provisions of the Treaty of Sèvres, including an independent Armenia with its western lands restored, had increased, and the West, ever self-interested, backed off.

The Republic of Turkey, in control of Anatolia and the strategic straits to the Mediterranean, was now in a position to offer inducements to those nations willing to make concessions to it. We have seen that Lenin seized the occasion to establish mutually agreed borders with Turkey. Trade and oil were inducements for the West. From hindsight we know that Turkey's oil reserves are limited, but in the early 1920s Turkey was thought to be the next Mesopotamia, and Western firms were anxious to gain access for exploration. This complex of economic and political pay-offs had its effect on the perception of Armenia and the Armenian question. By the mid-1920s, for example, *The Literary Digest, Current History* and *The New York Times*, which had earlier championed the Armenian cause, were publishing works on the genocide which equivocated in moral tone and diverged from the historical record. In 1927, the year the US established diplomatic relations with Turkey, *The New York Times* took the position on the genocide that bygones ought to be bygones.

With the onset of the Cold War, Turkey's strategic value to the West greatly increased. Turkey participated in the Korean War by contributing troops to the UN forces, and this paved the way for Turkey's entry into NATO. Now a linchpin in the Western alliance against the Soviet Union, Turkey was in a stronger position than ever before to influence Western politics, scholarship, and media on the Armenian question.[64]

Beginning with this period, we find increasing numbers of apologetic 'scholarly' writings which equivocate on the question of the genocide and in some cases quite openly proclaim an intent to assess Turkey in the light of that country's ability to promote US interests.[65] In 1977, revisionist histories of the the First World War period reached new heights with the publication of Stanford and Ezel Kural Shaw's *History of the Ottoman Empire and Modern Turkey.* The Shaws eschew voluminous US and European archival materials on the genocide and make selective use of Turkish materials to present a case of genocide denial. They go so far as to describe the wartime genocide of Armenians as a myth concocted by 'Entente propaganda mills and Armenian nationalists'.[66]

In the area of policy, the US government backed Turkey in its strenuous objection to a reference to the Armenian genocide in a report of the sub-committee of the United Nations Commission on Human Rights. This reference, known as Paragraph 30, was deleted in 1978 with US government support. The US State Department is loath to recognize the Armenian genocide as an historical event, despite ample documentation by its own envoys and consuls to the Ottoman Empire. On Nagorno-Karabagh, neither the Office of the President nor the State Department issued statements on human rights and self-determination in the territory, despite doing so for other peoples and regions of the former Soviet Union. The failure of the US to back self-determination for Nagorno-Karabagh and to raise the issue of human rights violations there should be seen as another expression of US support for Turkey, which has its own long tradition of support for Azerbaijan which pre-dates Sovietization in 1920.

As we have seen, the Soviet Union had its own reasons for courting Turkey, and the initial assignment of Nagorno-Karabagh to Azerbaijan was partially motivated by the search for security on its southern flank.

In summary, Armenians long presented the United States and the Soviet Union with unique problems which bear on the perception and definition of the matter of the genocide; many of these same considerations bear upon the matter of Nagorno-Karabagh and related issues in the late Soviet and the post-Cold War era. As a Soviet socialist republic and now an independent nation, Armenia has been at a disadvantage in competing with Azerbaijan's oil resources or Turkey's markets, minerals, and strategic location. As in the case of the genocide, the issue of Nagorno-Karabagh has been presented in Western and Soviet media and scholarship within a distorted framework shaped by superpower agendas. For example, in US press reports on Nagorno-Karabagh we find, in addition to the religious paradigm examined above, a reluctance to lend credibility to Karabagh Armenian grievances by presenting them as Armenian allegations, claims, and assertions rather than as facts. Statements by Azerbaijani officials were much more likely to be presented without qualifiers which undermined the credibility of statements.[67] The genocide was typically avoided as an issue in this body of reportage, but, when it did appear, it too was qualified. Paul Quinn-Judge in *The Christian Science Monitor*, for example, referred to the 'so-called massacres of 1915'.[68] We also find a consistent refusal to refer to the Armenian struggle for Nagorno-Karabagh as one for the self-determination of peoples. Instead the media insisted on labelling Armenian protests as a threat to Gorbachev's reform programme.[69]

As time and events have unfolded since 1988, we find old assumptions and biases repeated in different contexts. In 1992 the killing of Azerbaijanis by Armenian forces in Khojaly received front-page media coverage. The use of Khojaly by Azerbaijani forces for rocket attacks was seldom noted in media accounts. Also absent were reports from Helsinki Watch which indicated that, rather than having been massacred, Azerbaijani civilians had been shot in a crossfire as retreating Azerbaijani troops attempted to use them as human shields.[70] The massacre of Armenians at Maragha by Azerbaijani troops, also in 1992, received no Western media coverage at all.[71] We also find extensive criticism by Western governments and media of Armenian attacks on Lachin and Kelbajar but little or no mention of the destruction of Stepanakert by Azerbaijani rockets, the effects of the Azerbaijani blockade on Armenia, or the shelling and cross-border raids by Azerbaijan into Armenia itself.

Two nearly identical proposals which appeared in US publications in 1992 help to uncover the unstated assumptions which underlie much of the West's thinking on Nagorno-Karabagh. Former US State Department official Paul Goble, now with the Carnegie Endowment for International Peace in Washington, presented a plan for the resolution to the crisis in which Azerbaijan would retain Nagorno-Karabagh and Armenia would receive a corridor to the territory via the Lachin Strip. In return for the latter concession, Armenia would cede its southern province to Azerbaijan, allowing the long-sought pan-Turkic link between Turkey and Nakhichevan to the west and Azerbaijan to the east.[72] Shortly after Goble's proposal appeared in print, *The Nation* published a similar proposal in more ambiguous language in an article by Dilip Hiro, a Middle East specialist with numerous books to his credit. In Hiro's version, the fate of Nagorno-Karabagh is unstated while Armenian and Azerbaijani corridors are 'allocated' and 'maintained' without specification as to who should own them.[73]

To the uninitiated, the Goble–Hiro proposals have all the earmarks of objectivity and fairness. They seem to say that neither side is entirely right and that the truth, and therefore the solution, lies somewhere in the middle. Each side should, therefore, gain something and lose something as the price for peace. In Goble's version, the more specific of the two, Nagorno-Karabagh stays with Azerbaijan, Armenia gains territorial access to Nagorno-Karabagh through the Lachin Strip, and Azerbaijan gains territorial access to Nakhichevan and Turkey.

If one ignores history and geography, this seems like a fair-minded solution, one that has merit. However, the more one looks into the history behind the conflict, the more the 'solution' comes apart at the seams. The struggle is first and foremost a struggle for self-determination by Karabagh Armenians. Their grievances had built up over the course of decades and were capped by a risky but peaceful resistance to Azerbaijani authority beginning in 1988, followed by Azerbaijani attempts to impose its threatened rule by force. The Karabagh

Armenians responded by declaring independence, to which the Azerbaijanis responded with escalating violence and destruction of the territory in 1992. Given this sequence of events, Karabagh Armenians and their elected government are not going to return willingly to Azerbaijani rule in response to promises that a new Azerbaijani administration would eliminate the past abuses which drove the Karabagh Armenians to resist initially. The level of trust which would be required to render this a viable proposal is simply absent, particularly in the light of the fact that there is no provision for monitoring such a settlement and enforcing its provisions.

It is the case that Armenian access to Nagorno-Karabagh via the Lachin Strip would provide some cultural and commercial benefits to Armenia and the Karabagh Armenians, but Armenia (the only player in the Goble proposal to surrender any territory) would be more isolated than it is now by virtue of the loss of its Armenian–Iranian border, a frontier which some believe is the most promising for future Armenian development and security. However, access to the Lachin Strip would fail to compensate for the benefits Armenian's southernmost province would bring to Turkey and Azerbaijan. Among other gains, such a land transfer would allow for the construction of the Turkish-Caspian pipeline by what is acknowledged to be the least expensive, safest, and most secure route for the export of Azerbaijani oil, and there would be additional commercial and strategic benefits. It should also be noted – it is seldom noted in the Western media and is altogether ignored by the Goble–Hiro proposals – that the Lachin Strip was part of the original territory of Nagorno-Karabagh ceded to Azerbaijan by the Bolsheviks.

The Goble–Hiro proposals cannot be considered seriously because they are so prejudicial to Armenia and the Karabagh Armenians that they would be accepted only under the kind of duress resulting from a successful Azerbaijani invasion of Armenia and Karabagh. The benefits to Azerbaijan and Turkey are obvious. Azerbaijan would gain a favourable settlement, including a territorial link to its western province of Nakhichevan, at a time when the tides of a politically destabilizing war with the Armenians are beginning to shift against it. Turkey would have its long-coveted corridor to the east, and the settlement would extricate Turkey from a delicate situation in which there is domestic pressure for Turkey to aid its ally Azerbaijan at the same time that there are powerful domestic and international constraints on its ability to do so.

It is revealing that such a one-sided proposal could appear in two prestigious publications within a short period of time under the guise of being fair-minded and reasonable. It indicates the degree to which the historically generated 'obscurity' of Nagorno-Karabagh has created a blind spot when it comes to the right of Karabagh Armenians to defend themselves and to claim the right to self-determination.

Other Interested Parties: the US, Russia, Turkey, Iran, Great Britain, the UN and the CSCE

UNITED STATES

The Bush administration's emphasis on foreign policy did not extend to the Transcaucasus, and the Clinton administration, which assumed office in January 1993, shifted the governmental focus from foreign to domestic issues, in particular to national health insurance, unemployment, and the national debt. Yet we can discern some continuity in US policy and actions despite the change in administrations and parties in power. First, there has been the shipment of US government humanitarian aid to Armenia during the winters from 1991–1992 to 1993–1994. Second, the US has joined other non-combatant powers in insisting on the integrity of borders, and has vocally criticized the Karabagh Armenians for attacks on the Lachin Strip and Kelbajar, and, in 1993, for their conquest of broad areas of south-western Azerbaijan.[74] The US has been less vocal in its criticism of Azerbaijan for its economic blockade of Armenia and Nagorno-Karabagh and other forms of aggression; however, these Azerbaijani actions have been the basis of a ban on US aid to Azerbaijan which has been in effect since 1992.[75]

US commercial interests in the region are greatest with regard to Azerbaijani oil and natural gas, and what seems to be of primary consideration to the US is stability in the Transcaucasus and a favourable business investment climate rather than a particular solution to the struggle over Nagorno-Karabagh or political/territorial conflicts in neighbouring Georgia.[76] Continued armed conflict and probably a larger regional war, unless it were orchestrated for a specific objective, would not be in the US interest, and this is why it has joined in numerous internationally sponsored peace initiatives. To the extent that a Russian sphere of influence in these areas is compatible with these objectives, the US seems willing, within limits, to countenance it.

RUSSIA

The Russian presence in the southern Transcaucasus pre-dates the Bolshevik Revolution by a century. In 1991 that presence was deeply compromised by the dissolution of the Soviet Union and the assertion of Armenian, Azerbaijani and Georgian independence. The Georgians and Azerbaijanis attempted to forge an independent political path by refusing to join the CIS. The Armenians have traditionally been Russia's most reliable ally in the Transcaucasus, and the Armenians quickly joined the CIS and benefited for a time as the only Commonwealth member in the region.[77]

Russia undoubtedly retains ambitions in the Transcaucasus, seeking a military presence and influence over foreign policy in the three regional states, and oil and natural gas concessions in Azerbaijan.[78]

Russian President Boris Yeltsin views the region as a Russian sphere of influence, but he has been bedevilled by political and economic problems which in some ways rival those of the former minority republics. But in addition to the overthrow of the Elchibey government in Azerbaijan and the spectacular territorial gains of the Karabagh Armenians in 1993, the year was significant because Russia and Yeltsin emerged as strengthened players in the Transcaucasus. Georgia and Azerbaijan were brought into the CIS, and Russia became the leading force in brokering talks which included the Karabagh Armenians for the first time. This led to a ceasefire in early September 1993 which held for nearly two months. Since that time Russia has taken the lead in bringing parties together for talks, and of all the nations and international bodies with an interest in the conflict, only the Russians have been willing to commit troops to monitor a ceasefire.

Russia joins the US in taking the position that there should be no territorial changes. In late 1993 Russia began promoting broad autonomy for Karabagh within Azerbaijan as a solution to the crisis. This position of opposing territorial changes is consistent with Gorbachev's in the former Soviet Union and is designed with the same eye to the self-preservation of large multi-ethnic states at the expense of satisfying the grievances of minority peoples. The statement made by Gorbachev's top adviser Alexander Yakovlev is as apt now as it was several years ago when he told human rights activist Andrei Sakharov:

> The national structure of the state can't be changed in any respect. Any revision would create a dangerous precedent; there are too many flashpoints where ethnic passions could explode.[79]

Russia remains the pre-eminent regional power, and that has without a doubt kept Turkish ambitions in check. Russia maintains troops in Armenia and Azerbaijan (they left Azerbaijan in May 1993, but a small number had returned by the end of the year) and has taken a strong position in response to bellicose Turkish statements in the aftermath of victories by Karabagh Armenians in the spring offensives of 1992 and 1993.[80]

TURKEY

With the collapse of the Soviet Union, the US deferred to its NATO ally Turkey as the proper vehicle for extending Western influence in the Moslem states of the former Soviet Union. Turkey's performance, however, fell short of expectations for a number of reasons among which limited aid revenue and an inability to stand up to Russia are prominent. This has caused Turkey to fail both in meeting the economic aid and investment expectations of the newly independent Turcophone states, including Azerbaijan, and in more substantially aiding those states militarily. Whenever Turkey has spoken of employing military action to discipline Armenia, for example, Russia has made it clear that this would be viewed as unacceptable aggression on Turkey's part, and Turkey has backed down.

Turkey calls for the withdrawal of Armenian forces from all occupied Azerbaijani territory, and wants the Armenian government to recognize Nagorno-Karabagh as Azerbaijani. Turkey joins the other parties in calling for the maintenance of existing borders and, in addition, covertly seeks the fulfilment of its frustrated ambition to have a direct territorial link with Azerbaijan, the Caspian and Central Asia, where four of the five major ethnic groups – and new nations – are Turkic.

Armenia has attempted to create a working relationship with Turkey but been spurned. Turkey, for example, has rejected Armenian attempts to establish full diplomatic relations, and Armenia is the only former Soviet republic without an embassy in Ankara. Turkey has deployed heavy troop concentrations along the Turkish–Armenian border, bringing it face to face with Russian and Armenian troops. And after allowing the intermittent flow of international humanitarian aid across its territory to Armenia during the 1992–1993 winter, Turkey refused to allow the passage of any goods in 1993–1994.

While these are clearly hostile actions designed to assist Azerbaijan, they are also necessarily restrained actions because Turkey's larger ambitions face serious constraints. Turkey's desire to be admitted to the European Economic Community has already been set back as a result of the independence of the Eastern European nations and persistent questions about Turkey's human rights record, and any direct Turkish intervention in the Karabagh conflict would be damaging to Turkey's relations with the West. As a result, Turkey's involvement has been indirect and, to the degree possible, covert, with the intention that Azerbaijan should appear to achieve the necessary victories on its own and without Turkish intervention.

Following the Karabagh Armenian victories in the Lachin Strip and Shushi in May 1992, Turkish Foreign Minister Hikmet Cetin warned Armenia that 'Turkey will never allow a change by force in the legal facts of Nagorno-Karabagh. Armenia will be responsible for the grave consequences to arise from such an action.' This brought an immediate response from Yevgeni Shaposhnikov, Military Chief of the Commonwealth States, who warned that any Turkish intervention could spark a third world war.[81] Turkey backed down, but the Turkish defence of Azerbaijan was revived a year later after Karabagh Armenian forces seized the Kelbajar District and other areas of south-western and western Azerbaijan.

Turkish Defence Minister Nevzat Ayaz has denied the participation of any Turkish troops in the conflict, though he acknowledged that retired Turkish generals may have gone to Azerbaijan on their own initiative. At least one Turkish and one Arab newspaper reported more direct involvement. A story in

Cumhuriet on 5 July 1992 reported that ten Turkish generals were in Azerbaijan to train military forces there. On 10 July 1992 *Alshark-el-Aswat* reported the presence of over 1,000 Turkish military specialists, including 160 officers, in Azerbaijan. Alpaslan Turkesh, founder of the Turkish fascist Grey Wolves, acknowledged that his followers were fighting in Karabagh with Azerbaijani forces, though it was reported in late 1992 that they had returned to Turkey.[82]

Beginning with the Karabagh Armenian offensives which took Lachin and Kelbajar, Armenian forces have been subject to intense international criticism. In the case of the 1992 Kelbajar offensive, for example, US Secretary of State Warren Christopher called for an immediate withdrawal of Armenian forces. Turkish Prime Minister Suleman Demirel and President Turgut Ozal condemned the offensive, and Turkey's Ambassador to the United Nations called on the Security Council to take 'vigorous action' and used the example of the Kuwaiti crisis and the US-initiated international response as an example of the type of action he had in mind. Turkey joined Pakistan in co-sponsoring UN Resolution 822. Passed by the Security Council, it called for a ceasefire and the withdrawal of all Armenian forces from Kelbajar. Three subsequent resolutions also called for the withdrawal of Armenian forces from occupied areas of Azerbaijan, but there has been no mechanism of enforcement.

Overall, Turkey has been a loser in the region. Its importance to the West as an anti-communist bulwark ended with the fall of the Soviet Union, and this loss has only been partially compensated for by other services Turkey provides. Turkey's inability to intervene more directly and strongly on behalf of Azerbaijan has caused political embarrassment in Turkey and disillusionment in Azerbaijan. On the matter of Nagorno-Karabagh, Turkey is and will remain an important player, but one of secondary rank compared to Russia. Turkey supplies weapons and military advisers to Azerbaijan and works on Azerbaijan's behalf through the CSCE's Minsk Group and the UN. Turkey also provides hearty expressions of Turkish–Azerbaijani solidarity, joint Turkish–Pakistani UN resolutions condemning Armenia, and blustery threats directed at the Armenian government. In the autumn of 1993, a desperate Gaidar Aliev went to Turkey seeking more. Like his predecessor Abulfaz Elchibey, he did not get it.[83]

IRAN

Iran competes with Turkey for influence in the Middle East and Central Asia, and both have a keen interest in developments in the Transcaucasus. Iran is home to a large Azerbaijani minority in the north-west. These southern Azerbaijanis, who actually outnumber Azerbaijanis in the Republic of Azerbaijan, have shown no disloyalty to Iran, but there are militants to the north, in the Republic of Azerbaijan, who regard them as a captive minority within Iran and who harbour irredentist ambitions.

Regarding the Karabagh conflict, Iran intervened several times in 1992–1993 to negotiate ceasefires, but all were short-lived. Iran has been officially neutral while at the same time joining other nations in insisting on the integrity of borders and condemning Karabagh Armenian victories. Nevertheless, the Armenians see Iran as a more even-handed regional force than Turkey – a view not shared by the US government which seeks to employ Turkey to neutralize Iranian influence in the region.

Karabagh Armenian offensives in 1993 created hundreds of thousands of Azerbaijani refugees, many of whom crossed the border into northern Iran. The Iranian government fears the instability which may develop internally with the influx of so many Azerbaijani refugees fleeing into Azerbaijani areas of Iran. Thus Iran has viewed these developments with alarm and threatened, without elaboration, to 'take a more severe stand' if the fighting continued. The Iranians stopped short of military intervention, however, fearing the Russians – as does Turkey. Instead, the Iranians have tried to defuse the situation by sending stern messages to the Republic of Armenia in the hope that the Ter Petrosian government can pressure the Karabagh Armenians to accept a withdrawal, and they have re-routed many of the refugees out of Iran and into unoccupied Azerbaijan where they supply and operate refugee camps.

GREAT BRITAIN
Britain is Azerbaijan's second largest trading partner after Iran. The British have interests in oil equipment, communications and agriculture, and they are poised for further investment in banking and insurance. British Petroleum has been actively pursuing access to Azerbaijani oil and natural gas and leads a consortium of oil firms seeking a contract with the Azerbaijani government. The primacy of British investment interests is, perhaps, symbolically and practically represented by the fact that there is a British embassy in Baku but none in Yerevan. When the opportunity has presented itself, the British have been particularly vocal in their insistence that Karabagh is an Azerbaijani territory.

THE UN AND THE CSCE
There have been numerous attempts at international mediation of the Karabagh conflict. Some have been successful in imposing limited ceasefires, but most have been stillborn because the sponsoring agencies and nations have been unable to organize monitoring and enforcement mechanisms, or the proposals themselves have contained provisions unacceptable to one or the other of the parties. The Republic of Armenia has been most amenable to international settlement proposals since it is willing to settle for a recognition of the autonomy of Nagorno-Karabagh and further negotiations to define the form and direction of that autonomy. Azerbaijan refuses to accept the concept

of any autonomy with substance. The government of Nagorno-Karabagh sees international mediation efforts as problematic because it insists that the territory belongs to Azerbaijan. The Karabagh Armenians argue that, by defining as a precondition what should be the subject of negotiation, the settlement proposals deny the entire *raison d'être* of the Karabagh Armenian struggle.

As an example of the difficulties involved, we can consider the 3 + 1 Peace Initiative which was presented in the early summer of 1993. The name is taken from the three sponsoring parties – Russia, Turkey, and the US – and the umbrella organization, the Conference on Security and Cooperation in Europe (CSCE) and its nine-member Minsk Group, charged with negotiating a settlement.[84] The 3 +1 Initiative called for the withdrawal of Karabagh Armenian troops from the Kelbajar region and a 60-day ceasefire followed by negotiations. Azerbaijan accepted these terms immediately, and Armenia followed. The Karabagh Armenians turned the proposal down because it made no provision for their security. They had taken Kelbajar, they argued, specifically because it was used as a staging area for Azerbaijani rocket attacks and offensives against Nagorno-Karabagh. Now they were being asked to return Kelbajar according to a timetable in which there was a 16-day lapse between the withdrawal and the arrival of international observers and without any guarantee that the Azerbaijanis would not resume their attacks once the territory was returned to them. Thus the initiative failed.[85]

The UN passed four Security Council resolutions on Karabagh in 1993 (822 on 30 April, 853 on 29 July, 874 on 14 October, and 884 on 12 November). The resolutions differ in their details; for example, the later ones recognize Karabagh as a party to the conflict and call for Azerbaijani–Karabagh negotiations. In their overall thrust, however, they are strikingly similar. Each came in the wake of Karabagh Armenian victories, each has recognized Karabagh as an Azerbaijani territory, and each has called for the withdrawal of Karabagh Armenian forces. For this reason Azerbaijan has accepted them though with reservation about the provisions noted above. Armenia and Karabagh have also accepted them as opportunities for negotiation but see them as one-sided because (1) there is no recognition that the areas of occupied Azerbaijan were deployed as sites for rocket attacks on Armenia and Karabagh as well as full military offensives, (2) there is no mention of the crippling economic blockade of Armenia and Karabagh carried out by Azerbaijan, (3) there is mention only of Azerbaijani refugees and not Karabagh Armenian ones, and (4) there is no provision for monitors or other guarantees that occupied territories returned to Azerbaijan would not again serve as the basis for attacks on Karabagh or Armenia.

There seems to be general agreement by the US and the regional powers as well as the UN that the proper mediator for the conflict should be the CSCE.

Armenian and Azerbaijani representatives were brought together for talks in March 1992 in Helsinki. While these discussions yielded no immediate results, they did establish a dialogue which has been continuing. Representatives from Nagorno-Karabagh were admitted to the negotiations in 1993 after Azerbaijan set aside its objections that participation by Nagorno-Karabagh would convey recognition of the territory as an entity separate from Azerbaijan. CSCE proposals call for the withdrawal of troops from occupied territories and cease-fires, but not for the end of the economic blockades. Nonetheless, Armenia has accepted CSCE proposals and pressured the Karabagh Armenians to accept a CSCE proposal in June 1993 which was based on UN resolution 822. A CSCE proposal in October 1993 was rejected by Azerbaijan because it did not address the refugee problem, did not mention the Lachin Strip, did not call for an unconditional withdrawal of Karabagh Armenian forces (the proposal called for an end to the Azerbaijani rail and pipeline blockades as a precondition for withdrawal), and recognized Karabagh as a party to the conflict.

Despite these failures, the CSCE continues to provide a format for dialogue and seems open to working with other parties to find a settlement. Swedish diplomat Jan Eliasson, the current CSCE mediator, has recognized the renewed Russian presence in the region and expressed an interest in working with the Russians to resolve the crisis.

Escalating Violence

In Nagorno-Karabagh, the Azerbaijani government faces a local, indigenous Armenian majority with a strong historical claim to the land, which views Azerbaijani rule as illegitimate. The years of Azerbaijani economic blockade and the relentless shelling and raids by Azerbaijani forces have only strengthened Karabagh Armenian resolve to free themselves of Baku's rule. When the 1988 protests made it clear that the Karabagh Armenians wanted to end their forced connection to Azerbaijan, the Azerbaijani government moved to accelerate the shift in the demographic balance by terrorizing Armenian residents into abandoning the territory and by settling Azerbaijanis in their place. This continued until Yeltsin removed Russian forces from Karabagh in late 1991, and the Karabagh Armenians mobilized in self-defence.

This process of forced demographic change was documented by the human rights organization Helsinki Watch and also by a multinational delegation from the First International Andrei Sakharov Memorial Congress which visited Armenia and Azerbaijan in May 1991.[86] The delegation was headed by Lady Baroness Caroline Cox of the British House of Lords. The group repeatedly sought and was denied permission to visit Nagorno-Karabagh by the Azerbaijani government, but it was able to inspect Armenian and

Azerbaijani villages in border areas adjoining the two republics. The deportations from the Armenian village of Getashen, in Azerbaijan, were typical of what the observers found:

> During the deportations, there were numerous civil rights violations of several types. People were killed singly or multiply. There were beatings, rapes, forced abductions, and imprisonment. Property and livestock were stolen or bought for an insulting price, such as a car for two roubles. Voluntary requests to leave were obtained at gun point. Ears of girls were torn by forcible removal of earrings. We found no evidence, in spite of diligent inquiry, that anyone recently deported from Getashen left it voluntarily.
>
> Most of the witnesses told us that the beatings and killings were carried out by the Azerbaijan OMON (Azerbaijani Special Forces, or 'black beret units'). But the Soviet army organized the surrounding of the villages and taunted the villagers, 'Why have you not left already?' Then they stood aside while the OMON terrorized the villagers. The villagers were left on the Armenian side of the border with only the clothes they were wearing.[87]

Two months later, in July 1991, a follow-up delegation from the Andrei Sakharov Memorial Congress became the first international delegation to visit Nagorno-Karabagh. They found a number of types of human rights violations carried out by the Azerbaijani authorities including forced deportations, detentions, the abuse and harassment of civilians. including rape, and the closure and destruction of churches. One of the numerous case histories they collected follows:

> A young woman aged 20, Mrs Barseghian from the Berdadzor region: Mrs Barseghian said that on May 13, 1991 at 6:00 a.m. Soviet Interior Ministry troops and Azerbaijani OMON surrounded and entered the village to check passports. They tied her husband and brother-in-law's hands and threw them into a bus. They gave her a document which they insisted she should sign saying she was ready to leave the village voluntarily. She signed because she was terrified. She has one 14-month-old child. A soldier approached her child and took hold of his head and said, 'You are Armenian and therefore I must cut out your tongue.' She attacked the soldier and fought him off. The interpreter asked whether she had been raped and she remained silent. Several voices were raised in the hall to tell her to admit she had been raped because we needed to know. She then admitted that the soldier had raped her but that they had left the baby alone. Her husband and brother-in-law are still in jail.[88]

The declaration of independence by Karabagh's Armenians in late 1991 clearly indicated their commitment and ability to defy Baku, and the

Azerbaijani government responded with a tremendous escalation in violence by deploying helicopter gunships and GRAD rocket launchers, which fire 40 rockets at a time. Prior to the capture of Shushi by Karabagh Armenian forces, Azerbaijani forces rained down rockets on the capital city of Stepanakert and reduced the city of 60,000 to rubble. *The Christian Science Monitor* reported that:

> the population lives much of the day underground in cold basement cellars. A warren of rooms under one apartment is reserved for women and children who sleep three or four to a bed. The men lie in the corridors.[89]

Baroness Cox, who visited Nagorno-Karabagh dozens of times during 1991–1993, adds these poignant details:

> ... to compound the agony of the people caught in this besieged, bombarded city, the blockade has prevented the delivery of medical supplies .... Surgeons are operating with no anesthetics or analgesics, relying on vodka to provide some pathetically inadequate sedation for major trauma, including amputations and burns. The blockade also prevents the evacuation of the injured to hospitals in Armenia. The hospital and maternity hospital have been further damaged by shelling; mothers are giving birth in improvised wards in the basement of the Town Hall, but this has since been destroyed by shells; the fate of the mothers underneath is not known. The death rate among babies is increasing; many are born prematurely; many mothers do not have milk; and there are no supplies of baby formula.[90]

The work of human rights organizations serves to document actual conditions in Nagorno-Karabagh and Armenia. Unfortunately, these records run up against counter-viewpoints held by Western governments and promoted by the media. For reasons we have examined above, the West insists on the inviolability of borders, and its insistence blinds the observer to the politically motivated injustice of the 1921 decision to assign Nagorno-Karabagh to Azerbaijan. With the failure to call attention to this seminal decision, other distortions appear in its wake, and these distortions serve to further obscure the issues. Distortions include the failure to report that the Lachin Strip and the Shahumian District were part of the original parcel of Nagorno-Karabagh ceded to Azerbaijan, the framing of the discussion of the hardships endured by Armenia and Azerbaijan as a result of the conflict in a manner which ignores the tremendous inequality in the levels of suffering endured by the two ethnic groups, the under-reporting of the forced deportations and violence against the Karabagh Armenians, and the disproportionate attention given to Karabagh Armenian offensives in Lachin, Kelbajar, and other areas of Azerbaijan while Azerbaijani aggression against the Republic of Armenia has rarely been mentioned, and then only in passing. By largely ignoring the history of the conflict and the fundamental issue underlying it – the right of the Karabagh Armenian majority to define its destiny by exercising its collective right to self-determination – the media have obscured the facts and reduced the conflict to one of parity between warring ethnic groups: in other words, to yet another sad, inscrutable case of senseless ethnic bloodshed.[91]

In their analysis of the current situation in Nagorno-Karabagh, Baroness Cox and John Eibner conclude that there has been a tremendous asymmetry of violence in the struggle for the territory, and that the primary victims are the Armenians of Nagorno-Karabagh. While making it clear that the Karabagh Armenians are not beyond reproach and accepting that they have contributed to the toll of human suffering, Cox and Eibner nevertheless argue forcefully that Azerbaijan is the primary aggressor and cite five reasons for their conclusion:

1 Azerbaijan and the Soviet 4th Army carried out the brutal deportations of Armenians from Nagorno-Karabagh and the Shahumian District.

2 Azerbaijan has imposed economic blockades on both Armenia and Nagorno-Karabagh.

3 Azerbaijan initiated the use of GRAD rocket launchers, which greatly escalated the level of civilian casualties and destroyed housing, hospitals, and other essential facilities.

4 Azerbaijan deployed 500 kg and cluster bombs against civilian targets.

5 Azerbaijan is using ground-to-air missiles against civilians in Nagorno-Karabagh.[92]

Cox and Eibner's work was published before the bloodiest phase of the war from 18 December 1993 to early March 1994. Azerbaijani President Aliev announced after his election victory in October that re-taking Karabagh was his first priority. He hardened the Azerbaijani position, rejecting points earlier agreed to, by (1) withdrawing recognition of Karabagh as a negotiating party, (2) stating that the final decision on Karabagh lay with the Azerbaijani parliament and not the Minsk Group, and (3) insisting once again that withdrawal from the Lachin Strip serve as a precondition to a ceasefire and negotiations. Aliev also appealed for military assistance wherever he saw the likelihood of finding it, and he internationalized the conflict by introducing Afghan, Turkish, Ukrainian, and Russian mercenaries. On 18 December 1993, Aliev broke a Russian/Minsk Group initiated ceasefire and launched a major military offensive on all fronts.

The Karabagh Armenian forces are in rugged mountain terrain and are heavily dug in. To dislodge them, the Azerbaijanis need a 10 to 1 ratio of manpower and air support, and they can expect heavy casualties. To deal with these realities, the Azerbaijani offensive has been accompanied by new military tactics and political strategies designed to eliminate weaknesses in Azerbaijani military performance and to undermine the growth of popular opposition to the war. Because in the past Azerbaijani military units have often fled when faced with advancing Armenians, the Azerbaijanis are using so-called punitive units in this offensive. Azerbaijani ground forces are arranged in two parallel lines, and if the front unit seeks to retreat, its members are shot by the rear unit. Politically Azerbaijan has sought to reduce the impact of battlefield deaths by not claiming their dead and leaving them to be buried by the Armenians. This allows the government to create the false, but useful, impression that these dead soldiers are alive on the front, or are captives of the Armenians. Aliev has also ended the last semblance of democracy in Azerbaijan in order to intimidate any opposition into silence or to drive it underground. The press is heavily censored, opposition media have been closed, and opposition party activists have been jailed.

The Azerbaijani offensive failed to yield many concrete results for Azerbaijan. Aside from the capture of a few hilltops and villages, Azerbaijan's major victory has been the re-taking of the strategic town of Goradiz on the Azerbaijani–Iranian border. The real news in this offensive is found in the frightful casualty rates. There are reports of between 6,000 and 10,000 Azerbaijani deaths. The figures for the Armenians are 500 to 600, though 1,000 is probably more accurate. That figure breaks down to approximately 700 Karabagh Armenians and 300 from the Republic of Armenia. If these deaths are projected on to the US population during the Vietnam War era, we end up with the equivalent of 19,000 Republic of Armenia deaths, 250,000 Azerbaijani deaths, and over 1 million Karabagh Armenian deaths in a period of less than three months.[93]

Azerbaijan may not be able to sustain this level of casualties politically, and the Karabagh Armenians can certainly not continue to sustain them physically. In January 1994, the government of Nagorno-Karabagh increased the age of conscription from 18–43 to 18–50, and has men in their sixties on active duty. The Karabagh Armenians desperately want and need peace, but they are convinced that being forced back into Azerbaijan is the equivalent of death for their culture and community.

In their quest for peace they have offered Azerbaijan their occupied territories in return for the recognition of Karabagh's independence, but this offer has been spurned repeatedly as Aliev pursues a military victory. If Aliev can avoid a political backlash from continued high casualty rates, the Karabagh Armenians can be worn down, but if a settlement looks to be vindictive or even genocidal, Armenia will be drawn in rather than see the destruction of the Karabagh Armenians. In that instance we will have, instead of a settlement, an expanded war. But all predictions are risky in this situation fraught with ambiguity. Aliev is 71 years old, and no one else in Azerbaijan commands the loyalty he does. In his absence, Azerbaijan could once again fall prey to political disorder and even civil war. Nor can a coup in Armenia be ruled out entirely. And we must also consider the growing constituencies of ultra-nationalist forces in Turkey and Russia.

Whatever the short- and long-term outcomes, Donabedian and Mutafian have made a major contribution, providing the first complete English-language history of Nagorno-Karabagh. Their work places the struggle of the territory and its people squarely as one of the century's true, legitimate struggles for human rights and self-determination. This is an approach very much in keeping with the times, in which the old rulers and old frameworks have been cast aside. The Cold War is over, the Soviet Union is no more, and the Soviet minorities have stood on their feet and claimed the recognition they deserve. While too many journalists and foreign policy specialists in the West continue to be guided by Russocentrism and the ideological, political, and economic agendas of Turkey and the short-term benefits they feel the West can derive, this study stands as an important addition to a new and slowly evolving understanding of Nagorno-Karabagh and the larger Armenian question, one free of past encumbrances.

NOTES

1. Ronald Suny, *Armenia in the Twentieth Century* (Chico, California, 1983), p. 80.
2. The official Soviet viewpoint on nationalities is found in E. Bagramov, *The CPSU's Nationalities Policy* (Moscow, 1988).
3. Caroline Cox and John Eibner, *Ethnic Cleansing in Progress: War in Nagorno-Karabakh* (Zürich, London and Washington, 1993), p. 6. See also Celestine Bohlen, 'Blockade and Winter Deepen Misery in Armenia', *New York Times*, 7 February 1993, section 1, pp. 4, 12.
4. Cox and Eibner, *op. cit.*, p. 4. Catherine Bertini of the UN's World Food Programme describes the population of Armenia as 'extremely vulnerable' and 'on the verge of famine'. *Monthly Digest of News from Armenia* (Washington, DC, February 1994), p. 40. In its more prosaic language, the IMF writes of Armenia that 'it is clear that most of the population is experiencing severe hardship'. *Economic Review: Armenia* (Washington, DC, 1993), pp. 2–3.
5. The original version appeared as *Le Karabagh: une terre arménienne en Azerbaïdjan* (Paris, 1989) and the expanded version translated here by Levon Chorbajian was published as *Artsakh: Histoire du Karabagh* (Paris, 1991).
6. Robert Hewson, 'The Meliks of Eastern Armenia', *Revue des Etudes Arméniennes*. Part I, vol. IX, 1972; part II, vol. X, 1973–1974; part IV, vol. XIV, 1980.
7. Louise Nalbandian, *The Armenian Revolutionary Movement: The Development of*

Armenian Political Parties through the Nineteenth Century (Berkeley and Los Angeles, 1963).

8. In the light of the fact that the Turkish state continues to deny that a genocide was committed against the Armenian people and goes so far as to promote revisionist histories to deny it, it is useful to reference at least a portion of the work documenting the genocide. Permanent People's Tribunal, *A Crime of Silence: The Armenian Genocide* (London, 1985); Vahakn N. Dadrian, 'Genocide as a Problem of National and International Law: The World War I Armenian Case and Its Contemporary Legal Ramifications', *Yale Journal of International Law*, vol. 14, no. 2, summer 1989, pp. 221–334; Vahakn N. Dadrian, 'The Naim–Andonian Documents on the World War I Destruction of Ottoman Armenians: The Anatomy of a Genocide', *International Journal of Middle East Studies*, vol. 18, 1986, pp. 311–360; Leslie A. Davis, *The Slaughterhouse Province: An American Diplomat's Report on the Armenian Genocide, 1915–1917* (New Rochelle, NY, 1989); and Levon Marashlian, *Politics and Demography: Armenians, Turks, and Kurds in the Ottoman Empire* (Cambridge, Massachusetts, Toronto and Paris, 1991). Richard Hovannisian's *The Armenian Holocaust: A Bibliography Relating to the Deportations, Massacres and Dispersion of the Armenian People, 1915–1923* (Cambridge, Massachusetts, 1981) remains a useful source. Three recent studies break new ground: Raymond H. Kevorkian and Paul B. Paboudjian, *Les Arméniens dans l'Empire ottoman à la veille du génocide* (Paris, 1992) is a documented compilation of Armenian communities in Anatolia on the eve of the 1915 genocide, Donald E. Miller and Lorna Touryan Miller, *Survivors: An Oral History of the Armenian Genocide* (Berkeley and Los Angeles, 1993) is based on lengthy interviews with genocide survivors, and Vahakn N. Dadrian's *Documentation of the Armenian Genocide in German and Austrian Sources* (New Brunswick, NJ, 1994) compiles a large body of archival material.

9. Edmund M. Herzig, 'Armenians' in Graham Smith, ed., *The Nationalities Question in the Soviet Union* (London and New York, 1990), p. 148.

10. Shireen L. Hunter, 'Azerbaijan: Search for Industry and New Partners' in Ian Bremmer and Ray Taras, eds, *Nation and Politics in Soviet Successor States* (Cambridge, 1993), p. 251.

11. Issues which should be added to those already noted include de-Russification; economic, cultural, linguistic, and educational autonomy; international recognition of the genocide; the right to veto central government projects; the creation of separate Armenian military detachments; the depletion of the waters of Lake Sevan; and the right to display the tricolour flag of the 1918–1920 Republic of Armenia.

12. Nora Dudwick, 'The Karabagh Movement: An Old Scenario Gets Rewritten', *The Armenian Review*, vol. 42, no. 3/167, 1989, p. 67.

13. *Ibid.*, p. 67.

14. Nora Dudwick, 'Moments That Will Live Forever: The First Year of the Karabagh Movement', paper presented at the Karabagh/Artsakh Conference, Columbia University, New York, 11 February 1989, p. 4.

15. *Ibid.*, p. 9.

16. Pierre Verluise, *Arménie: La Fracture* (Paris, 1989).

17. The newspapers consulted were *The New York Times, The Washington Post, The Los Angeles Times, The Boston Globe,* and *The Christian Science Monitor.*

18. Levon Chorbajian, 'Karabagh and the US Media', paper presented at the meetings of the International Association of Mass Communications Research, Bled,

Yugoslavia, August 1990. As an example of errors in reporting, the US papers noted on several occasions that the transfer of a territory from one republic to another was without precedent in the Soviet Union when in fact there had been numerous changes. It was only in a British paper that one could discover that 'there is a precedent: the Crimea was transferred from Russian to Ukrainian jurisdiction in 1954' (Angus Roxburgh, 'Gorbachev in Desperate Dash to Resolve Armenian Crisis', *The Sunday Times*, 6 March 1988). It was also in the British press that we found the lone instance of media advocacy of the reunification of Karabagh with Armenia: see 'Gorbachev's Armenian Dilemma', *The Independent*, 26 February 1988.

19. The media frequently employ religious reductionism for the presentation of long-standing and nuanced territorial disputes. Consider the cases of Israelis and Palestinians in the Middle East and Protestants and Catholics in Northern Ireland.

20. Elizabeth Fuller, 'The Azerbaijanis in Georgia and the Ingilos: Ethnic Minorities in the Limelight', *Central Asian Survey*, vol. 3, no. 2, 1984, pp. 75–85.

21. Leslie Davis, *op. cit.*, pp. 58, 82, 175–176.

22. Shireen Hunter, *op. cit.*, pp. 248–249.

23. Tamara Dragadze, 'Azerbaijanis' in Smith, *op. cit.*, p. 163. In its extreme version the claim is made that the Sumerians, Chaldeans, Iranian Parthians, Kurds, and Medes were Turkic. See Shireen Hunter, *op. cit.*, p. 234. Many scholars discount such claims and argue that large numbers of Turkic peoples settled in the eastern lowland portions of the Transcaucasian isthmus only in the eleventh century AD See Tadeusz Swietochowski, *Russian Azerbaijan, 1905–1920* (Cambridge, 1985), p. 1 and Audrey Altstadt, *The Azerbaijani Turks* (Stanford, 1992), p. 7. The view of Azerbaijani historians that Nagorno-Karabagh is Azerbaijani land is not unanimous. For a revealing dissenting view, see George Bournoutiani, *A History of Qarabagh: An Annotated Translation of Mirza Jamal Javanshir Qarabagh's Tarikh-e Qarabagh* (Costa Mesa, CA, 1994).

24. Dragadze, *op. cit.*, p. 164 and Altstadt, *op. cit.*, pp. xi, 2–6.

25. Altstadt, *op. cit.*, p. 196. This issue is addressed by Donabedian and Mutafian in their text.

26. *Ibid.*, pp. 100, 196.

27. *Ibid.*, p. 208.

28. Dragadze, *op. cit.*, p. 174.

29. Altstadt, *op. cit.*, pp. 127 and 199. Altstadt warns of the risks of relying on Soviet statistics, but she goes on to provide comparative indicators of social development for Azerbaijan, Armenia, Nagorno-Karabagh, and the Soviet Union on such items as hospital beds, libraries, and apartments, etc. per 100,000 population. According to Altstadt's figures, Nagorno-Karabagh ranked higher than Azerbaijan on eight dimensions, Armenia on seven, and the Soviet Union on five. Altstadt, p. 199.

30. *Ibid.*, pp. 125–128 and 199. Altstadt's position fails to explain why the Armenian population in Nagorno-Karabagh declined as a percentage of the region's total throughout the entire period of Azerbaijani control and especially from 1940 up to the beginning of the current crisis in the late 1980s.

31. It should be noted that many of these Azerbaijani luminaries are from Ganja – part of historic Artsakh, but not part of Nagorno-Karabagh.

32. The Armenian government has also pressured Karabagh to accept CSCE ceasefire proposals which fell short of providing international monitors to prevent Azerbaijani aggression. Yerevan also urged the Karabagh Armenians not to take the city of Aghdam or expand their gains to the Iranian border. For their part, the Karabagh Armenians ignored pressures from the Republic of Armenia to curb their

offensives in the summer and fall of 1993. Behind these refusals stand the history of major power duplicity in the fateful years after the First World War and the inability of any major power (although the Russians have been moving in this direction) to commit troops to guarantee a ceasefire.

33. *The Military Balance, 1993–1994* (London, 1993), pp. 71–73.
34. *The Military Balance* (1992–1993), (London, 1992), p. 59.
35. GRAD missile launchers deploy 40 missiles at a time. The weapon takes its name from the Russian word for hail.
36. 'Police Kill 6 Protesters in Azerbaijan', *Boston Globe*, 7 March 1993, p. 17 and 'Unwilling Recruits', *AIM*, vol. 4, no. 4, April/May, 1993, p. 12. In south-eastern Azerbaijan on the Iranian border, a short-lived Talish-Mughan Autonomous Republic was declared in August 1993. In a neighbouring conflict, the Russians backed Abkhazian separatist forces in Georgia to discipline the independent-minded government of Eduard Shevardnadze to the point where a desperate Shevardnadze had to accept Georgian membership in the CIS. He had earlier vowed that Georgia would forge its own path outside of the Commonwealth.
37. 'Ex-Kremlin Figure Returns to Power in Azerbaijan', *New York Times*, 16 June 1993, p. A14.
38. Armenia is considered in this section for the same reasons it was presented in the military section.
39. *Economic Review: Armenia* (Washington, DC, 1992), p. 2.
40. Armenia does have coal deposits, but extracting them would involve considerable deforestation in what few forests the country possesses. Alternative underground coal gasification technologies are prohibitively expensive. Similarly, expansion of hydroelectric capacity is very time-consuming employing local technologies, and prohibitively expensive using imported ones. *Ibid.*, p. 49. See also John Tedstrom, 'Armenia: An Energy Profile,' *Report on the USSR*, 21 February 1991, pp. 18–20.
41. *Economic Review: Armenia* (1992), *op. cit.*, p. 2. Desperation caused by the effectiveness of the Azerbaijani blockade has led the Armenian government to consider re-activating its nuclear plant despite the risks and start-up costs estimated at US$15 million. International assistance in upgrading the plant has been obtained, and there are plans to re-open the plant during 1995.
42. *Ibid*, p. 48.
43. *Ibid.*, p. 6. The cost of the economic blockade is estimated to have cost Armenian industry 800 million roubles in 1991, the equivalent of 6.5 per cent of the country's NMP. *Ibid.*, pp. 4, 6. The IMF estimates a further drop in GNP of 50 per cent for 1992. *Economic Review: Armenia* (Washington, D.C., 1993), pp. 2–3.
44. Carolann S. Najarian, 'When Artsakh Is Free, It Will Be a Great Victory over Injustice', *Armenian Mirror Spectator*, 24 April 1993, p. 7.
45. This opposition is based on three types of grievance: economic hardship, opposition to what some see as President Ter Petrosian's conciliatory policies towards Turkey, and opposition to the government's insistence that the question of Nagorno-Karabagh is a dispute between Baku and the Karabagh Armenians. The latter two positions are seen as a sell-out by nationalist forces.
46. See Tigran Xmalian, 'The Gridlock: Yerevan's Inability to Govern', *AIM*, vol. 4, no. 3, March 1993, pp. 10–11.
47. *Economic Review: Azerbaijan* (Washington, DC, 1992), p. 71.
48. *Ibid.*, p. 3.
49. *Ibid.*, pp. 14, 18.
50. *Ibid.*, p. 15.

51. *Economic Review: Azerbaijan* (Washington, D.C., 1993), pp. 29–31. These revenues enable Azerbaijan to purchase the services of mercenaries from Afghanistan, the Ukraine and Russia, and weapons from China, Israel and the Ukraine.

52. *Economic Review: Azerbaijan* (1992), *op. cit.*, pp. 14–16. Corporations which have signed or have been pursuing deals are Amoco, Apache, Chevron, McDermott, Pennzoil and Unical (US); British Petroleum; Ramco (Scottish); Statoil (Norwegian); and Turkish Petroleum.

53. *Ibid.*, p. 53; *Economic Review: Armenia* (1992) *op. cit.*, p. 25.

54. Dragadze, *op. cit.*, pp. 169–170; Smith, *op. cit.*, p. 371.

55. Altstadt, *op. cit.*, p. 208.

56. Dragadze, *op. cit.*, pp. 168–169.

57. *Economic Review: Azerbaijan* (1992), *op. cit.*, p. 9.

58. The settlement of large numbers of Russians in the minority republics and the deportation of minorities to Central Asia and Siberia also sowed the seeds of later conflicts.

59. See Ronald Suny, 'The Revenge of the Past: Socialism and Ethnic Conflict in Transcaucasia', *New Left Review*, no. 184, October–November 1990, pp. 5–34 for a superb discussion of these issues.

60. Bagramov, *op. cit.*, *passim*.

61. Bremmer and Taras, *op. cit.* pp. 11–12; Alexander J. Motyl, *Sovietology, Rationality, Nationality: Coming to Grips with Nationalism in the USSR* (New York, 1990), Chapter 1. In making this point, we must acknowledge, nonetheless, the political use of Soviet minorities as a means of highlighting the 'failure' of Soviet nationality policy as well as the activities of Western national security agencies in funding dissident national exile groups, targeting national populations for print and electronic media, training leadership cadres, funding guerrilla movements, and the like.

62. See Motyl, *op. cit.*, as an exception.

63. Henry Morgenthau, *Secrets of the Bosphorus: Constantinople, 1913–1916* (London, 1919); Arnold Toynbee, *The Treatment of Armenians in the Ottoman Empire* (London, 1916).

64. Turkey received nearly $8 billion in US military aid during the period 1946–1985, ranking fourth among recipients and third for the period 1984–1990. 'Turkey in the Age of Glasnost', *Middle East Report*, September–October 1989, vol. 19, no. 5, p. 24.

65. Lewis Thomas and Richard Frye, *The United States and Turkey and Iran* (Cambridge, Massachusetts, 1951), p. 8.

66. Vol. II, *Reform, Revolution, and Republic: The Rise of Modern Turkey, 1808–1975* (New York, 1977), pp. 315–316. See note 8 for a refutation.

67. Chorbajian, *op. cit.*

68. Paul Quinn-Judge, 'Rumbles in Soviet Armenia', *The Christian Science Monitor*, 6 June 1988.

69. The British press, despite shortcomings, was much more willing to take positions which would be contrary to the desires of NATO ally Turkey than the US newspapers. 'Gorbachev's Armenian Dilemma', *The Independent*, 26 February 1988, advocated that Armenian demands for Nagorno-Karabagh's union with the Armenian SSR be met in the name of justice. For other examples of reporting on Nagorno-Karabagh which runs against the current in the US press, see Mary Ellen Bortin, 'Moscow Says Final "No" to Redrawing Soviet Borders', *The Independent*, 24 March 1988; Andrew Wilson, 'Gorbachev Faces Ethnic Chernobyl', *The*

Observer, 27 March 1988; Norman Davies, 'Soviet Empire and Colonial Ingratitude', *The Independent*, 7 April, 1988; and Tim Kelsay, 'Turks Tread Softly on Treaty Rights to Intervene in Soviet Conflict', *The Independent*, 22 March 1988.

70. Cox and Eibner, *op. cit.*, pp. 56–58.

71. *Ibid.*, p. 58.

72. Paul Goble, 'Coping with the Nagorno-Karabagh Crisis', *The Fletcher Forum of World Affairs*, vol. 16, no. 2, summer 1992, p. 26.

73. Dilip Hiro, 'The Question of Azerbaijan', *The Nation*, vol. 255, no. 7, 14 September 1992, p. 243.

74. Aside from interests based on alliances, it is worth noting that the US, Britain, Turkey, Iran, and Russia all face threats of greater or lesser proportion from national minorities of their own, some of whom seek autonomy or even national independence – the US from Native Americans, Afro-Americans, and Puerto Ricans; Britain in Northern Ireland, Wales, and Scotland; Turkey and Iran from the Kurds; and Russia from a large number of groups who have only begun to mobilize around such issues as language rights, taxation, investment policy, environmental integrity, conscription, and the control of timber, mineral, energy, and water resources. An insistence on territorial integrity (that is, that Azerbaijan should keep Nagorno-Karabakh) therefore contributes to the ideological repertoire of the US, Britain, and the regional powers for the maintenance of their putative turf against the claims of minorities.

75. The Clinton administration's foreign aid reform bill submitted to Congress in February 1994 seeks a repeal of the ban.

76. Although there have been proposals to run the pipeline from Azerbaijan through Georgia to the Black Sea or via Iran to Turkey or the Persian Gulf, the Armenian route to Turkey and the Mediterranean is both the most direct and the least expensive to construct.

77. Armenian Russophilia, born of isolation and vulnerability, has not always been rewarded. Often at key junctures, the Russians have preferred to court the Turks, Azerbaijanis, and others at Armenian expense, knowing the Armenians had nowhere else to go.

78. Ronald Suny, 'The New Safety Net: Russia Redefines Its Terms of Hegemony,' *AIM*, December 1993, pp. 21–22 and Jon Auerbach, 'Russia Tightening Its Grip on Former Republics', *Boston Globe*, 6 December 1993, pp. 1, 13.

79. Andrei Sakharov, *Moscow and Beyond, 1986–1989* (London, 1990), p. 49.

80. At the same time that Aliev has made concessions to the Russians and courted them, he is wary of their presence. He has refused to allow Russian troops to be stationed on the Azerbaijani–Iranian border and in the conflict zone between Karabagh Armenian and Azerbaijani forces.

81. 'Turkey Warned in Enclave', *Boston Globe*, 21 May 1992, p. 2.

82. 'Fascist Grey Wolves Spearhead Attack Against Armenians in Artsakh', *Armenian Mirror Spectator*, 25 July 1992, p. 1; 'Ankara Promises to Assist Turkish Republics and Train Their Armies', *Armenian Mirror Spectator*, 11 January 1992, pp. 1, 16; and 'Turkish Mercenaries in Artsakh', *Armenian Mirror Spectator*, 11 April 1992, pp. 12–13.

83. Turkish Prime Minister Tansu Ciller threatened Armenia with an immediate invasion if the Armenians intervened in Azerbaijan's western province of Nakhichevan. Armenia has no intention of launching such an invasion and would be mad to do so. Ciller's threat, therefore, should be seen for what it is: namely, posturing for the domestic audience.

84. The Minsk Group members are Belarus, the Czech Republic, France, Germany, Italy, Russia, Sweden, Turkey, and the US.
85. The proposal would have failed in any case since Azerbaijan was in the midst of the coup which brough Aliev to power.
86. Cox and Eibner, *op. cit.*, p. 41.
87. 'Report of an International Delegation from the First International Andrei Sakharov Memorial Congress to Armenia and Azerbaijan', 25–31 May 1991, unpublished manuscript. Delegates were from Great Britain, Japan, Norway, the USA, and the USSR. *See also* Cox and Eibner, *op. cit.*, pp. 46–48.
88. Cox and Eibner, *op. cit.*, pp. 48–50.
89. Daniel Sneider, 'Karabagh Residents Hunker Down for War', *The Christian Science Monitor*, 16 March 1992, p. 6.
90. 'Unspeakable Fate for Armenians If Artsakh Falls', *Armenian Mirror Spectator*, 29 February 1992, p. 6.
91. We note that self-determination, long championed – albeit selectively by many – as a hallmark of international justice, is now under attack. See Amitai Etzioni's ode to the haves over the have-nots in which he writes, 'Self-determination struggles ... have largely exhausted their legitimacy as a means to create more strongly democratic states.' Amitai Etzioni, 'The Evils of Self-Determination', *Foreign Policy*, no. 89, winter 1992–1993, pp. 21–35.
92. Cox and Eibner, *op. cit.*, pp. 66–67.
93. These figures are based on the following numbers: a US population of 220 million and 55,000 deaths, an Azerbaijani population of 7 million and 8,000 deaths, an Armenian population of 3.5 million and 300 deaths, and a Karabagh Armenian population of 150,000 and 700 deaths.

2
INTRODUCTION

Patrick Donabedian & Claude Mutafian

'Is Armenia burning?' That was the headline in a Parisian daily in the spring of 1988. This Soviet republic, the sole remnant of historic Armenia, was the scene of a major first in the USSR: hundreds of thousands of demonstrators putting forward a series of ecological, cultural, and national demands in a country which claimed to have peacefully and definitively resolved the question of nationalities. This was an extraordinary awakening, facilitated, of course, by the Gorbachev reforms. But it was an awakening accompanied by anti-Armenian pogroms, hypocritically labelled in the USSR, as in the West, as 'inter-ethnic conflicts'. Carried out by the Azerbaijani Turks, these pogroms revived the spectre of the genocide of 1915 which had eliminated the major part of Armenia from the map. Just before the horrifying earthquake of December 1988, they provoked a dual wave of emigration: Armenians driven out of Azerbaijan and Azerbaijanis fleeing Armenia.

Why was there this sudden outburst? One of the reasons is a small territory, nearly the size of the state of Delaware, whose name was unknown to the general public until it was displayed in the newspapers: Karabagh. This Turkish name ('the black garden') designates a region administered by a Turkish Soviet Republic (Azerbaijan). But the population, 80 per cent Armenian in the mountainous zone (Mountainous Karabagh), reminds us that it was part of the ancient Armenian province of Artsakh. Subjugated to Turkish khans in the service of Persia in the eighteenth century, integrated into the Russian Empire in the nineteenth century and, finally and arbitrarily, attached by Moscow to Azerbaijan in 1921, Mountainous Karabagh never ceased seeking its reunification with Armenia. While the Turks and Persians, from the west and east, deployed their substantial forces to subjugate and liquidate the Armenian presence, the Armenian *montagnards* fought fiercely for centuries to protect this fortress, a national bastion rich in tradition and heroic deeds.

Why such intense and relentless conflict over a small mountainous area? In fact, the problem should be posed in a number of contexts: Turkish–Armenian (Pan-Turkic plans to destroy the whole of Armenia), Azeri–Armenian (the forced co-existence of two peoples who have never been allowed to settle their border disputes independently), Islamic–Christian (religious opposition, in principle secondary, but easily stirred up), Turkish–Soviet (the border between the USSR and NATO member Turkey, which is linguistically linked to Azerbaijan), and Iranian–Soviet (Iran being Shiite, as are the Azerbaijanis, and also sharing a border with the Soviet Union). To this we must add the internal Soviet dimension. Until recently a centralized state ('the last empire'), it has collapsed, its decay accelerated by demands for autonomy and then independence by the republics, long-standing national resentments and innumerable ecological, economic, social and demographic problems.

Aggravated by a chain of emigrations and violence, the problem of Mountainous Karabagh was further intensified by a surge of nationalism as the republics of the Soviet Union began to search for sovereign status. Yet when the problem came out into the open in 1988, it was posed in political terms: the population of a region, in theory autonomous, but in reality stifled for seventy years, formulated a demand for self-determination conforming to the constitution, the new Gorbachevian spirit, and prevailing international standards. Against this demand, the trustee republic (Azerbaijan) asserted the pre-eminence of its rights over the territory, which it also presented as a national sanctuary. To itemize its refusal and to negate the rights of the indigenous population, it has gone so far as to rewrite history. In the pages that follow, readers will see for themselves how questions of ethnic origin and ancient and medieval history have transcended the bounds of academic dispute and become charged with nationalist passions and weighed down by a climate of intolerance and hostility.

The Karabagh crisis reveals the deep conflicts which tore at the Soviet empire, but also a certain ongoing colonialist trait of the regime. In effect, rather than settling the dispute while there was still time, the central government – by its indecision, procrastination and, probably, its provocation – allowed the situation to deteriorate. The government continued to be directed by imperialist attitudes. It failed to deploy force to protect civilian populations, and instead acted, first, to impose an arbitrary order which could only exacerbate tensions and, second, to safeguard its vital interests when it felt them to be seriously threatened. It favoured, as much from incompetence as from Machiavellianism, what has recently been referred to as the 'Lebanonization' of the region. Was it not to neutralize aspirations towards autonomy and democracy, seen to be dangerous, and to justify their presence, that Soviet rulers encouraged the misrepresentation of a political demand as an inter-ethnic conflict?

Today, events follow an impetuous course, highly unpredictable and changing before we can offer an interpretation. The past lends itself better to analysis. Some say that everything began in February 1988. But was this explosion unforeseen and fortuitous? As we will see, that is not the case. The turbulent history of Karabagh reveals the roots of problems and allows us better to understand the unchaining of passions.

3

THE HISTORY OF KARABAGH FROM ANTIQUITY TO THE TWENTIETH CENTURY

Patrick Donabedian

Karabagh and Mountainous Karabagh

The 'Autonomous Region of Mountainous Karabagh' (4,388 square kilometres) occupies only one part, essentially the mountainous part, of a region of Transcaucasia known as Karabagh since the fourteenth century.[1] The Azeri, that is to say the eastern Turkish, pronunciation, like the Armenian, is 'Gharabagh'. This name seems to refer to the fertility of the land, favourable to the cultivation of fruit despite the altitude of the mountainous section: *kara* means black and *bagh* garden or vineyard.[2] The name was applied initially to two ancient north-eastern provinces of historic Armenia, Artsakh (also called Tsavdek in the early Middle Ages, and later, Khachen) and Utik (Otena). These provinces stretched between Lake Sevan to the north-west, the Kura (Kur, Cyrus) River to the north, and the Arax (Araxes) River to the south, and were part of the Kingdom of Greater Armenia until the beginning of the fifth century.[3] They then became part of the Persian province of Arran or Albania, and were successively occupied by Arabs, Seljuk Turks, Mongols, Turkmens, Ottoman Turks, Safavid Persians, and the Russians.

The geographical area of Karabagh was reduced over time, and in the modern period it only corresponds to the ancient province of Artsakh (about 10,000 square kilometres). The present Autonomous Region of Mountainous Karabagh corresponds to the western portion of ancient Karabagh, including a portion of the upper course of the Tartar (or Terter or Trtu) River and the mountains further to the south. The lower south-eastern part (the Plain of Mil or Mughan), which is next to the lowlands on the right bank of the Kura River at an angle formed by the confluence of the Kura and the Arax, is sometimes called the Karabagh Plain or (since the turn of the century) Lower Karabagh. Since 1920 some have invoked an alleged natural economic tie unifying upper and lower Karabagh.[4] In reality, there is a much more obvious link between the mountainous region of Karabagh and the Armenian Plateau of which it is the eastern extremity. This mountainous area, with an average altitude of 1,300 metres, includes the present area of the Autonomous Region but also the lands which are contiguous to the west and north-west – that is to say, the following districts of the Republic of Azerbaijan: Lachin, Kelbajar, Kedabek (Gedabek), Dashkesan, Shahumian and (a portion of) Khanlar. On the contrary, the area extending further to the east is geographically different: it is made up of plains and steppes which descend towards the Caspian Sea.

This region is inhabited, essentially, by Armenians, Kurds, and Turks. The Armenian population is in the majority in the principal zone of the mountainous region (that is to say in the Autonomous Region of Mountainous Karabagh) and, until 1988, in the neighbouring districts in the north, sometimes called Upper Gandzak. The 1989 census indicates that in the Autonomous Region of Mountainous Karabagh, 158,000 of the 188,000 inhabitants are Armenian. They speak an eastern dialect of Armenian. The Kurds are established in the lowlands of the east and in the Lachin Strip separating the Republic of Armenia and the Autonomous Region of Mountainous Karabagh. They are no longer enumerated in the statistics of the Republic of Azerbaijan, but they are still numerous. Finally the Turks, referred to according to the epoch (we will see why later) as Caucasian Tatars or Azerbaijanis (Azeris), are centred in the lower northern and eastern zones and speak a Turkic language called Azeri.

Besides foreign domination, up until the Russian conquest in the nineteenth century the population of Mountainous Karabagh was under the authority of the local nobility: Armenian (or Armenian–Albanian) princes from the end of antiquity to the Middle Ages, Armenian *meliks* from the sixteenth to the nineteenth centuries and Turkish khans from the mid-eighteenth century to the start of the nineteenth.

The Eastern Provinces of Armenia until the Fifth Century

The first historical evidence concerning this region of Transcaucasia dates from the Urartian epoch (ninth to sixth centuries BC). The province of Urtekhe or Urtekhini,[5] situated at the western extreme of the future Artsakh, south-east of Lake Sevan, was part of the territories conquered in the eighth century BC by the Urartian king Sarduri II (760–735 BC). He had extended the frontiers of the kingdom from his capital of Tushpa or Van in western Armenia to Transcaucasian Armenia. We can recognize in the name Urtekhe the prototype of the Armenian name Artsakh and possibly also of the name Orkhistene given by the Greek geographer Strabo.[6] After the fall of Urartu (sixth century BC), the region came under the domination of the Medes and Achaemenian Persians.

The historian Movses Khorenatsi (an Armenian source from the fifth century AD according to some, and the eighth century AD, according to others) indicated that the province of Utik (along with Artsakh with which it was contiguous on the south) was part of the Armenian Kingdom of the Ervandunis (or Orontids) between the fourth and second centuries BC.[7] Certain authors estimate that when King Artashes (189–160 BC) brought about the unification of the Kingdom of Greater Armenia, Caucasian tribes, probably Albanians, living in Artsakh and Utik were brought in by force.[8] This thesis is said to be based on Strabo, but, in reality, when he describes the conquests Artashes carried out at the expense of the Medes and Iberians – and not the Albanians – he says nothing of Artsakh and Utik, since these provinces were certainly already a part of Armenia.

Be that as it may, the same Strabo attests that by the second or first century BC the entire population of Greater Armenia (Artsakh and Utik included) spoke Armenian.[9] This homogeneity is confirmed by archaeological finds: excavations carried out between Lake Sevan and the Kura River have brought to light an ancient culture characterized by its 'jar burials' (at the end of the first millennium BC) which practised the traditions of the Armenian plateau and was distinguished from the culture called Yaloylu Tepe in Caucasian Albania on the north bank of the Kura.[10] Strabo reports, moreover, that these eastern regions were wealthy and militarily powerful, since they furnished the Armenian kings with a large cavalry force.

The seventh-century AD Armenian atlas *Ashkharhatsuïts* cites Artsakh as the tenth province of Greater Armenia and Utik as the twelfth province, and notes their princes (the princes of Gardman, Utik, Second Siunik, and Tsavdek) on lists of nobles and military figures of the Armenian court.[11] The seventh-century Armenian historian Sebeos attests that there were two cities with the name Tigranocerta (Tigranakert) which were founded by the Armenian King Tigran (Tigranes) II (95–55 BC), one in Artsakh and one in Utik.[12] Speaking of the third century AD, the fifth-century Armenian author Agathangelos specifies that the Armenian kings had a winter residence at Khaghkhagh in Utik.[13] Converted to Christianity, as was the rest of the country, at the beginning of the fourth century, the eastern provinces of Artsakh and Utik remained a part of the Armenian Kingdom until its fall in 428 AD.[14] As reported by pseudo-P'awstos Buzand, as a result of victories by the Persian King Shahpuhr II against Rome at the end of the decade of the 360s, the eastern regions of Armenia were annexed by Albania, then allied with Persia. By virtue of Roman victories at the start of the 370s, however, General Mushegh Mamikonian soon returned these territories to Armenia, then allied with Rome, and restored the Armenian–Albanian frontier at the Kura River.[15]

Before A. Mnatsakanian's clarification of the meaning of the term Albanian, which differs by time period, several authors, including Brosset, Hübschmann,

Marquart, Toumanoff and Trever, transposed to antiquity and the first centuries AD a situation which appeared only after the fall of the Armenian kingdom in 428.[16] They believed that the picture given by the sources after the fifth century in which Artsakh and Utik were in the heart of Albania, could be applied to earlier periods. In fact, as we will see below, numerous historical witnesses invalidate such a conception. Some authors also supposed that the name of the province of Utik, at the eastern extreme of Armenia, was taken from an ethnic group, probably Albanian, the Udi or Uti: a tribe of Udi extraction would have lived on the right bank of the Kura and been Armenianized very early, participating in the ethno-genesis of the Armenian people.[17]

Relying on that, certain historians of the Baku school have tried to show that the territories extending between Lake Sevan and the Kura (which would include Karabagh) have belonged, since antiquity, not to Armenia but to Caucasian Albania – which, in their view, is the ancestor of the Soviet Republic of Azerbaijan.[18] In reality, many ancient Greek and Roman writers (Strabo, first century BC–first century AD; Pliny the Elder, first century AD; Plutarch, first–second century AD; Ptolemy, second century AD; Dio Cassius, second–third century AD) as well as Armenian sources (in particular Agathangelos, Koriun, pseudo-P'awstos Buzand, fifth century; the Gahnamak and Zoranamak documents or the List of Thrones and the Military List, the atlas *Ashkhar-hatsuïts*, seventh century; Movses Khorenatsi) confirm that until the fifth century AD these territories were part of Armenia and that the Kura served as the northern frontier of Armenia and separated it from Caucasian Albania.[19]

The Caucasian Albanian state was established during the second to first centuries BC and, according to Strabo, was made up of 26 tribes. It seems that their language was Ibero–Caucasian. By the end of antiquity, Albania encompassed the area between the Kura, the Caucasus Mountains, and the Caspian Sea. Its capital was Kabala (Kapaghank in Armenian).[20] During the first centuries AD Albania, like Armenia, was governed by an Arsacid (Arshakuni) dynasty, installed by the Persians.[21] The Albanians fiercely resisted the Roman armies, and the country was, it is thought, largely independent until the fifth century AD with the exception of the Caspian shore, which it conceded to the separate Massagetae Kingdom in the third and fourth centuries.[22]

Artsakh and Utik in Albania

The situation of Artsakh and Utik changed after Armenia was partitioned in 385 or 387[23] between the Eastern Roman Empire (soon after the Byzantine Empire) and Persia: the Sasanids put an end to the Armenian Kingdom in 428, and divided Transcaucasia into three new administrative entities. That began a new period in which Artsakh (the future Karabagh) and Utik were politically cut off from Armenia and annexed to another entity. The entire eastern portion of Transcaucasia was reorganized into a province (*marzpanate*) called Arran or Albania (Aghuank or Aghvank in Armenian). This included, between the Kura and the Caucasus, the Kingdom of Albania, the ethnic groups along the Caspian and, between the Arax and Kura Rivers and Lake Sevan, the two territories now detached from Armenia: Artsakh and Utik.[24] It is estimated that this new entity was created, in fact, around the middle of the fifth century: Utik, a royal possession, was probably separated from the Armenian Kingdom with its fall in 428, while Artsakh, a princely possession, would only have been annexed to Albania after the anti-Persian uprising in 451.[25]

The term Albania was now applied to areas further to the south-west. The political formations situated in the east, on the shores of the Caspian Sea (Lupens, Massagetae), broke off and were no longer known as Albania. On the contrary, the Christian Kingdom of Caucasian Albania, which the Persians had tolerated until 461, would continue in the west in what had been part of Armenia, and in the process it would be strongly influenced by the Armenians.[26] Thus the term Albania changes its meaning, becoming purely geographical and taking over a part of Armenia. It is this transformation which the author of *Ashkharhatsuïts* (seventh century) had in mind. He specifies that Artsakh and Utik are 'now detached from Armenia and included in Albania', and he takes care to distinguish this new entity from the old 'Albania, strictly speaking', situated north of the Kura.[27] Summarizing these changes, Anasian writes that after the partition of Armenia, half of what is supposed to be Albania, land or population, represents Armenia, Armenians, and Armenianness. It is this major fact and determinant which, up to the present, has escaped the specialists or been disregarded by them.[28]

In this new Albania, the provinces of Artsakh and Utik played a major role. Moreover, it was to Utik, at Partav, that the Albanian capital was transferred around the start of the sixth century (according to A. Akopian). A winter residence of the Armenian kings in Utik was now designated to serve the same function for the King of Albania.[29] Probably because it was more homogeneous than the tribes living north of the Kura, the Armenian element was progressively able to impose its language and culture.[30]

The Descendants of Arran

During the epoch of the Vardanians (mid-fifth century AD), Armenia and the rest of Transcaucasia were faced with a Persian Sasanid offensive which sought assimilation and *mazda*-ization. Albania was an active force in this struggle and contributed its cavalry forces and a rear base for Armenian troops: its king,

Vache, won fame by opposing the kings of the eastern regions – Lupens, Massagetae, and Balasakan, who fought the Armenians – before abdicating. According to the historian B. Ulubabian, he was a member of the Arranshahik line.[31] We recall that at the beginning of our era the Persians established the Arsacid dynasty in Albania, but alongside it there existed, it seems, local Armenian princes from an old family which would later be called Arranshahik (or Erranshahik). This family constitutes one of the longest dynasties in Transcaucasia.[32] According to a legendary tradition reported by Movses Khorenatsi, the eponymous founder of this dynasty, Arran, was a descendant of Sisak, the ancestor of the Siunids, himself the grandson of the ancestral eponym of the Armenians, Hayk. The first Arsacid king of Armenia, Vagharshak, entrusted to Arran the responsibility for the north-east extremity of the kingdom, and it is from him that the great princely families of these regions would descend.[33] The name Arran came under Persian influence to become Arranshahik ('little king of Arran').[34] It was found in the name of several districts of Artsakh and Utik. According to B. Ulubabian, it designated at one time the territory of the two provinces.[35] From the fifth century the Persians and the Arabs applied it to all of eastern Transcaucasia, extending its range to the north-east, the opposite of Albania which shifted to the south-west. In the passage from Movses Khorenatsi cited above (note 33) an Armenian etymology is attributed to the Armenian name Aghuank (Aghvank) of Albania. This is one of the pieces of evidence proving that after the fifth century there was an identification between the Armenian provinces of Artsakh-Utik and the name Albania-Aghuank which covered them.[36]

Following Vache, who resisted the Persians but was forced to surrender his crown in 451 AD and enter the Church, another famous figure appeared, one who is equally considered an Arranshahik: his nephew Vachagan the Pious.[37] Vachagan was able to take advantage of the weakening of Sasanid authority to restore, at the end of the fifth and the beginning of the sixth centuries, the Kingdom of Western Albania on the territories of Artsakh and Utik, as well as on a section of the northern bank of the Kura River.[38] His reign was one of rapid expansion. Vachagan opened numerous schools and wrote a code of laws. He brought holy relics from Etchmiadzin and, according to the historian Movses Daskhurantsi, he built as many churches as there were days in a year.[39] Many of them served as centres for large monastic complexes which endured throughout the Middle Ages.

Church and Language in Albania

Albania was converted to Christianity at the start of the fourth century by the Armenian evangelizer St Gregory the Illuminator who named a certain

Thomas of Satala bishop.[40] In about 330, the grandson of St Gregory, Grigoris, head of the eastern provinces of Armenia, was in turn designated bishop for the Kingdom of Albania. He met his death while proselytizing the extreme north-east of this country near Derbend (Darband, Derbent in the present-day Daghestan) in 338, and his body was brought back to Artsakh. The mausoleum which was dedicated to him stands as the oldest dated monument in Mountainous Karabagh. It is found in the monastery of Amaras where the church was started by St Gregory and completed by St Grigoris himself. He was buried there and on his tomb, in 489, King Vachagan the Pious had a funeral chapel constructed which is still open to visitors.[41] According to tradition, this same monastery housed the first school in Artsakh, opened early in the fifth century by the inventor of the Armenian alphabet Mesrop Mashtots, who was intensely active in teaching there.

In his *History of Albania*, Movses Daskhurantsi preserves the legendary stories of an apostle Eliza who came directly from Jerusalem in the first century to convert the Albanians, and of the adoption of Christianity by King Urrnair about 370. But, as A. Akopian demonstrates, this is a matter of fabrication long postdating the baptism of Albania.[42]

It was natural, therefore, that the Albanian Church, like that of Iberia (until 608), should pledge fidelity to the Armenian Church.[43] The three churches joined at the Councils of Dwin (sixth century) to refute the dyophysite dogmas of the Council of Chalcedon and to distance themselves from Greek Orthodoxy.[44] In 552 the headquarters of the Albanian Church was moved from Derbend to Partav. Following Khazar incursions, as indicated by Movses Daskhurantsi, this transfer coincided with the political-geographic centralization we referred to above.[45] It also highlighted the Armenian influence on the Albanian church, whose jurisdiction extended over Artsakh and Utik. One of the consequences of this was that Armenian progressively supplanted Albanian as the language of church and state. Although Mesrop Mashtots provided the Albanians with an alphabet, the Albanian language disappeared.[46] In Albanian, there remain only a few fragments of inscriptions dated from the sixth and seventh centuries, which were found for the most part at Mingechaur, on the north bank of the Kura.[47] Further evidence comes from Arab writers of the tenth century who indicate, rather enigmatically, that 'Arranian is spoken in the land of Barda'a (Partaw) ... in Arran'. Nevertheless, the Albanian language disappeared.[48] One of its remainders, it seems, is the language of the Udi ethnic group whom we have referred to above as the probable descendants of the Albanians (the last members of this group lived in two locales in northern Azerbaijan until 1988, when they were driven out, and in a village in Georgia). Regarding Albanian writings, which certainly existed, none have come down to us.[49]

In the portion of the country extending from the south bank of the Kura, on the contrary, Armenian never ceased to exist. For the seventh and eighth centuries we have an interesting account concerning the existence of an Armenian dialect spoken in Artsakh: in a grammar book, the Armenian author Stepanos Siunetsi advises those wishing to master the Armenian language to learn the 'peripheral dialects', one of which is 'Artsakhian'. This evidence is restated in the fourteenth century by the scholar Essayi Nshetsi.[50] Moreover, the Armenian dialect of Karabagh remains very hardy; by virtue of the size of the area covered and the number of speakers, it is the most important Armenian dialect.[51]

The transfer of the ecclesiastical seat to Partav in 552 coincides, according to B. Ulubabian, with the founding of an Albanian Catholicossate or, at least, with the strengthening of this institution. The Bishop Abbas of Mets Arrank in Artsakh became (552–595) 'Catholicos of Aghuank (Artsakh and Utik), the Lupens (north bank of the Kura), and of Chor (land of the Massagetae up to Derbend)'. As tradition would have it, the Catholicoi-Archbishops of Albania received investiture from the Catholicos-Patriarch of Armenia.[52] However, they sometimes manifested impulses toward independence. Thus at the end of the sixth century and the beginning of the seventh, under Byzantine influence, the Iberian Church (Gregorian) separated from the Armenian in 608, and the Albanian patriarch was himself tempted by dyophysite doctrine. For a brief period this patriarch separated himself from the Armenian, taking with him the Bishop of Siunik, but he was returned to the Armenian fold by the Catholicoi Abraham (608–615) and Komitas (615-628).[53] Between the eighth and tenth centuries other analagous attempts were made; notably, at the start of the eighth century, by Archbishop–Catholicos of Albania, Bakur-Nerses. The danger of this dissent appeared so grave to Patriarch-Catholicos Elia of Armenia (703–717) that he did not hesitate to appeal to Caliph Abd el Malik to put an end to it.[54]

The vigorous reactions of the Armenian patriarchs are recorded in all regions of Armenia within the context of their struggle against Chalcedonism which they considered a dangerous menace. These are interpreted in a highly tendentious manner by certain Azerbaijani historians who, without any foundation, try to present this action as an anti-Albanian crusade in which Armenian prelates and princes 'destroyed the literary monuments of Arran' and 'with their crossed flag annihilated the people of historic Albania'.[55]

Following the 'Albanian Episode': Arab Occupation

At the start of the seventh century the Mihranid dynasty, in origin Persian, established itself in Utik, then seized Artsakh, and held them for about two centuries.[56] As reported by Movses Daskhurantsi, the Mihranids supplanted the Arranshahiks by massacring large numbers of them, but they ended by coming under the influence of their environment, converting to Christianity, and becoming heavily Armenianized.[57] In the beginning they controlled only the lone canton of Gardman (in Utik). Under Varaz-Grigor (628–637) and under Jivanshir (637–683) they took control of the Armenian portion of Albania and then of all the old marzpanate, and recognized the authority of the Caliph. From the Emperor of Byzantium, Heraclius, they received the title of Presiding Prince (according to C. Toumanoff) which became hereditary within their family.[58] Thus they inherited the appellation Albania which had already become conventional.

This name had lost all political meaning since it no longer referred to the marzpanate once the Arabs had put an end to the Sasanid state. It was now applied almost exclusively to Artsakh and Utik and began to be synonymous, in Armenian sources of this period, with the terms 'the eastern portion of Armenia' and 'the north-east province'.[59]

Having conquered Transcaucasia in the seventh and eighth centuries, in the eighth and ninth centuries the Arabs formed, under the name Arminiya, a vast administrative unit grouping Armenia, a portion of Georgia, and, up to the banks of the Caspian, Arran or Albania.[60] The Arab governor of Arminiya (*vostikan* in Armenian) had two residences, one at Dwin in Armenia and the other at Partav in Albania. This latter country, however, remained under the control of the Mihranids, who held on until the start of the ninth century. They disappeared when their last representative, Varaz-Trdat, was murdered in 821.[61]

The family which regained the reins of power in western Albania (Artsakh and Utik) was the Arranshahik. They have been incorrectly merged by C. Toumanoff and other writers with the house of Siunik.[62] Certainly these two neighbouring provinces of eastern Armenia, Siunik and Artsakh, were effectively linked. Among the evidence, we have the legend of Arran, descendant of Sisak, and the toponymic relationships (cantons named Haband in both provinces, Artsakh sometimes called Little Siunik or Second Siunik, the existence in Artsakh of a canton called Sisakan-i-Kotak, which is to say Little Siunik in Pahlavi).[63] At the start of the ninth century it is Arranshahik Atrnerseh, son of Sahl, prince of Khachen (in Artsakh) who marries the last Mihranid princess Spram and inherits power over the entire region.[64] His father, the powerful and courageous Sahl Smbatian (Sahl ibn Sunbat in Arab sources), lord of northern Artsakh, appeared in the first half of the ninth century, as the governor of all of Arminiya (Arran-Albania included). This is not, whatever some may say, a Siunid or Bagratid, but a local dynast, Arranshahik, and the name Siunik which sometimes appears in his titles must certainly be understood as Little Siunik, and is explained, perhaps, by his conquest of the south-east shores of Lake Sevan.[65] Arab sources of the period recognize him unambiguously as an Armenian prince.[66] One of his relatives, the lord of Dizak (southern Artsakh), Essayi, father of Movses (Issa abu Musse) is also mentioned as waging war against the Arabs.[67]

Losing control over the mountainous regions, the Arabs held on to their power in the lowlands, in the rich lands of the Kura Valley: at Barda'a (Partav) and Ganja (Gandzak) and further to the east. With the weakening of the caliphate, at the end of the ninth and during the tenth century, eastern Transcaucasia, or the eastern portion of the old marzpanate of Albania or Arran, gave rise to several local Moslem emirates: those at Ganja, Shirvan, and Derbend. Among them, the Shahdadid emirs at Ganja, in origin Kurdish, played a role which cut across the history of the region during the tenth and eleventh centuries. Replaced in turn by the Seljuks, they constituted a permanent menace to the Christian principalities and established a Moslem population on the north-east border of Artsakh-Utik.[68]

The Kingdoms and the Seljuk Invasion

In Armenia, too, the weakening of Arab domination in the ninth century favoured the expansion of local powers. In particular, the Bagratid princes reinforced their position and extended their possessions to re-establish the Armenian kingdom.[69] Paradoxically, in eastern Armenia, at the same time that the Albanians were undergoing rapid Armenianization (the majority moved to Islam in eastern Albania), the Armenian élites in Artsakh and Utik were adopting a form of Albanian patriotism or particularism. They planned to employ this as an ideology in their resistance – as in the resistance of other large Armenian provinces, Vaspurakan and Siunik – to attempts by the Bagratids to centralize power.[70]

The descendants of the Arranshahiks attained the level of royalty during the ninth and tenth centuries. They established two Armenian–Albanian kingdoms on their lands in Artsakh. Dizak, in the south, had only a brief existence. Among the descendants of Essayi of Dizak, only his grandson Gagik is reported to carry the title of king, in the year 1000.[71] Khachen, in the north, was more important. It included most of Artsakh and the south-east basin of Lake Sevan (until the ninth century a part of Siunik, today Zangezur, the south-east portion of the Republic of Armenia). On the other hand, further to the east Utik began to escape the control of local princes, its eastern territories having been conquered by the Shahdadid Emir of Gandzak while the north-west section was occupied by the Armenian Bagratids of Tashir or Lorr.[72] By virtue of that annexation, the latter took for themselves the title of Kings of Albania.[73]

In Khachen, the principal figure of the second half of the ninth century was 'The Prince of Siunik and Albania', Grigor-Hamam 'Arevelktsi' (the Oriental), grandson of Arranshahik Sahl Smbatian. Movses Daskhurantsi reports that, at the same time as Prince Ashot Bagratuni restored the Kingdom of Armenia in 885, Grigor-Hamam created the vassal Kingdom of Khachen.[74] This time the title Kingdom of Albania was more justified. Indeed, having brought together a large part of the territories of Artsakh and western Utik, Grigor-Hamam extended his authority from the shores of Lake Sevan to the city of Partav, as well as to certain territories on the north bank of the Kura (Cambysen).[75] This king is also celebrated for his vast literary production in Armenian. Indeed, he is considered to be the same Hamam who was an important contemporary grammarian, poet, theologian, and musician.[76]

The four sons of Grigor-Hamam divided his possessions. Atrnerseh (910–956) founded on the north shore of the Kura the Kingdom of Shake-Cambysen (Heret in Georgian) with its centre at Shake, today known as Shaki (in northern Azerbaijan). Georgian influences caused this area to convert to Chalcedonism in the second half of the tenth century.[77] In the eleventh century the kingdom passed into the hands of the Bagratids or Kiwrikids of Lorr and was attached by them to neighbouring Kakheti before being incorporated into Georgia in 1104.[78] Another son of Grigor-Hamam, Sahak-Sevada, established himself at Parissos, in northern Artsakh, and attached several districts in Utik. One of them, Gardman,[79] encroached upon the royal domains and Sehak-Sevada was disciplined by his son-in-law and suzerain, King Ashot Bagratid.[80] His son Hovhannes Senekerim succeeded him and, it seems, tried like his father to escape the authority of his lords. According to Movses Daskhurantsi, he re-established the kingdom of Albania and was recognized by the Arabs and the Byzantines.[81] This small Kingdom of Albania-Parissos or Gardman-Khachen fell in 1003 to the combined attacks of King Gagik of Armenia and Emir Fadl of Ganja (Padlun in Armenian), and was divided between them around the middle of the eleventh century.[82] Finally, the two other sons of Grigor-Hamam held some territories in Khachen.

All of these small kingdoms and princes were, in principle, vassals of the Bagratid Kingdom of Armenia, whose monarchs would periodically reimpose their supremacy by force over territories which extended to the Kura.[83] The fact that the tenth-century Byzantine Emperor Constantine Porphyrogenitus mentions 'the Prince of Khachen in Armenia' among the Armenian political figures with whom he had a correspondence[84] demonstrates that this entity was considered a part of Armenia. It should be noted that this term Khachen is derived from the Armenian word *khach* (cross), and is applied most often, from the tenth to the thirteenth centuries, to the former Artsakh and future Karabagh. It reproduces the name of the district and, above all, the fortress which served as the centre for the local princes.[85]

The annexation of the Bagratid Kingdom by the Byzantines, who became masters of their capital at Ani in 1045, left Armenia defenceless against a formidable danger, the advance of the Seljuks. These Turks, Islamicized since the tenth century, took control of Iran around the mid-eleventh century, seizing Baghdad in 1055, and then attacked Byzantium. Led by Alp Arslan, the Seljuks took Ani in 1064, defied the Emperor Roman Diogenes at Mantzikert in 1071 and occupied nearly all of Armenia and eastern Transcaucasia; and in 1075 they supplanted the Shahdadids in the emirate of Ganja.[86] All that remained of the Armenian Kingdom were the secondary principalities at Tashir and Siunik, and these soon disappeared in turn.

Siunik is particularly interesting because certain Khachen princes played an eminent role in the last period of its history, at the time of the Seljuk conquest. This kingdom, separated from the Bagratid Kingdom in 987 and reduced to its southern region of Baghk (Ghapan, Kapan), was spared the first time by Turkish invaders. Its royalty was linked by marriage to the princes of Khachen, and it appealed to them from time to time in safeguarding the kingdom. The first to reign at Ghapan in Siunik was Senekerim, from the Arranshahik line of Khachen-Parissos.[87] He was designated the successor to the last King of Siunik, Grigor III, his brother-in-law, who died without an heir.[88] With the approval of the conciliatory Seljuk Sultan Melik Shah, son of the conqueror Alp Arslan, Senekerim assumed his throne on the death of Grigor and reigned from 1072 to 1094 or 1096. His son Grigor, who succeeded him, left his daughter as his only heir. Once again a new Prince of Khachen arrived, Hasan Gerakaretsi.[89] After the execution of Grigor IV by the Seljuks in 1166, this Hasan reigned for several years in what remained of Siunik. But this kingdom was ravaged by the Eldiguzid (Ildenizid) princes (*Atabegs*) of Azerbaijan (northern Iran). Hasan fled in 1170 'to his more inaccessible principality of Khachen, which with other small enclaves hidden in the heart of the mountains, made up all that remained of the Kingdom of Greater Armenia'.[90] Thus ends the interlude of Siunik. It illustrates the role of refuge and bastion which Khachen-Karabagh would often play in Armenian history.

We have seen above that there was a particular sense of Armenian–Albanian identity which expressed itself in Khachen during the period of the kingdoms. The best representative of this tendency is the historian of Albania, Movses Daskhurantsi (or Kaghankatvatsi), who lived at the end of the tenth century, probably in the Kingdom of Parissos.[91] In his *History of Aghvank* (of Albania) written in Armenian around 980, he glorifies the history of his country and stresses its strong ties with Armenia. At the same time he seeks to establish the ancient origins of the Albanian Church and its right to autocephalous status.[92] Focusing on the Armenian portion of the country, Moses Daskhurantsi is silent on the Islamization of the eastern portion of former Albania, which is treated in tenth-century Arab sources.[93]

Indeed, eastern Albania, with the disappearance of its Christian kingdoms and the establishment of its Moslem emirates, ceased to exist as such, and its population assimilated in part (in the western regions) with the Armenians and Georgians, but above all it was Islamicized through mixing with Arab residents, and then Turks.[94] This Caucasian substratum, converted to Islam, would be augmented by Iranians and, above all, by Turks to give birth to the ethnic group Azerbaijani (Azeri). Once known as Tatars, their language is Turkic and their religion is Islam, Shiite since the sixteenth century by virtue of Safavid tutelage. They constitute the people of present-day Azerbaijan. The Seljuk invasion proved decisive, for it was the first and principal staging point in the process of Turkification of the populations of eastern Transcaucasia and the northern Iranian province of Azerbaijan.[95]

'Albanian': An Ambiguous Concept

Thus ended the 'Albanian episode' in the history of the eastern provinces of Armenia. After the Seljuk invasion and the fall of the Christian kingdoms, these regions continued to shelter Armenian princes, heirs of the Arranshahiks. They were able to consolidate and re-integrate the Armenian orbit in the thirteenth century. Indeed, in the absence of the centralizing power of the Bagratids, the separatist tendencies of the lords in the peripheral regions also disappeared.[96]

These developments brought about a new change in the meaning of the name Albania. Initially, as we have seen, ancient Albania was situated north of the Kura; then, from the fifth to the seventh century, a second Albania or Marzpanate of Arran added Armenian territories south-west of the Kura to Albanian territories in the north-east then in the process of Armenianization. In the third stage we have the exclusive adoption of the name Albanian by the Armenians on the south-west bank at the same time as the Islamization and de-Albanianization of the north-east territories. In the fourth and final stage, beginning with the year 1000, the name Albania is only used by Armenian authors and takes on an essentially regional-ecclesiastical meaning.

In the Islamic sphere, the designation Albania does not exist; the largest part is called Arran and the eastern section, Shirvan.[97] Armenian historians continued to use the term Albania in a sense purely conventional, geographic, and non-ethnic, in order to designate the provinces of Artsakh and Utik. Above all, after the year 1000, they gave the term a limited ecclesiastical meaning. From then on, in Armenian sources, 'Albanian' referred to the Christians of former Albania, that is to say the Armenians of Artsakh and Utik and the descendants of Armenianized Albanians.[98] For this reason the name remained attached to the patriarch in charge of Armenians in eastern Transcaucasia (the present-day Republic of Azerbaijan). This patriarch had his seat in the monastery of

Gandzasar in Artsakh (Mountainous Karabagh), and until the nineteenth century held the title of 'Catholicossate of Albania', even though Albania, strictly speaking, had long since ceased to exist.

The complex relationships between the intermingled concepts of Albanian and Armenian call for care and prudence on the part of historians. Of course, it is highly prejudicial to scientific inquiry (and society itself), to impose politically expedient and tendentious interpretations on such complex historical questions. Nevertheless, historians of the Baku school[99] try to minimize and denigrate the Armenian factor[100] in an Albania they portray as having an uninterrupted history and an ethnically homogeneous population.[101] They present this Albania as a direct precursor of contemporary Soviet Azerbaijan. According to this perspective, everything in Armenia (not only Artsakh and Utik but also Siunik) which was at one time or another linked to entities called Albania is, in reality, Albanian, which, in the spirit of these historians, means Azerbaijani. How are we to understand, in this schema, the national momentum which has driven and continues to drive the Armenians in these areas? How are we to understand the thousands of works of art and culture created there – the 1,700 architectural monuments counted in Mountainous Karabagh?[102] This national dynamic could only be, according to them, an illusion, a result of forced assimilation, manipulation, and extremism.

A Christian Albanian–Azerbaijani culture is created out of the works and monuments of the Armenians. To that end, everything is declared to be Albanian–Azerbaijani: the churches which are in no way distinguishable from those in the rest of Armenia, except for specific provincial characteristics, and are covered with Armenian inscriptions;[103] the innumerable *khachkars*, the stone crosses which clearly belong to the body of Armenian art (in Baku, they have been re-baptized with the Turkish name *khachdash*);[104] and the medieval authors from these regions, not only Movses Daskhurantsi but also Mkhitar Gosh (twelfth century) and Kirakos Gandzaketsi (thirteenth century), even though they assert their Armenian identity.[105] We can easily make out the objective of such an interpretation: to demonstrate that the population's links with Armenia are not historically based since it is fundamentally a question of Albanians, that is to say Azerbaijanis. The objective is to show that the Armenian-ness of Karabagh is only a myth and that the 'Albanians' who live there have no reason to challenge their membership of the Republic of Azerbaijan.

The Princes of Khachen after the Seljuks

After the dislocation of the centralized Seljuk Empire of Melik Shah at the end of the eleventh century, there came a troubled period marked by incessant confrontations between generals, emirs, and Seljuk sultans, as well as between indigenous princes and Turkish chieftains, which would last until the second half of the twelfth century. The region was administered, along with the rest of north-east Armenia and northern Iran (Azerbaijan), by the Emir of Gandzak, Turkish since 1075.[106] The Armenian lords were particularly undermined in the old Utik; they lost a great deal in Artsakh as well, but were not completely eliminated there.[107] Three princely families from the Arranshahik dynasty remained in this province, from now on more often referred to as Khachen. In the west, to Lake Sevan, the princes of Tsar had their seat at the fortress of Handaberd. In the north, the princes of Haterk (Upper Khachen) were established on the left bank of the Tartar River, with their spiritual centre at the monastery at Dadivank. Finally, in the south, the princes at Khokhanaberd or Lower Khachen held the centre of the province around Gandzasar.[108] Elsewhere there were several secondary families and new Turkish lords.

In the second half of the twelfth century, the decline of Seljuk power allowed the Georgians to move in the direction of Armenian lands, and the Georgian–Armenian military alliance to be strengthened. Beginning with the end of the twelfth century, the Zakarian princes (*Mkhargrdzeli* in Georgian), ranking Armenian dignitaries in the Georgian court, liberated the major part of Bagratid Armenia on behalf of the court and held effective control over it.[109] They reconquered, among other areas, all of Artsakh and Utik, including Partav, with the exception of the city of Gandzak which remained in Turkish hands.[110] Armenian nobles and generals in the service of the Zakarians received their old domains or were granted new ones for their participation in the Georgian–Armenian military campaigns.

The three branches of Khachen – Tsar, Haterk, and Khokhanaberd – were re-established or confirmed in their rights, while another regional family, the Khaghbakians, installed themselves in northern Siunik in the Vayots- Dzor.[111] The inscription left by Prince Hasan of Haterk at the monastery of Dadivank in 1182 seems to indicate that some did not await the call of the Zakarians to combat and liberate themselves from the Turks. He had fought, victoriously he says, for 40 years, or since 1142.[112] Probably this was also the case for the lords at Khokhanaberd, whose principality of Lower Khachen is confirmed by Mkhitar Gosh as autonomous in the second half of the twelfh century, with its spiritual centre at Gandzasar.[113] Vakhtang, who reigned during the first half or middle of the twelfth century, was followed by his son Hasan (the use of Arab first names was something of a fashion among the Armenian nobility) until about 1200. He was succeeded by his son, Vakhtang-Tangik, who died in 1214. He was the father of the great Hasan-Jalal (1214–1261) who will be our focus further on.[114] The considerable importance of Khachen in the Georgian– Armenian ensemble is confirmed by the fact that the main Armenian figure in this period, the Grand Prince Sarkis Zakarian, gave two of his daughters in marriage to princes from this province.[115] One of them, Khorishah, had married Vakhtang-Tangik.

The leading family among the three was the one from Haterk.[116] In this period, one found there the Vakhtangian princes (offspring of a certain Vakhtang-Sakarr) who had the same names as the princes from Khokhanaberd and who succeeded to the throne in a parallel manner. Confusion among specialists is due to these homonyms and parallel successions.[117] Vakhtang of Khokhanaberd was surnamed Tangik (Vakh-tang-ik) to distinguish him from the first prince of the region, his contemporary and distant relative, Vakhtang of Haterk who also died in 1214. The father of the latter, Hasan of Haterk, was known not only for his forty years of struggle, noted above, but also for his retreat with his wife to the monastery of Dadivank. He is sometimes known as Hasan the Monk.[118] Mkhitar Gosh, author of the celebrated Code of Laws (*Datastanagirk*), took refuge with Vakhtang of Haterk in 1184. At his request, Vakhtang and his brothers contributed in 1191 to building the monastery at Nor-Getik (present-day Goshavank in the north-eastern Republic of Armenia).[119] When Vakhtang died (1214) his patrimony was left without an heir and was reunited with Tsar. As for his wife, Arzu-Khatun, she had erected in the memory of her husband and deceased son the principal church at the monastery of Dadivank.[120] In accordance with the Armenian tradition of the hereditary transmission of prelacies, the Vakhtangians of Haterk kept as their privilege the charge of the abbey of the monastery at Dadivank.

As the head of the principality of Tsar, we find at the end of the twelfth century another Prince Hasan, married to another daughter of Sarkis Zakarian, Dop. Probably due to the death of her husband, Dop took over leadership of the domain which grew by virtue of its unification with Haterk.[121] The fact that she was the sister of Generalissimo (*Amir Sipahsalar*) Zakare and of the regent (*atabek*) of Georgia, Ivan, may explain such a transfer. What is remarkable is that her descendants took her name, a woman's name, and called themselves Dopian. At the beginning of the thirteenth century the Dopians controlled all of the north and west of Khachen. But the Mongol invasion would soon cause major changes, bringing the princes of Lower Khachen to the fore.

A Grand Armenian Prince under the Mongols

Liberated from the Seljuks only shortly before, the Armenian vassal principalities in Georgia suffered the first and exceedingly violent incursions by the Mongols, Kipchaks, and Khwarazmians from 1220 to 1232. Still suffering from the after-effects of these first and terrible ravages, they were not able to face the Mongol invasion of 1235–1236. The Georgians and Armenians were unable to organize a defence of their nations against this surge. After 1236 the Mongols were the masters of eastern Georgia, all of the Armenia of the Zakarians, and also of Shirvan.[122] The Turkish emirate of Gandzak fared no better, and its capital was destroyed in 1232.[123] The invaders established their base in the Kura Valley and in the Mil/Mughan Plain. The Armenian provinces (Artsakh-Khachen) retained their administrative structure, remained attached to eastern Georgia and together formed the 'vilayet of Gurjistan'. Further to the east, the emirates of Arran (Kura Valley) and Shirvan each formed a vilayet. Finally, south of the Arax, in north-western Iran, extended the vilayet of Azerbaijan.[124]

In Khachen, Prince Grigor of Tsar, vassal to Avag Zakarian, probably lost the northern territories of the region (Haterk) which were recovered, we do not know how, by his relative and neighbour in Lower Khachen. At least, this is what we learn from an engraved inscription by Prince Hasan of Khokhanaberd on the church at Gandzasar in 1240.[125] Indeed, it describes him as 'the Legitimate Autocrat of the Country of Upper and Grand Artsakh'. He probably held Haterk among his possessions, perhaps even prior to the Mongol invasion, and imposed his authority over the lords of Tsar.[126] Hasan-Jalal's titles (see below) reflected his position as the First Prince of Khachen.

Despite his three names, all of them Arab – Hasan (handsome), Jalal (glorious), and Dawla (wealthy)[127] – this prince was certainly Armenian. Indeed, his contemporary Kirakos Gandzaketsi described him as 'The Great Prince Hasan, who is flatteringly called Jalal, a man pious, honest, and Armenian'.[128] He was certainly one of the principal figures in Armenian political and cultural life in the thirteenth century. He succeeded his father in 1214 and was able to maintain a degree of autonomy in Khachen. After trying to resist, he submitted to the Mongols around 1239 and worked hard to establish good relations with them in return for their favour. With this objective in mind he gave his daughter Ruzukan in marriage to the Mongol chief Bora-noyin. Nor did he neglect his relationships with his peers and compatriots. He married his two other daughters to the wealthy merchant Umek and to Tarsayij Orbelian of Siunik.[129] Like all of the princes now subordinate to the Mongols, he had to participate in their military campaigns, but his particular strength was in the area of diplomacy where he played the role, to a degree, of representative of all of Armenia. Thus, in 1244, he facilitated contacts between Cilician Armenia and the Mongols, who accepted an embassy from King Hetum.[130] Through his friendship with the Mongol Prince Sartakh, who was a Christian and looked after his co-religionists, Hasan-Jalal undertook two journeys: the first in 1251 to the father of Sartakh, the Khan Batu of the Golden Horde (the Mongol state in Russia), north of the Caspian, and a second (1255–1260) as far as Karakorum to see the Great Khan

Mangu.[131] Desiring to protect his domains from tax levies but also to elude the domination of the Zakarians, he secured for Khachen the status of a *tuman*, a separate administrative unit reponsible directly to the Khan. This privilege, which conferred a considerable degree of autonomy, was granted by the Mongols with a view to exercising better control over their territories by dividing the princes. They made the same concession to the other large areas in north-eastern Armenia: the three Zakarian principalities and the Orbelian principality in Siunik.[132] Hasan probably participated in an anti-Mongol uprising. He was imprisoned in northern Iran at Qazvin and was martyred there in 1261.[133]

Sources and inscriptions proclaim Hasan-Jalal-Dawla as the 'Grand Prince of Khachen, Legitimate Autocrat of the Country of Artsakh, Prince of Princes in Royal Splendour, the Great King, the King of Aghvank'.[134] He was equally a great builder, not only in Khachen (churches of Gandzasar and Vajarr), but also in the centre of eastern Armenia where he had the monastery of Kecharis restored in 1248.[135]

The history of Hasan-Jalal and his activities in architecture, and those of his descendants known as Jalalians or Hasan-Jalalians, are abundantly documented by Armenian inscriptions which cover the walls of monuments erected in Khachen during this period of rapid expansion in the thirteenth century.[136] The monastery at Gandzasar, built near the Jalalian residence between 1216 and 1261, was one of the spiritual and temporal centres of the principality. The richly sculpted decor is distinguished by several portraits of patron princes, including, probably, Hasan-Jalal.[137] In theory, dependent on the pre-eminent Catholicossate of Armenia, the monastery at Gandzasar became the seat of the 'Catholicossate of Albania' from the fifteenth century until 1815.[138] The head of the monastery and then the office of Catholicos were hereditary within the Jalalian family from that point on.

The Long Ordeal of the Mongol and Turkmen Occupations

After the death of the Grand Khan Mangu in 1259, the Mongol Empire fragmented. In the south-west Ilkhan Hulagu (1256–1265), founder of the Ilkhanid dynasty, created a new Mongol state which included Iran and Transcaucasia. The capital was at Tabriz in Iranian Azerbaijan. The vilayet of Gurjistan remained unchanged, including, as always, Khachen. Already very difficult because of the heavy tax burden, the situation of Christian peoples deteriorated further at the start of the fourteenth century with the conversion of the Persian Mongols to Islam. Added to that was the lengthy war between the Ilkhanids and their compatriots of the Golden Horde based in Russia, with Transcaucasia as the arena of conflict.[139] But this suffering was only a prelude to that brought on by the anarchy following the Mongol decline in the middle of the fourteenth century and then the terrible devastations of Tamerlane at the century's end.

The Mongol occupation had disastrous socio-economic effects on Armenia. The peasantry was exterminated or deported, and those who remained were ruined. The nobility was likewise decimated or undermined economically. The cities were in ruins. Ethnic integrity was weakened through the emigration of indigenous peoples and the settlement of Kurds in the south and Turks in the east. Nomadism developed at the expense of agriculture and rich lands were transformed into pasture.[140] Khachen, contiguous to the Plain of Mil (named the Plain of Karabagh after the fourteenth century), was not spared. According to Kirakos Gandzaketsi, the Tatar–Mongol hordes, after their seasonal warfare, spent the winter on the plain and left in the spring either for new combat or across Khachen on their way to their pastures and summer camps near Lake Sevan.[141]

Despite these incessant upheavals, when the majority of the Armenian grand families progressively disappeared from the political arena, the two branches of the princes of Khachen, the north-east and the south, continued to exist. The inscriptions and the colophons of the manuscripts, which are our only sources for this period, show that the Jalalians, although weakened, remained in possession of Lower Khachen during the fourteenth and fifteenth centuries and maintained their primacy over the Dopians of Tsar. They simply returned to the Dopians, it seems, the northern district of Khachen: Haterk.[142] Certainly their power was very much reduced. In a colophon from 1417 the superior of the monastery at Gandzasar deplores the situation whereby the princes of Khachen are 'in the hands of lawless people' and 'the House of Armenia is thus weakened'.[143] But we have to believe that the Jalalians were able to offer a measure of security in their domains since, near the end of the fourteenth century, the idea was born (though not realized) of transferring to Gandzasar the seat of the central Armenian Catholicossate, then in Cilicia.[144]

The Dopians also remained in their domains of Tsar, augmented by Haterk. One of them, Prince Grigor, was declared in a colophon at the start of the fourteenth century 'Prince of Armenians, Lord and Baron of Little Siunik (North Khachen), Handaberd, and Akana, and the Mountain Regions of Lake Guegham (Sevan)....'[145] More or less the same description was applied a century later, in 1430, to a Dopian of that period: 'Lord and Baron of Little Siunik, Akan, Haterk, and Handaberd, and of Lake Guegham....'[146] Tsar is also mentioned on the sad occasion of the first invasion by Tamerlane in 1386; its fortresses were taken and the family of Hasan Dopian was put to the sword.[147]

Unprecedented destruction accompanied the invasions of Tamerlane

(1386–1405) followed by a period of internal disputes which benefited the Turkmens known as the Black Sheep (Karakoyunlu) who established their power in northern Iran, Iraq, and Armenia (1410–1468).[148] These bloody confrontations between the Timurids (successors to Tamerlane) and the Karakoyunlu lasted until 1434 and brought with them a series of massacres, destructions, deportations, and famines. The reign of Turkmen Jihan Shah (1437–1467) brought a relative lull to eastern Armenia.[149] Deciding to temporarily favour certain Armenian regions, Jihan Shah allowed the re-establishment of a pan-Armenian Catholicossate in Etchmiadzin in 1441.[150] It is of particular interest to us here that he confirmed the possessions of the Princes of Khachen and accorded them the title of *melik* ('king' or 'prince' in Arabic). Robert Hewsen presents the reasons for this action, which was particularly important in the history of Karabagh:

> Jehan-shah established a row of tiny buffer territories along the northern frontier of his realm which ran through the old Armenian lands of Siwnik and Artsakh. These territories were placed under the rule of local dynasts descended from Armenian princely houses and to whom were given the title 'melik' together with broad autonomy ….[151]

Alas, the lull was of short duration. Succeeding the Black Sheep, Turkmens known as the White Sheep (Akkoyunlu) imposed their power over Armenia and Iranian Azerbaijan (1468–1502) and warred with the Ottoman Turks, bringing new devastation and oppression.[152] The long ordeal continued.

The Armenian Meliks under Persian Occupation

Having survived the invasion of Tamerlane and the Turkmen occupation, the descendants of the Jalalians (Lower Khachen) and the Dopians (Upper Khachen and Tsar) also overcame the anguish of the Turco-Persian wars of the sixteenth century and preserved their ancestral lands. They somehow or other maintained Armenian authority over Mountainous Karabagh. This region was the only part of Armenia to preserve indigenous, hereditary Armenian power and a degree of national sovereignty without interruption until the late Middle Ages. Cut off on the west from the rest of Armenia (though linked to Siunik), equally cut off on the east from the Plain of Mil, Armenian Karabagh lived by withdrawing unto itself and practising autarky. Thanks to the fertility of its valleys, it was, as Robert Hewsen reminds us, economically self-sufficient, having to import only salt.[153]

From the sixteenth to the eighteenth centuries several great Armenian families of princely ancestry held small islands of independence in eastern Armenia. Five of them, who were related, formed a coalition in the mountains and valleys of the former Artsakh-Khachen. In the eighteenth century these were called the 'Melikates of Khamsa' (*khamsa* is the Arabic word for five).[154] The Hasan-Jalalians remained the masters of Central Khachen and kept their hereditary monopoly over the Catholicossate of Gandzasar which gave them particular prestige among the meliks. From the same dynasty the Avanians or Eganians were the meliks of Dizak in the south of the region. Related to the Jalalians, the Dopians were split into two branches: the Beglarians or Abovians were the meliks of Gulistan in the north while the Shahnazarians were established in the south as the meliks of Varanda. Finally, the fifth house of meliks were the Israelians of Jraberd (actually north of the Autonomous Region of Mountainous Karabagh). The only 'foreigners', they were, in point of fact, originally tied to the region since they descended from a dynasty of Khachen, the Khaghbakian-Proshians who, as we saw above, settled in Siunik in the thirteenth century.[155] These melikates were not the only ones in eastern Armenia, and in the seventeenth century we might mention eleven others, but, along with those in Siunik, these were the most powerful and strategically the most important.[156]

At the conclusion of the terrible Ottoman–Persian wars in the sixteenth century and after incessant attacks and counter-attacks which ruined and de-populated a large part of Transcaucasia, including Karabagh, the territory came under the authority of the Safavid Shahs of Persia. The campaigns of Shah Abbas I at the start of the seventeenth century were decisive in this conquest.[157] This was particularly devastating for eastern Armenia whose population in the border regions was deported to Iran by the tens of thousands, under harsh conditions, during the winter of 1604–1605.[158]

The Safavids practised scorched-earth tactics on lands which could be of use to the Ottomans at the same time that they took measures to strengthen the borders of their state. These territories were placed in the charge of governors or *beglarbegs*. The territories in Transcaucasia were divided into three *beglarbegates*: from west to east, Yerevan-Nakhichevan (called Shukur-Saadi), Karabagh-Gandzak (from Lake Sevan to the Arax and Kura rivers), and Shirvan (between the Kura and the Caspian Sea).[159] Within these three provinces there were or were created local authorities with more or less the following divisions: in the plains and lower zones, the Persian authorities established or recognized a series of Moslem khanates, and in the mountainous areas they confirmed what remained of the authority of the Armenian lords. Here is what Robert Hewsen has to say about the subject:

> The Persians set up a series of hereditary Khanates whose rulers were Muslims ... the Khanate of Karabagh, the southern lowland area between the plateau (Karabagh properly called) and the Kur; the Khanate of Ganja, the lowland area just north of the Khanate of Karabagh; the Khanate of

Erevan ... and the Khanate of Nakhitchewan.... In between this horseshoe-shaped encirclement of essentially low-lying jurisdictions lay the plateau of Siwnik-Karabagh and upon this plateau lay the independent melikdoms.... Only those of Karabagh and, to a certain extent, those of Siwnik were truly autonomous while under Persian suzerainty.[160]

Henceforth, in this region which interests us, we have to recognize two neighbouring but distinct areas, each of which can lay claim to the name Karabagh: one in the Armenian highland, in the hands of the meliks, and the other, to the east, between this highland and the Kura, in the hands of the Moslem khan.[161]

In 1603 the Armenian nobles received official confirmation of their titles as meliks from Shah Abbas. In contrast to those in Siunik and elsewhere who depended, if only partially, on the Persian governors in the beglarbegate of Gandzak, the meliks of Karabagh were granted a large measure of autonomy in matters of defence, internal politics, justice, and taxes. In peacetime, each had to contribute a military force of one to two thousand men which could be considerably augmented when it proved necessary, most notably when they had to defend the Persian frontiers against Ottoman attacks.[162] The importance of these powers, even though diminished, should be stressed in the case of Armenia which had lost its sovereignty long before and found itself divided between the Ottoman Empire and Safavid Persia, its population stripped of protection. Under these conditions, the meliks constituted the only authority capable of opposing external threats and maintaining national traditions. It should be understood that Karabagh, where the Armenian nobility survived up until the modern period, was an important reference point for national identity. It is often referred to as the 'bastion of the Armenian political and cultural conscience'.[163]

Rebirth of the Idea of Independence

In the melikates of Karabagh and in the neighbouring province of Siunik, under the aegis of the two Catholicoi at Etchmiadzin and Gandzasar, the national renaissance and the idea of recreating an independent Armenian state took shape in the seventeenth and eighteenth centuries. This state would be allied with Georgia and protected by Russia. After a secret meeting held in Etchmiadzin in 1677, steps were taken at the start of the eighteenth century by Israel Ori, Bishop Minas, and the Catholicos Essayi Hasan-Jalalian in the courts of Europe, Russia, and Georgia with the intention of liberating Armenia from the Ottomans and the Persians.[164]

The missions and extraordinary adventures of Israel Ori, son of a melik of Karabagh, merit special attention. He arrived in Europe as a very young man and spent three years in Venice, served in the army of Louis XIV, was captured by the English and then released. He tried to convince the German Prince Johann-Wilhelm of Lower Palatinate to liberate Armenia and assume the crown. He then saw Pope Innocent XII and the Emperor of Austria and was charged by them to investigate the possibility of action in Armenia with Russia. Arriving in Moscow, he tried finally to convince Czar Peter the Great through numerous reports on the Caucasus and Persia where he had been sent with the rank of colonel. He stressed the opportunities for Russia in a Transcaucasian and Armenian campaign which could rely heavily on local forces.

Indeed, in Karabagh a unified military force was being organized at the same time that the popular militias in Siunik were organizing under the direction of Armenian General Davit Bek, sent for this purpose from Tiflis by the Georgian King Vakhtang.[165] During the first decades of the eighteenth century we find, in Armenian Karabagh, an average of 10,000 permanently mobilized men led by *yuzbashis* (centurions, lieutenants) from the melikates for the purpose of repulsing Ottoman and Persian troops in the hope of an advance by Peter the Great's army, or for joining Persia to fight the Ottomans. The monastery at Gandzasar was the organizational centre for all of this political and military activity.[166] Russia favoured these developments by dangling the prospect of the creation of an Armenian state.

Precisely at this time the Safavid Empire weakened following the Afghan revolt in 1722. This left a void which the Russians, who had just resolved their problems with the Swedes in 1721, and the Ottomans sought to profit from to realize their ambitions with regard to the Caucasus and the Caspian Sea.[167]

Encouraged by the Caucasian campaign of Peter the Great, who had penetrated as far as Derbend and Baku in 1722, the Armenians in Karabagh and Siunik rebelled against the Persian occupation and enjoyed a brief period of independence during the 1720s. In order to facilitate the progress of Russian troops in 1722, the King of Georgia, the Catholicos of Gandzasar, and the meliks brought together a Georgian–Armenian army of over 40,000 men near Gandzak.[168] But the hour had not yet struck for such a Russian advance into Transcaucasia. The Czar preferred to avoid a confrontation with the Ottoman armies. The latter entered Georgia in 1723 and then marched on Karabagh. They were stopped once near Gandzak by local forces which included, it is interesting to note, Georgian troops and those of the Armenian meliks, but also Moslem militia (Shiites) from Gandzak.[169] Fighting in Karabagh and Siunik continued under the direction of Davit Bek and his successor Mkhitar until the Persian armies re-established the Shah's authority over these lands around 1730.[170]

The meliks of Karabagh moved closer to the Persians, who did not remove them for the freedom they experienced during fifteen years of struggle: on the contrary, Nadir Shah rewarded them for their military assistance. The coalition of the five meliks, called Khamsa, with Melik Egan of Dizak at its head, was officially given a new administrative status, distinct from the beglarbegates of Yerevan, Gandzak, and Shirvan, and linked directly to the central Persian authorities.[171]

The uncertain beginnings of the liberation movement, followed by the uprising in Karabagh and Siunik, were short-lived, lasting only eight years from 1722 to 1730. Nevertheless, they firmly anchored the idea of struggle for independence, and demonstrated the growing importance of the Russian factor in the destiny of the region.

The Eighteenth Century: The Turks Enter Mountainous Karabagh

The coalition of Armenian nobles in Karabagh proved its effectiveness during the first decades of the eighteenth century, as we have seen. But around 1750 a breach took place due to the ambitions of one of the meliks, who broke the union and allowed a Turkish chief to gain a foothold in Mountainous Karabagh for the first time. In the melikate of Varanda, the murder of Melik Hovsep Shahnazarian by his younger brother Shahnazar, who took power, provoked armed opposition by the other four meliks. The usurper needed the help of an outside force, which he found in the Turk Panah Ali, chief of the Jivanshir tribe.[172]

This tribe, which was nomadic in the Plain of Karabagh or Mughan, had set its sights on the pastures of the Karabagh plateaux and valleys. But until now the meliks had been successful in keeping Panah Ali's desires in check. In 1722 the Jivanshir were opposed by the Armenian militias and defeated by them.[173] The situation changed with the death of Nadir Shah of Persia in 1747. The ensuing disorders allowed Panah to impose his authority in the plains and to take the title of Khan of Karabagh.[174]

The split among the meliks presented an unforeseen opportunity to complete his penetration of the plateau country. Panah brought Melik Shahnazar into his service and installed himself in the melik's domain of Varanda, forcing him to cede the fortress of Shosh, the future city of Shushi or Shusha. In the early 1750s, in the heart of the mountainous Armenian retreat, the khanate of Shushi-Karabagh was created.[175] Having taken Varanda, Panah Ali Khan soon took control of the melikate of Khachen. He forced the meliks of Gulistan and Jraberd to flee to Gandzak, and he considerably weakened the melik of Dizak. He also extended his authority to all of Siunik up to the border of Nakhichevan.[176] The resistance of the meliks was not, however, totally broken and they increasingly looked to Russia.

With the death of Panah in 1763, his son Ibrahim continued the politics of his father with energy, finesse, deceit, and cruelty. He tried, if not to extend the borders of the khanate, at a minimum to consolidate his frontiers in the face of sudden changes in Russian military strategy in the Caucasus in the second half of the eighteenth century, complicated relations between Russia and Persia, and the actions of the Armenian meliks. It seems that at first, in 1767, he tried to placate the Armenians by allowing the nobles of Gulistan and Jraberd to return to their lands and recover their rights.[177] But very soon his attitude changed.

Meanwhile new plans for the liberation of Armenia were being developed in patriotic circles, actively represented in St Petersburg by the Archbishop of Armenians in Russia, H. Arghutian (Argutinski-Dolgoruki) and by the Count H. Lazarian (Lazarev). At the heart of these plans was Karabagh which was to be liberated from Persian domination, and its representative the Khan, to make up the core of the future Armenia. The meliks and the Catholicos of Gandzasar maintained regular contact with these circles, secret in theory, but in reality followed by the Khan.[178]

After 1780, advisers to Empress Catherine II of Russia – Prince G. Potemkin and Generals Suvorov, P. Potemkin, and Count Zubov – laid plans for Transcaucasia after the Russian occupation. They foresaw the establishment of a Russian protectorate over the Georgian Kingdom and the creation of an Armenian state out of the khanate of Karabagh. For their part, the meliks and the Catholicos increased their urgent requests (1781, 1783, 1784) for a Russian military intervention.[179] Each time this was postponed (notably in 1784) because of revolts by Caucasian *montagnards* incited by Turkey or continued Russian hope of obtaining Transcaucasia without war.[180]

Cleverly hedging between Persia and Russia and short-circuiting Armenian initiatives by himself pledging allegiance to Russia, Khan Ibrahim of Karabagh created a free hand to settle his accounts with the Armenian leadership.[181] In 1781 he had Melik Essayi of Dizak killed, and in 1784 he had the meliks of Gulistan and Jraberd imprisoned (they escaped). The melik of Dizak and, in 1786, the Catholicos of Gandzasar were also killed.[182] Thus began a particularly sombre period in the history of Karabagh. Ibrahim's persecutions were followed by famine, devastation, and massacres by Persian troops, epidemics, and forced emigration (above all towards Georgia). All of this depopulated Armenian Karabagh.[183] From 1795 to 1797 the region was further devastated by the incursions of the cruel Persian Shah Agha Mohammad Khan. Furthermore, the Armenians received no benefit from the Russian expedition, which came to a sudden halt in 1796 with the death of Catherine II.[184] To these ordeals we must add the famine of 1797 and the epidemic of 1798. The appeal for assistance by the meliks of Gulistan and Varanda to Paul I in 1799 only resulted in a new wave of Armenian emigration (smaller than the earlier one) in the direction of southern Georgia.[185]

Several years later, when the khanate was annexed by Russia and the Khan was killed, the melikates were considerably reduced in size without totally disappearing. We note that the Russo-Persian Treaty of Gulistan in 1813 carried the signatures of the five meliks.[186] At this time Karabagh could be numbered in several tens of thousand inhabitants (see below).

Armenians and Turks in Karabagh

There had been a Moslem presence on the northern, eastern, and south-eastern peripheries of the mountains of Karabagh since the Arab occupation, and certainly since the ninth and tenth centuries and the creation of the Shahdadid emirs (Kurdish in origin) in the city of Gandzak and on the Karabagh (Mil, Mughan) Plain. The Moslem population consisted of Islamicized Albanians, Arabs, Iranians, and Kurds. After the Seljuk invasion, the Turkish tribe Oghuz or Ghuzz occupied ancient Albania or Arran in the eleventh and twelfth centuries up to the Kura Valley and imposed their language there without, however, penetrating the Armenian mountains.[187] Under the Mongols, Timurids, and Turkmens (thirteenth to fifteenth centuries), thousands of turcophone nomads settled in the lowlands of Mughan and contributed to Turkifying the area along with all of eastern Transcaucasia and northern Iran (Azerbaijan).[188]

The Turkification of these territories administered by Persia was accelerated after the sixteenth century by the arrival of nomadic Shiite Turkish tribes from Anatolia after the adoption of Shiism as a state religion in the Safavid Empire at the same time that Sunni orthodoxy grew stronger in the Ottoman Empire.[189] In the sixteenth century in the Karabagh Plain up to the eastern border of Armenian Karabagh, there were 24 Kurdish tribes and 32 Turkish tribes, of which the Jivanshir was the principal one.[190] As we have seen, it was only after 1750 that a Moslem Turkish element (Azeri) settled in Shushi in the heart of ancient Artsakh or medieval Khachen. Several decades later there was a reverse population flow as a portion of the Armenian population in the north (melikates of Jraberd and Gulistan) emigrated to Georgia in the wake of persecution by Ibrahim Khan and the series of misfortunes mentioned above.

In spite of these developments, the Moslem presence in Mountainous Karabagh was numerically very small. Until then and even after the decline of the Armenian principalities, the population was verified as being Armenian throughout the period of the Middle Ages. A thirteenth-century Persian geographer pointed out that 'the population of Khachen is Armenian', and a German witness from the fifteenth century, Johann Schiltberger, unequivocally confirmed that Karabagh 'is found in Armenia', adding that 'the Armenian villages are forced to pay tribute to infidels'.[191]

By the end of the Middle Ages, the situation had not changed, and in the eighteenth century the population in the mountain areas, which, as we have pointed out above, could provide thousands of soldiers, contained a very large Armenian majority. That is confirmed by official Ottoman, Georgian and Russian documents from that period.[192] In a 1793 report to Empress Catherine II on the future submission of Ibrahim Khan, Prince G. Potemkin wrote:

> As soon as the opportunity presents itself, we must consider entrusting the administration of this region which is made up of Armenians to one of their nationals and, in this manner, recreating a Christian state in Asia which would conform to the commitments by your Imperial Highness made through myself to the Armenian meliks.[193]

We have seen, however, that many Karabagh Armenians went into exile in the late eighteenth century. This decline is reflected in a decree by Paul I which records the Armenian population of the region in 1797 as eleven thousand families while an 1823 document mentions only 5,107 Armenian households.[194]

In the nineteenth century peace returned once again after Russian annexation. The refugees returned and the numbers rose. Throughout the nineteenth century the Armenian population steadily increased, maintaining an overwhelming Armenian majority in Mountainous Karabagh.[195] We have precise data at our disposal for the years 1823, 1832, 1850, 1873, 1886 and 1897 which show that the Armenian population increased from 30,850 in 1823 to 106,363 in 1897, while the population of Moslem turcophones or 'Tatars' went from 5,370 to 20,409. The latter were primarily concentrated in Shushi, the regional capital. The Armenians made up an average of 84 per cent of the population for the region including Shushi, and 94 per cent in the rural areas.[196]

Contrary to what certain Azerbaijani authors would have us believe, it clearly was not the transfer to Russian territory of Armenians from Persia (deported there, we should recall, by Shah Abbas), authorized by the Russo-Persian Treaty of Turkmenchai (1828), which transformed this region into an Armenian land at a single blow.[197] It is true that, in conformity with Article 15 of this treaty, about 45,000 Armenians from northern Persia crossed the Arax River into eastern Armenia in 1828–1829.[198] Of these refugees, however, only 400 families settled in Mountainous Karabagh.[199] This migration only slightly increased the Armenian majority, which was already very large. We conclude this line of argument by noting that at the start of the twentieth century the Armenian Bishop of Karabagh (whose jurisdiction covered an area larger than present-day Mountainous Karabagh) counted 222 churches serving 224 villages and over 200,000 parishioners.[200]

The Nineteenth Century: Russia Enters the Scene

During the second half of the eighteenth century Karabagh faced a serious threat to its national political equilibrium which reinforced the pro-Russian orientation of the Catholicos of Gandzasar and the Armenian nobles. As for the Khan, he turned his attentions to Persia, and even to the Ottoman Empire, while he pretended to hope for Russian suzerainty. After a long approach, after several decades of anxious waiting and numerous commitments which endangered the Armenian communities, Russia finally launched a decisive offensive at the start of the nineteenth century against the Persians in Transcaucasia.

From eastern Georgia, which had been annexed by Czar Alexander I in 1801, the Russian army seized Gandzak in 1804. In 1805 General Tsitsianov forced Ibrahim Khan to cede Karabagh and then conquered the other provinces of eastern Transcaucasia in 1806. These acquisitions were ratified by the Treaty of Gulistan in 1813.[201] To the great disappointment of the Armenians, the khanate of Karabagh remained so until 1822 when it was superseded, along with the melikates, to create the Province of Karabagh.[202] As for forms of property relations and land usage, they would remain unchanged for many decades.

Hostilities soon broke out again at the initiative of Persia which was encouraged by the British, now worried about the Russian advance. During the second Russo-Persian conflict, Armenians from all the regions, with the Archbishop Nerses Ashtaraketsi at their head, fought resolutely on all fronts with the Russians, convinced that their destiny was at stake. The Armenian volunteers played an especially important role in the defence of Shushi in June–September 1826.[203] Indeed, this war ended with the Russian annexation of the khanates of Yerevan and Nakhichevan, and was sealed by the Treaty of Turkmenchai in 1828.[204]

Now all of eastern Armenia was under Russian control, and the Armenian leadership waited for Russia to satisfy their long-standing national aspirations, a satisfaction they felt they had earned. Armenian notables in Russia grouped around the 'Armenian patriots', represented, as always, by the Lazarians and Arghutians. In 1827 they submitted a plan to the government for the unification of Armenian lands, which unquestionably included Karabagh, with the intention of creating a national homeland. But this project was rejected by the administration of Czar Nicholas I, which opposed the creation of ethnically homogeneous units. The only concession to Armenian demands was the creation of the Armianskaia Oblast (Armenian Province) in 1828. It only included the old khanates of Yerevan and Nakhichevan. The Guberniia of Erivan (Yerevan) was created on the same territorial basis as the previous oblast in 1849. All other Armenian territories were left out of these borders.[205]

This 'divide and rule' politics was designed to neutralize national demands by mixing and opposing ethnic groups, and it presided over the successive divisions of conquered territories. Mountainous Karabagh was an integral part of the eastern Armenian plateau and was ethnically more homogeneous than the other Armenian territories, but it was annexed before them and remained separated from them. It was attached to the steppes and plains which would become the Soviet Republic of Azerbaijan in the twentieth century. With them it was included in a unit successively called the Caspian Province (1840), the Guberniia of Shemakha (1848) and finally the Guberniia of Elisavetpol (1867).[206]

Under Russian Administration

By the decree of 9 December 1867 Transcaucasia was divided into five guberniias: Kutayis, Tiflis, Erevan (Yerevan), Elisavetpol, and Baku.[207] Karabagh was integrated in the Guberniia of Elisavetpol (the name given to the city of Gandzak or Ganja, renamed Kirovabad during the Soviet period and once again Ganja in 1989). Christian Armenians and Moslem Turks (called Tatars: the term Azerbaijanis was not yet in existence) found themselves together in the province of Elisavetpol, as they were in the provinces of Yerevan and Baku. But in Karabagh the differences between the ethnic groups were more pronounced than elsewhere because Armenian Karabagh had long been isolated, had maintained a homogeneous population, and had better preserved its identity.

Here more than elsewhere, language, religion, and mode of life separated the two ethnic groups. Traditionally, the Armenians were sedentary peasants and also bourgeois entrepreneurs. The Tatars were originally what many of them remained during the nineteenth century, semi-nomadic herders led by military lords interested in enlarging their territories. The slow evolution of socio-economic relations did not alleviate this tension, which contained the seeds of future conflicts.[208]

An economic analysis of Mountainous Karabagh done at the beginning of the twentieth century by an Armenian intellectual stressed the urgent necessity of diversifying trade routes and, in particular, building a vehicular mountain road from the Lake Sevan basin to Karabagh.[209] This project, which would have expanded the old Dwin–Partav commercial route of the Middle Ages, was never undertaken. Nevertheless, the study allows us to consider briefly the economies of Mountainous and Lower Karabagh in the nineteenth century. The Tatars on the steppes practised animal husbandry and cultivated rice, cotton, fruit and vegetables. The seasonal migration of livestock constituted the sole link between the Tatars and the Armenian mountains where they went during the summers. These migrations posed a serious problem for the Armenian peasantry, whose fields and vineyards were regularly damaged. The Armenian *montagnards* cultivated wheat, vineyards and mulberries, and raised animals within the villages. They also kept bees, harvested timber and produced local crafts. To export the copper, pure alcohol, brandy and silk that they produced, the Armenians needed lines of communication. The Armenian roads leading to the regions of Yerevan and Siunik (Zangezur) were difficult to use and offered poor market prospects. The road to Tabriz, heavily used during the Persian period, maintained a degree of importance. But it was only the road opening to the east which offered an outlet to the Russian market. The Russians took advantage of the ease of exploitation to develop the Caspian coast, which is tied to the Volga River. Only having access to the Shushi–Evlakh route and the railway linking Tiflis and Baku, Mountainous Karabagh had no other choice but to turn to the east, toward Baku, and to bypass the steppe known as Lower Karabagh. In other words, there was no economic link between Mountainous and Lower Karabagh, a situation which did not change during the twentieth century.

In addition to the administrative divisions, Armenian ecclesiastical affairs were regulated by the *Polojenie* (Statute) of 1836. The unified structure which was denied to the secular leadership was granted to the Church, perhaps to enhance control. The Catholicossate of Gandzasar, whose last incumbent had been lowered to the rank of archbishop-metropolitan in 1815, was henceforth only a bishopric. Karabagh became one of six dioceses for the Armenians in Russia and was placed under the direct jurisdiction of the Catholicos of Etchmiadzin.[210]

Mountainous Karabagh remained part of the Guberniia of Elisavetpol from 1868 to 1917. Sheltered from Ottoman and Persian aggression, it experienced a measure of development during the nineteenth century, and the city of Shushi became one of the principal Armenian and Tatar centres. As much due to its level of cultural activity as to its number of inhabitants, Shushi surpassed all other cities in eastern Armenia, the rest being only modest market towns. After Tiflis and Baku, it ranked third in Transcaucasia, overcoming even the provincial capital of Elisavetpol. In 1826 Shushi had 15,188 Armenians and 11,595 Tatars.[211] Numerous books and over a dozen newspapers and magazines were published there in Armenian. Five churches were built during the nineteenth century while the Turks erected three mosques (two of them in 1875 and 1885). The latter are the only Moslem architectural monuments in the entire Autonomous Region of Mountainous Karabagh.

Ambiguity in the Term 'Azerbaijani'

In anticipation of certain misunderstandings concerning the history of eastern Transcaucasia, it may be useful to summarize the historical components of the term 'Azerbaijani'.[212] We begin by recalling that the geographical term

'Azerbaijan' is the Arab form of the Greco-Iranian name Atropatena, Atrpatakan in Armenian, which designated a northern region of Iran. One of Alexander the Great's generals, Atropate, founded a state there in 321 BC which inherited his name. As with 'Atropatena', the term 'Azerbaijan' (Adharbayjan) was employed by the Arabs to refer to the northern region of Persia where the two principal cities were Tabriz and Ardabil. Arab geographers clearly distinguished this territory south of the Arax from the countries to the north, Armenia and Arran (ancient Albania).

Under the Seljuks, Mongols, and Turkmens, the region of Tabriz was the centre of states ruling over Transcaucasia. This explains why sometimes, though rarely, medieval Moslem historiography contains references to Azerbaijan extended to Barda'a and Nakhichevan. Nevertheless there remained a clear distinction between the region called Azerbaijan in the south and the territories located north of the Arax between the Kura Valley and the Caspian Sea: to the east, Shirvan; to the west, the ancient Arran with the city of Gandzak/Ganja, where a new name appeared, that of Karabagh (Karabagh-i-Arran), to designate the area between the Arax and the Kura up to their juncture.

We have seen that northern Persia and Transcaucasia were Turkified by the arrival, in several waves, of Oghuz and Turkmen tribes. In the sixteenth century their influence was augmented by the influx of Turkish Shiite nomads into the lands of the Persian Safavid Empire. This confessional dimension, namely their Shiism, became important in the ethnogenesis of these Turkish communities that were called Azeri, and it explains why they deliberately moved closer to Persia. Having assimilated, though not totally, the substrata of the Albanian population to the north and of the Iranian population to the south, these turcophone tribes imposed their language, Azeri (the name of the old Iranian language spoken in northern Persia until the Middle Ages). The word Azeri (Adhari) refers to the northern Iranian province of Azerbaijan and is employed also as an ethnonym for peoples speaking this language, not only in Iranian Azerbaijan but also in Transcaucasia.

After the Russian conquest of Transcaucasia, the turcophone populations of the former Persian khanates were called 'Caucasian Tatars' (as in Crimea, where the Turks were called 'Crimean Tatars').

It is in September 1918 that the term Azerbaijan was applied for the first time to eastern Transcaucasia. The Turkish army under the command of Nuri Pasha entered Baku, and Turkish generals and local leaders baptized Azerbaijan, the republic born several months earlier out of the former guberniias of Elisavetpol and Baku. This borrowing of the name of a neighbouring Persian province gave expression to the designs of Turkish nationalists on northern Persia. Once this new state was created and named, the new term Azerbaijani, which should apply to all citizens, rapidly assumed a restrictive meaning designating only the former Tatars, the Azeris. The indigenous ethnic groups who survived Turkification became minorities. In addition to the Armenians we cite the Udis, probable descendants of the ancient Albanians who still numbered several thousand in northern Azerbaijan until 1988; the Kurds who were numerous in Karabagh and who number several tens of thousands even if they are no longer enumerated by the official census;[213] the Tats, an Iranian ethnic group numbering 20,000 in the north-east of the republic; and, finally, the Talish, another Iranian group whose language, forbidden, is related to the old Iranian Azeri and who number several tens of thousands in the south-east of the republic, in the vicinity of Lenkoran.

At one time or another these lands had been controlled by the khans. Then they were included in the Russian guberniias of Elisavetpol or Baku. Now, independently of the ethno-cultural identity of their populations, all these territories were proclaimed Azerbaijan, the term applied in a collective ethnonymic sense, and this was the case for Mountainous Karabagh as well. The term 'Azerbaijani' began to be applied to the cultural heritage of these regions, merging the Moslem heritage and, for the past twenty or thirty years, the prior and neighbouring legacies of Albania and the Armenian provinces.

A Brief Survey of Art History

The art created in Artsakh or Khachen constitutes one of the important chapters in the history of Armenian art, from which it cannot be dissociated. It has progressed through the same major stages from the adoption of Christianity early in the fourth century through to the end of the Middle Ages and on to the nineteenth century. As in the rest of Armenia, the principal expression of this medieval art has been ecclesiastical architecture.[214] Numerous monuments, chapels, churches, and monastic complexes are preserved despite the total absence of maintenance over the past seventy years (those in the Autonomous Region of Mountainous Karabagh represent only a small part of this architectural legacy). Works in Karabagh obey the same plans and are built according to the same techniques as those in the rest of the country.

Volcanic rock is the principal material. Mixed with lime, it forms the nucleus for the walls which are then covered with facing. The exterior facing can consist of carefully cut blocks for the large buildings in cities or in monasteries such as Gandzasar. But it was also common practice, as in several outlying provinces, to use stone less carefully cut for more modest structures, creating a more rustic appearance. The inscriptions on these façades appear exclusively in the Armenian language and often provide precise dating, the names of the patrons, and sometimes even the name of the architect.[215]

There are several monuments which have come down to us from the paleo-

Christian period and from the early Middle Ages. Among them is the type of martyrium represented at Amaras (Martuni District) by the mausoleum of St Grigoris (489): a vaulted burial chamber equipped with two lateral vestibules which serves as the crypt for a church dating from a later period. Several chapels from this period consist of simple vaulted rooms (single nave) with an apse on the east sometimes flanked by two small rooms (Targmanchats near Dashkesan, probably fifth century). The basilica at Tsitsernavank in the Lachin District (probably fifth or sixth century) is the best-preserved example in Armenia of a basilica with three naves.[216] Churches with a cupola built on a radiating or cruciform floor plan were numerous in the rest of Armenia during the seventh century and are as well represented in Karabagh: the chapel at Vankasar (Aghdam District, seventh century), where the cupola and its drum rest on the central square of a cruciform floor plan; Okhte Drni (Hadrut District, probably fifth to seventh centuries) with roughly cut and bonded walls enclosing a quatrefoil interior with four small diagonal niches. We note, however, that certain plans frequently employed in other regions of Armenia during the seventh century are not, to our knowledge, found here. These include the chamber with a cupola supported by wall braces (Aruj), the cruciform plan with a cupola on four free-standing pillars (St Gayane), the radiating type with four rooms in a rectangle (St Hripsime).

Curiously, few of the monuments are precisely dated from the post-Arab period and that of the kingdoms (ninth to the eleventh centuries), very productive periods in the other Armenian provinces. The structures we can place in this period are chapels on the cruciform plan with a cupola (Varazgom, Lachin District, and Khunisavank, Gedabek District) and churches with a single nave (Poladlu and Parissos, Gedabek District).

On the other hand, during the post-Seljuk period and the beginning of the Mongol period (end of the twelfth, and the thirteenth century), architecture flourished, especially in the construction of monasteries. These were the active centres of culture and art, with their scriptoria where manuscripts were copied and illuminated. They also served as refuges for the population and were always fortified. Churches with a single nave continued to be constructed in numbers. At the monastery of Yeghishe Arakyal or Jervechtik, Martakert District, we find eight single-naved chapels aligned from north to south. Less common is the type of free cross plan with a cupola found in the Chapel of St Saviour in the Martakert District. Several monastic churches of the thirteenth century adopted the model used most widely throughout the country: the church with a cupola, in the inscribed cross plan with two or four angular rooms. This is the case for the monasteries at Dadivank (1214), Gandzasar (1216–1238), and Gtichavank (1241–1246). In the case of the two latter churches, the cone over the cupola is umbrella-shaped, a picturesque form widespread in Armenia from the eleventh century on.

Like all Armenian monasteries, those in Khachen reveal great geometric rigour in the layout of their buildings. The monastery at Dadivank (Kelbajar District, twelfth–thirteenth centuries) is remarkable. Indeed, the monastic complex is sufficiently well preserved to leave no doubt that it was one of the grandest and most complete monasteries in all of medieval Armenia. Its approximately twenty buildings are divided into three groups: ecclesiastical, residential and ancillary.[217] Characteristic of Armenian monastic architecture of the thirteenth century is the *gavit* or *zhamatun* which is found on the west façade of the churches and serves as narthex, mausoleum and assembly room. Some appear as a simple vaulted room or a gallery open to the south (Dadivank, St James of Mets Arrank or Mets Irants); others have an asymmetrical vaulted room on pillars (Gtichavank), and still others feature a quadrangular room with four central pillars supporting a pyramid dome (Dadivank). In a fourth type of gavit, the vault is supported by a pair of crossed arches (Horrekavank, Bri Yeghtsi). The gavit at Gandzasar (1261) is distinctive in the latter group by virtue of its superior quality of workmanship. Its layout corresponds exactly to that of Haghpat and Mshkavank (northern Armenian Republic). At the centre of the ceiling, the cupola is illuminated by a central window which is adorned with the same stalactite ornaments as Geghard and Harrij (monasteries in the Republic of Armenia dating from the early thirteenth century).

After an interruption from the fourteenth to the sixteenth centuries, architecture flourished again during the seventeenth century. Bastions of spiritual and cultural life, the monasteries were restored and enlarged. In this period we frequently find a single church at the centre of a walled quadrangle (Amaras). As in other regions of Armenia, there are numerous monastic and parish churches constructed according to a relatively simple layout featuring a basilica with one, two, or three pairs of pillars. The nineteenth century is distinguished by the merging of innovation and a return to the grand national monuments from the past. Thus when it was decided to construct the Cathedral of Our Saviour, called Ghazanchetsots (one of the grandest churches in all of Armenia), in 1868–1888 in Shushi, it was to Etchmiadzin, the most important sanctuary for Armenians, that they looked for inspiration, at least for the plan.

More exposed to destruction, monuments from civil society are less numerous and less well preserved. Only ruins remain of the medieval fortresses. From the seventeenth and eighteenth centuries, several palaces of the meliks should be noted, especially the Beglarian Palace in Gulistan (Martakert District). In the eighteenth and nineteenth centuries Moslem monuments appear. They are linked to the creation of the khanate of Shushi, and as we have seen above, the only three mosques in Mountainous Karabagh were built in this city.

We should also mention some Moslem mausoleums from the Mongol epoch (fourteenth century) on the periphery of Mountainous Karabagh in the districts of Fizuli, Kubatly, and Lachin. The mausoleum at Khachen-Dorbatly (1314), not far from Aghdam, reveals a great similarity in sculpted decor to an Armenian funerary church of the same period, the chapel at Eghvard. Perhaps these two works are by the same artist, who signed 'Shahik' in Armenian and 'Shahenzi' in Persian?[218]

The churches' stone façades lent themselves to sculptures, which are particularly important in thirteenth-century monuments. The forms are the same as those found throughout Armenia: sculpted bands around the doors and windows, blind arcature running along the façades and the drum of the cupola, and animal reliefs above the openings. Special mention should be made of the abundant sculpted decor on two churches: Dadivank, where we see the donors displaying a model of the church, and, above all, Gandzasar, where the donors are shown on the drum with two of them holding the model above their heads. Attention should be paid to the great care which went into the construction of the church at Gandzasar, the spiritual and temporal centre of the main principality of the region. In its decor we find elements which relate it to two other Armenian monuments from the early thirteenth century: the colonnade on the drum resembles that at Harrij (1201) and the great sculpted cross at the top of the façades, probably of Georgian origin, is also found at Kecharis (prior to 1214).

Khachkars, stone slabs decorated with a cross, represent a special chapter in the history of Armenian sculpture and are unique to this country. In the first stage of their history, this type of monument already existed in Artsakh – as attested by one of the earliest dated samples of Armenia, in a village on the eastern shore of Lake Sevan (Mets Mazra, 881) which was part of the dominion of the princes of Khachen.[219] A very large number of khachkars are also found in Mountainous Karabagh. Several thirteenth-century examples are particularly refined. We note the two khachkars of Gtichavank, dating from about 1246, one of which, preserved at Etchmiadzin, shows the two bishops who founded the monastery. There are also the two plaques embedded in the bell tower at Dadivank (1283), which are veritable laceworks in stone.

More so than mural paintings, of which nothing remains except a few fragments from the interior of the main church at Dadivank, we have a fair number of illuminated manuscripts, especially from the thirteenth and fourteenth centuries. There were over thirty scriptoria at the time, including those at Gandzak, Gandzasar, Khoranashat, Targmanchats and Erits Mankants. Recently conducted research identifies a group of illuminated works specific to the Artsakh-Utik region (or Artsakh-Sevan).[220] The works in this group come from the north-east provinces of Armenia and are close, in their linear and unadorned style, to those of Siunik, but also to the miniatures from Vaspurakan (southern Armenia). They show the same naïve faces with large curved eyes under the long lines of eyebrows. The compositions are simple and monumental, often with an iconography that is original and distinct from Byzantine models.

It is not possible to discuss all the minor arts here, especially the metalworking arts which were developed in ancient Artsakh. We know that in the tenth century dyed fabrics and rugs from this region were highly valued by the Arabs. Al-Muqadasi wrote that 'They are without equal.'[221] Two accounts by the thirteenth-century Armenian historian Kirakos Gandzaketsi mention embroideries and altar curtains by his contemporaries the Princesses of Khachen, Arzu and Khorishah.[222] The abundance of rugs produced in the modern period is rooted in this solid tradition. Indeed, recent research has begun to highlight the importance of the Armenian region of Artsakh–Karabagh in the history of rugs known as Caucasian.[223] Among woven works by Karabagh Armenians , we note several types. Rugs in an 'eagle' or 'sunburst' pattern, a sub-type of Armenian rug featuring dragons, whose centre of manufacture from the eighteenth century was Jraberd (Chelabert), have characteristic large radiating medallions. There were also rugs with serpents or clouds ('cloudbands'), with octagonal medallions comprising four pairs of serpents in an S shape, and rugs with a series of octagonal, cross-shaped or rhomboid medallions, often bordered by a red band. Artsakh-Karabagh is also the source of some of the oldest rugs bearing Armenian inscriptions: the rug with three niches from the village of Banants (1602, erroneously dated 1202 by several authors), the rug of Catholicos Nerses of Albania (1731), and, perhaps, the famous 'Guhar (Gohar) Rug' (1700). We should add, finally, that most rugs with Armenian inscriptions come, it seems, from Karabagh.[224]

NOTES

1. The Turkish name 'Karabagh' does not appear in historical sources prior to the fourteenth century. It makes its appearance after the arrival of Turkish tribes in Transcaucasia in the eleventh century. We see it for the first time in the fourteenth century in *Georgian Chronicle, 1207–1318*, translated into Armenian by P. Muradian (Yerevan, 1971), p. 112. See also the *Kartlis Tskhovreba* (History of Georgia) (Tbilissi, 1959), vol. II, p. 240. The name is also mentioned by a fourteenth-century Persian historian, Hamd Allah Mustawfi of Qazwin, *The Geographical Part of the Nuzhat al-Qulub*, translated by G. Le Strange (Leiden, 1919), pp. 172–4. The term Karabagh has been examined by B. Ulubabian, *The Principality of Khachen between the Tenth and Sixteenth Centuries* (Yerevan, 1975), pp. 40–4.

2. According to G. Galoyan *et. al.*, *Mountainous Karabagh: Historical Handbook* (Armenian Academy of Sciences, Yerevan, 1988), p. 8, this name can be traced to

the Persian toponym *Bagh-i-Siyah* (black garden) which corresponds to *Bagh-i-Safid* (white garden), where the adjective 'black' refers to the mountainous and relatively wooded character of the region. The name 'black garden' is also attributed to the region's mountainous terrain, covered with forests and vineyards: L. Alishan, reprinted in M. F. Brosset, *S. Orbelian, Histoire de la Siounie*, translated by M. F. Brosset (St Petersburg, 1866), p. 61; *Encyclopedia of Islam*, new edition (Leiden, 1978), see 'Kara Bagh'. The name refers to the richness of the soil, according to R. Hewsen, 'The Meliks of Eastern Armenia', *Revue des Etudes Arméniennes*, Paris, part I, vol. IX, 1972, p. 288.

3. The study of the historical geography of ancient Armenia is based on, among others, the Armenian world atlas *Ashkharhatsuïts*, a work of the early seventh century published in French as A. Soukry, *Géographie de Moïse de Corène* (Venice, 1881). It was revised by S. Eremian, *Armenia According to Ashkharhatsuïts* (Yerevan, 1963). Also see T. Hakopian, *Historical Geography of Armenia*, 2nd edition (Yerevan, 1968) and H. Hübschmann, *Die Altarmenischen Ortsnamen* (Strasbourg, 1904).

4. This alleged link is one of three reasons employed by the Caucasian Bureau of the Communist Party for its decision of 5 July 1921 to justify the annexation of Mountainous Karabagh by Azerbaijan; *Mountainous Karabagh: Historical Handbook, op. cit.*, p. 33 (see Appendix VB). The argument is repeated, notably by I. Aliev, *Mountainous Karabagh: History, Facts, and Events* (Baku, 1989), pp. 3 and 103.

5. G. Melikishvili, *Urartian Cuneiform Inscriptions* (Moscow, 1960), p. 310, note 161, and p. 446; N. Arutiunian, *Biainili (Urartu)* (Yerevan, 1970), pp. 263–4.

6. Strabo, *Geography*, compiled and translated by F. Lasserre (Paris, 1975), book XI, chapter 14, 4 (coll. G. Bude, vol. VIII, p. 122). The filiation of Urthekhe-Artsakh was proposed by G. Kapantsian (Ghapantsian) *Chetto-Armeniaca* (Yerevan, 1931), p. 104, cited in *Mountainous Karabagh: Historical Handbook, op. cit.*, p. 7.

7. Movses Khorenatsi (Moses of Khoren), *History of the Armenians*, translated into English by R. Thomson (Cambridge, MA, London, 1978), book II, chapters 44–5, pp. 184–5.

8. This thesis has been advanced or treated by Marquart, Marr, Grousset, Adonts, Leo, Orbeli, Trever, Eremian and Toumanoff. It is discussed and refuted by H. Anasian, 'Une mise au point relative à l'Albanie caucasienne (Aluank)', *Revue des Etudes Arméniennes*, Paris, vol. VI, 1969, pp. 325–7; B. Ulubabian, *Studies in the History of the Eastern Province of Armenia, 5th–7th Centuries* (Yerevan, 1981), pp. 59–62, 112–14; A. Akopian, P. Muradian, and K. Yuzbashian, 'A Contribution to the Study of the History of Caucasian Armenia', *Patma-Banasirakan Handes* (Review of History and Philology of the Armenian Academy of Sciences), Yerevan, no. 3, 1987, p. 177; A. Akopian, *Albania-Aghuank in Greco-Latin and Ancient Armenian Sources* (Yerevan, 1987), p. 14.

9. Strabo, *op. cit.*, book XI, chapters 14, 5 (Bude, vol. VIII, p. 123).

10. A. Akopian, *op. cit.*, pp. 15–16, 82.

11. *Ashkharhatsuïts* (*op. cit.*, cf. note 3), Soukry, ed., p. 33 of the Armenian text and p. 44 of the French text; Eremian, *op. cit.*, pp. 109–110. See the List of Thrones or Gahnamak and the Military List or Zoranamak in N. Adonts, *Armenia in the Period of Justinian*, revised translation by N. Garsoian (Lisbon, 1970), pp. 191–5; also, *ibid.*, pp. 230 and 73*: the list of Princes given by Agathange.

12. Sebeos, *History*, chapter 38; Armenian edition by G. Abgarian (Yerevan, 1979), p. 125; French translation by Fr. Macler, *Histoire d'Héraclius par l'évêque Sebêos*,

(Paris, 1904), p. 82. Cf. S. Krkyasharian, *Essays on the History of Cities in Armenia and Ancient Asia Minor* (Yerevan, 1970), p. 113; *History of the Armenian People* (Yerevan, Armenian Academy of Sciences, 1971) vol. I, p. 574; G. Svazian, 'Artsakh in Historical Sources', *Lraber* (a journal for the social sciences, Armenian Academy), Yerevan, no. 11, 1989, p. 4.

13. Agathange, *History of the Armenians*, chapter 2, para. 28 (French translation in V. Langlois, *Collection des historiens ... de l'Arménie*, vol. I, Paris, 1867, p. 119).

14. It is estimated that these provinces constituted a part of Armenia after the division in 385 or 387 until the first quarter or half of the fifth century. See below, note 25.

15. P'awstos Buzand, *History of Armenia*. book IV, chapter 50; book V, chapters 4, 8, 12, 13; French translation by Langlois, *op. cit.*, vol. I (Faustus de Byzance, *Collection historique*), pp. 266, 281–2, 287–8; English translation by N. Garsoian, *The Epic Histories Attributed to P'awstos Buzand* (Cambridge, MA, 1989), pp. 167, 189–90, 193, 199–200; J. Marquart, *Eransahr nach der Geographie des Ps. Moses Chorenaci* (Berlin, 1901), p. 170. See B. Ulubabian, *Studies, op. cit.*, pp. 116–18, for the explication of a passage by this same P'awstos concerning the decade of the 330s and situating Amaras (Artsakh) 'in the vicinity of Aghouank on the frontiers of Armenia'; misinterpreted, this passage may appear to contradict the facts cited above.

16. A. Mnatsakanian, *On the Literature of the Country of Aghvank* (Yerevan, 1966 and 1969); reported on in French by H. Anasian, *op. cit.*, pp. 299–330.

17. A. Mnatsakanian, *op. cit.*, pp. 250–254 (Armenian edition); A. Akopian, *op. cit.*, pp. 72–82; A. Akopian, P. Muradian, and K. Yuzbashian, *op. cit.*, p. 179.

18. I. Aliev, *op. cit.*, pp. 19, 27, 54; K. Aliev, *Caucasian Albania from the First Century BC to the First Century AD* (Baku, 1974), pp. 83–123; Z. Buniyatov, *Azerbaijan from the Seventh to the Ninth Centuries* (Baku, 1965); F. Mamedova, *Political History and Historical Geography of Caucasian Albania* (Baku, 1986).

19. These sources are reviewed in A. Mnatsakanian, *op. cit.*, pp. 31–5; H. Anasian, *op. cit.*, pp. 303–5; and especially A. Akopian, *op. cit.*, pp. 21–7 and 96–8. See Strabo, XI, 14, 4; Pliny the Elder, *Natural History*, book VI, chapter 15 (translated into French by A. de Grandsagne, vol. V [Paris, 1830], p. 32); Plutarch, *Lives*, vol VIII, Pompey, chapter 34, 1–4 (coll. G. Bude, Paris, 1973), pp. 206–7; Ptolemy, *Geography*, book V, chapter 12 (ed. C. Muller, vol. I, part 2e [Paris, 1901], pp. 931–2); Dion Cassius, *Roman History*, book XXXVI (English translation by E. Cary, vol. III [London, 1969], coll. Loeb, pp. 92–3); Agathange, *op. cit.*, chapter 2, para. 28 and chapter 112, para. 795 (French translation in V. Langlois, *Collection des historiens ... de l'Arménie*, vol. I [Paris, 1867], pp. 119 and 171); P'awstos Buzand, *op. cit.*, book III, chapter 7 and book V, chapter 13 (French translation in Langlois, *op. cit.*, pp. 215 and 288; English translation by N. Garsoian, *The Epic Histories*, pp. 73 and 200); *Ashkharhatsuïts, op. cit.*, book V, chapter 21 (ed. and trans. by A. Soukry [Venice, 1881], p. 29 of the Armenian text and p. 39 of the French text). Concerning the Gahnamak and Zoranamak lists see note 11. The frontier between Armenia and Caucasian Albania has also been investigated by B. Ulubabian, *Studies, op. cit.*, pp. 113–14; A. Akopian, P. Muradian and K. Yuzbashian, *op. cit.*, p. 175; A. Novoseltsev, 'Regarding the Political Frontier Between Armenia and Albania in Ancient Times', in the collection *Kavkaz i Vizantiya* (Yerevan, 1979), I, pp. 10–18; Sh. Smbatian, 'The Southern Frontier of Caucasian Albania Reconsidered', *Lraber*, Yerevan, no. 10, 1989, pp. 3–17.

20. Aside from the historic sources and, notably, *The History* by Movses Daskhurantsi (or Kaghankatvatsi), the study of Caucasian Albania was founded until the 1960s on the works of Barkhudariantz, Manandian, Marquart, Shanidze, Eremian and Trever. This body of work was supplemented and updated by the research of A. Mnatsakanian, *op. cit.*; cf. H. Anasian, *op. cit.* This research has been developed, among others, by Ulubabian and Akopian. The Azerbaijani viewpoint is found in the books cited in note 18 and severely criticized by the Armenian Academy and the Institute of History of the Academy of the USSR (see note 99).

21. On the Arsacids of Albania see B. Ulubabian, *Studies, op. cit.*, pp. 136–7 and 144–5; C. Toumanoff, *Studies in Christian Caucasian History* (Washington, 1963), p. 258, note 362; C. Toumanoff, *Manuel de généalogie et de chronologie pour l'histoire de la Caucasie chrétienne* (Rome, 1976), pp. 79–80 and 587.

22. On the Massagetae, see A. Akopian, *op. cit.*, pp. 98–108.

23. The traditionally accepted date for the partition of Armenia is 387 but E. Danielian suggests 385. See 'The Date of the Partition of Armenia: 387 or 385?', *Patma-Banasirakan Handes*, Yerevan, no. 1, pp. 203–14.

24. J. Marquart, *op. cit.*, p. 118, interprets this transfer in an imprecise manner when he writes that 'after the partition of Armenia, the Albanian king seized the 12 districts of Artsakh and the 8 districts of Utik'. The explication in the *Encyclopedia of Islam* (*op. cit.*, see 'Arran', p. 660) is more precise: 'Before 387 AD, the land between the two rivers was considered part of Armenia, comprising the provinces of Ardzakh, Uti, and P'aitakaran. After the division of Armenia between the Greeks and the Sasanids in 387 AD, the first two provinces went to Albania/ Arran…. This is one reason for much confusion in the designation of Arran.'

25. B. Ulubabian, 'Concerning the Administrative and Political Situation in Northeast Armenia before the Marzpanate', *Banber Erevani Hamalsarani*, Yerevan, no. 2, 1975, pp. 149–64; B. Harutiunian, 'The Administrative and Political Situation in the Northeast Regions of the Kingdom of Greater Armenia, 387–451', *Banber Erevani Hamalsarani*, Yerevan, no. 2, 1976, pp. 77–95; A. Akopian, *op. cit.*, pp. 110–14. This is confirmed by the fact that the princes of Artsakh (Tsavdek) and Utik (Gardman) are still mentioned in documents concerning Armenia during the first half of the fifth century. See B. Ulubabian, *Studies, op. cit.* According to G. Svazian, *op. cit.*, p. 8, the Marzpanate of Arran was formed only after 461, after the disappearance of the Albanian Kingdom.

26. On these matters see B. Ulubabian, *Studies, op. cit.* and A. Akopian, *op. cit.* For a summary of Akopian's work see *Revue des Études Arméniennes*, Paris, vol. XXI, 1988–1989, pp. 485–95.

27. *Ashkharhatsuïts*, Soukry, *op. cit.*, pp. 29 and 33 of the Armenian text and pp. 39 and 44 of the French text; Eremian, *op. cit.*, pp. 105 and 109–10; Sh. Smbatian, *Movses Kalankatuatsi, History of the Country of Aluank*, Russian translation with commentaries (Yerevan, 1983), pp. 179–80, note 23. This definition of ancient Albania as the 'true Albania' is adopted by J. Marquart, *op. cit.*, p. 118: 'Das eigentliche Albanien, d.h. das Landzwischen dem Kur and dem Kaukasus.' A very clear differentiation between 'Armenian Aghuank' on one side of the Kura and 'Aghuank of Shirvan' on the other is made by E. Dulaurier in his translation of *La Chronique de Matthieu d'Edesse* (Paris, 1858), pp. 409–10, note 4.

28. H. Anasian, *op. cit.*, p. 307.

29. Eghishe, chapter 3, (Elishe, *History of Vardan and the Armenian War*, translated by R. Thomson [Cambridge, MA, 1982], p. 127) and Movses Daskhurantsi, *History of Albania* (Aghuank), book II, chapter 2 (English translation by C.

Dowsett, *Movses Dasxuranc'i, The History of the Caucasian Albanians* [London, 1961], p. 67; cf. B. Ulubabian, *Studies, op. cit.*, pp. 115 and 139; J. Marquart, *op. cit.*, p. 118.

30. H. Anasian, *op. cit.*, p. 308.

31. Vache appears on the list of Albanian kings compiled by M. Daskhurantsi (book I, chapter 15) who confesses that he cannot specify their lineage. C. Toumanoff (*Manuel, op. cit.*, pp. 79–80 and 587) places him among the Arsacids, B. Ulubabian (*Studies, op. cit.*, p. 150) among the local dynasts, descendants of Arran and called Arranshahik. If we accept that Vachagan the Pious was an Arranshahik (see below), it must logically follow that the same is the case for his paternal uncle, Vache (M. Daskhurantsi, book I, chapter 14 and 17); A. Akopian (*op. cit.*, p. 243, no. 4), however, disputes this relationship.

32. On the Arranshahik dynasty see A. Mnatsakanian, *op. cit.*, pp. 73–9; B. Ulubabian, *The Principality, op. cit.*, pp. 56–9 and 86–7; B. Ulubabian, *Studies, op. cit.*, pp. 129–197. Although the name Arranshahik was not used as a dynastic name until the seventh century, it is generally recognized that this dynasty, which Movses Daskhurantsi presents as the 'ancient Armenian line of Erranshahik' (book II, chapter 17; Dowsett translation, p. 108), descended from Arran (see below) and had existed in antiquity before the arrival of the Arsacids, been supplanted by them, but reappeared after their disappearance and outlived the Persian Mihranids of the seventh to ninth centuries and continued its existence: C. Toumanoff, *Studies, op. cit.*, pp. 257–8, note 362; C. Toumanoff, *Manuel, op. cit.*, pp. 22, 68–72, 587–90.

33. Movses Khorenatsi, *op. cit.*, book II, chapter 8; English translation by R. Thomson, pp. 139–40; Movses Daskhurantsi, *op. cit.*, book I, chapter 4; Dowsett translation, p. 4; J. Marquart, *op. cit.*, p. 120.

34. A. Musheghian, 'Pseudo-Albanian Literature and Its Apologists', *Lraber*, Yerevan, 1989, no. 8, p. 23 indicates that in 554 the Syrian author Zachary the Orator names 'Little King of Arran', the literal translation of 'Arranshahik', lord 'of the country of Arran, in this same country of Armenia'!

35. B. Ulubabian, *Studies, op. cit.*, pp. 51–3.

36. B. Ulubabian, *The Principality, op. cit.*, p. 57; B. Ulubabian, *Studies, op. cit.*, p. 115.

37. Like Vache II, Vachagan III the Pious is considered an Arsacid by Toumanoff and an Arranshahik by Ulubabian (see note 31 above). The latter (B. Ulubabian, *Studies, op. cit.* p. 141) does not truly demonstrate his case but, nevertheless, two arguments are in his favour: (1) M. Daskhurantsi (book I, chapter 17, the translation of his passage by Dowsett, p. 27, should be corrected by his note 1, pp. 27–8) reports that under the Persian King Vologese, the lords of Aghuank named Vachagan, 'of the royal house of their nation', to reign over their lands, and one can reasonably suppose that Daskhurantsi meant by that the local line of Arran; (2) the domains and centres of activity of Vachagan correspond essentially to the right bank of the Kura; cf. A. Akopian, *op. cit.*, p. 243, note 4. According to A. Akopian. *op. cit.*, pp. 187–8, however, questions concerning the historicity of Vachagan the Pious remain.

38. On the reign of Vachagan see B. Ulubabian, *Studies, op. cit.*, pp. 155–64 and 187–97.

39. Movses Daskhurantsi, book III, chapter 23 (chapter 22 in the Dowsett translation, p. 225).

40. The baptism of Albania, immediately following that of Armenia, and coinciding

with that of Iberia, is studied by A. Akopian, *op. cit.*, pp. 124–7.

41. On this monument see M. Hasratian, 'L'ensemble architectural d'Amarass', *Revue des Etudes Arméniennes*, Paris, vol. XII, 1977, pp. 243–59. These events were recorded by M. Daskhurantsi, book I, chapters 14 and 23 (Dowsett translation, pp. 21–3 and 45).

42. M. Daskhurantsi, book I, chapters 6 and 9, book II, chapter 48, book III, chapter 24 (Dowsett translation, chapters 24–33, pp. 5, 7–8, 117, and 228); A. Akopian, *op. cit.*, pp. 126–7, 129–30, note 25 and p. 184.

43. On the pre-eminence of the Armenian Church over the Albanian and the rule of consecration by which the Albanian Catholicos is invested by the Armenian, see B. Ulubabian, *Studies, op. cit.*, p. 203; A. Akopian, *op. cit.*, pp. 140–2; Sh. Smbatian, *M. Kalankatuatsi, History, op. cit.*, pp. 183–4, 217–19, 223, and 229. This is affirmed by numerous testimonies in the sources, notably in M. Daskhurantsi, book I, chapter 9, book II, chapter 48, book III, chapters 4, 7–9, 22, and 24 (Dowsett translation, chapter 22, numbered 21, pp. 8, 176, 191–6 and 220–1; chapter 24, numbered 23, pp. 229–31). As an example we cite book III, chapter 8, where the Catholicos of Albania declares to the Armenian Catholicos, 'we recognize before God and before you, Patriarch, that the consecration of the Albanian Catholicos must be carried out by the chair of St. Gregory [the Armenian Church], with our agreement, as it has been since the epoch of St. Gregory, for it is the source of our enlightenment'. (Dowsett translation, p. 195, corrected and completed by notes 2 and 3, p. 195). Several passages in S. Orbelian, *History of Siunik* (chapters 7, 26, 31 and 43; Brosset translation, pp. 16, 67, 85, and 137–9) reveal the following hierarchy: (1) Patriarch-Catholicos of Armenia, (2a) Archbishop-Catholicos of Albania, (2b) Bishop-Metropolitan of Siunik. In the eighteenth century the Catholicos of Gandzasar still received his investiture from Etchmiadzin. M.-F. Brosset, *Collection d'Historiens Armeniens* (St Petersburg, 1874–1876), vol. II, p. 193.

44. On the participation of the Albanian bishops at the Council of Dwin in 506, see A. Akopian, *op. cit.*, pp. 127–9.

45. A. Akopian, *op. cit.*, pp. 135–6. Movses Daskhurantsi, book II, chapter 4 (Dowsett translation, p. 70) attributes the move of the ecclesiastical seat to Partav to the devastating Khazar (or Hun) incursions. Extrapolating from this fact and having stated that as of the fifth century the term Aghuank is used in Armenian sources to refer to the south bank of the Kura, M.-F. Brosset imagines a massive Albanian migration to the south-west: 'The ancient Aghuans, Albanians, moved ... south toward the Kura. Later they crossed this river and established themselves in the Qarabagh Plain, the Armenian provinces of Artsakh, Utik, and Phaitacaran'. S. Orbelian, *History of Siunik*, translated by M. Brosset (St Petersburg, 1864), p. 8, note 1; the same author continues, 'Later, the Khazar incursions drove them to the South'. *Idem*, introduction, 1866, p. 137. This thesis is found later in R. Grousset, *Histoire de l'Arménie* (Paris, 1947), p. 99, note 2 and J. M. Thierry in *Revue des Etudes Arméniennes*, Paris, vol. XV, 1981, p. 291.

46. On the progressive replacement of Albanian by Armenian, see A. Akopian, *op. cit.*, pp. 137–40.

47. On these inscriptions and deciphering them, see A. Abrahamian, *Deciphering Caucasian Armenian Inscriptions* (Yerevan, 1964); A. Shanidze, *The Language and Literature of the Caucasian Albanians* (Tbilissi, 1960); S. Muraviev, 'Three Studies of Caucasian Albanian Literature', in *Annual of Ibero-Caucasian Linguistics*, Tbilissi, vol. VIII, 1981, pp. 222–325 (especially pp. 260–93).

48. These testimonies (Al-Istakhri cited by Ibn Hawkal and Al-Muqadasi) are reported in J. Marquart, *op. cit.*, p. 117; *Encyclopedia of Islam*, under 'Arran'; B. Ulubabian, *Studies*, *op. cit.*, pp. 71–2; A. Akopian, *op. cit.*, p. 140, note 65; Akopian, Muradian and Yuzbashian, *op. cit.*, p. 172; G. Svazian, *op. cit.*, p. 13.

49. A. Mnatsakanian, *op. cit.*, pp. 87–95; G. Vorochil, 'De l'histoire de l'Albanie caucasienne et de l'écriture albanaise', in *Bedi Kartlisa, revue de Kartvélologie*, Paris, vol. XXXII, 1974, pp. 280–1; Akopian, Muradian and Yuzbashian, *op. cit.*, p. 173. B. Ulubabian, *Studies*, *op. cit.*, pp. 94–107 and A. Musheghian, *op. cit.*, p. 17 highlight the absurdity of the Azerbaijani thesis according to which Albanian literature would have been destroyed by the Armenian priesthood. According to G. Dumezil, 'Une chrétienté disparue, les Albaniens du Caucase', *Mélanges Asiatiques*, Paris, 1940–1941, fasc. I, pp. 125–6, the Islamization of the Albanians is responsible for the disappearance of their literature. 'Between the 7th and 10th centuries the work of the evangelists was destroyed by Islam and with it went the books and even the alphabet they employed.'

50. B. Ulubabian, *Studies*, *op. cit.*, pp. 73–9; H. Anasian, *op. cit.*, p. 307, note 41.

51. For an introduction to Armenian dialectology see H. Adjarian, *Classification des dialectes arméniens* (Paris, 1909). On the dialect of Karabagh see Adjarian, pp. 25–32 and B. Ulubabian, *Studies*, *op. cit.*, pp. 54–8.

52. B. Ulubabian, *Studies*, *op. cit.*, pp. 201–4.

53. Movses Daskhurantsi, book II, chapter 48, book III, chapters 3–9 and 24 (Dowsett translation, chapter 24 numbered 23, pp. 176–8, 189–97, 228–31); Stepanos Orbelian, *History of Siunik*, chapters 22, 25, and 26 (M. Brosset translation, pp. 53–4, 61–3, and 65–7); R. Grousset, *op. cit.*, pp. 266 and 269; J. Mecerian, *Histoire et institutions de l'Eglise arménienne* (Beirut, 1965), pp. 71–2; B. Ulubabian, *Studies*, *op.cit.*, pp. 204–5; Akopian, Muradian, and Yuzbashian, *op. cit.*, pp. 183–4; A. Akopian, *op. cit.*, pp. 191–4 and 253–4 (Akopian questions the historicity of the Albano-Siunikian schism in the late sixth and early seventh centuries).

54. Movses Daskhurantsi, book III, chapters 3–8 (Dowset translation, pp. 189–96); Stepanos Orbelian, chapter 52 (Brosset translation, pp. 158–65); J. Muyldermans, *La domination arabe en Arménie, extrait de l'Histoire Universelle de Vardan* (Louvain-Paris, 1927), p. 99; J. Laurent, *L'Arménie entre Byzance et l'Islam*, M. Canard's revised edition (Lisbon, 1980), pp. 318–19; R. Grousset, *op. cit.*, pp. 312, 390–1, 470–2, 479–80; A. Ter Ghevondian, *Armenia and the Arab Caliphate* (Yerevan, 1977), pp. 80–2; B. Ulubabian, *Studies*, *op. cit.*, pp. 267–71.

55. Z. Buniyatov, *op. cit.*, pp. 97 and 101. Among the numerous refutations of these assertions are A. Ter Ghevondian, *Armenia*, *op. cit.*, p. 82; Sh. Smbatian, *Movses Kalankatuatsi, History*, *op. cit.*, pp. 228–230, note 26; A. Musheghian, *op. cit.*, p. 17; H. Anasian, *op. cit.*, p. 301, note 19. These tendentious interpretations take a pathologically anti-Armenian direction in the work of certain disciples of Buniyatov. Thus one may read in a brochure published by the Institute of History of the Academy of Azerbaijan: 'Following this dirty [sic] intrigue [the reaction of the Armenian Pontif to the attempted split], the Arabs put an end to the sovereignty of Albania, and the Albanian Church was subordinated to the Armenian. That was the beginning of a progressive de-ethnicization of the Albanian nation. Thus the darkest [sic!] forecasts were realized. The Armenians (for the nth time) began to oppress the Albanians.' I. Aliev, *op. cit.*, p. 62.

56. On the Mihranids, Mihranians, or Mihrakans see C. Toumanoff, *Studies*, *op. cit.*, pp. 216 and 258; Toumanoff, *Manuel*, *op. cit.*, pp. 397–400 and 589–90; B.

Ulubabian, *Studies, op. cit.*, pp. 234–60; H. Svazian, 'Aghvank and the Mihranian Line', *Lraber*, Yerevan, no. 9, 1980, p. 91–101. Brosset confuses the Mihranids and the Arranshahiks, S. Orbelian, *Histoire, op. cit.*, II, 1866, p. 62, note 1, p. 137, note 2, p. 183.

57. M. Daskhurantsi, book II, chapter 17 (Dowsett translation, pp. 108–9); H. Anasian, *op. cit.*, pp. 316–17.

58. C. Toumanoff, *Studies, op. cit.*, p. 216; C. Toumanoff, 'Aransahikides ou Haykides? Derniers rois de Siounie', *Handes Amsorya* (Vienna, 1976), p. 172, note 10; R. Hewsen, 'The Meliks', *op. cit.*, p. 309.

59. A. Mnatsakanian, *op. cit.*, pp. 84–6.

60. For Arminiya and the Arab period, see *Histoire des Arméniens*, under the direction of G. Dedeyan (Toulouse, 1982), chapter 5, pp. 185–214; *Encyclopedia of Islam*, under 'Arminiya', pp. 635–8; J. Laurent, *op. cit.*

61. M. Daskhurantsi, book III, chapters 20 and 23 (Dowsett translation, chapter 20, numbered 19, p. 214, and chapter 23, numbered 22, p. 226); S. Orbelian, chapter 34 (Brosset translation, p. 96, and the introduction, p. 24); R. Grousset, *op. cit.*, p. 349; C. Toumanoff, *Manuel, op. cit.*, p. 232. M. Daskhurantsi and S. Orbelian write that the murderer of Varaz-Trdat, Nerseh of Siunik, 'seized all of his property'. But we must conclude that this is an exaggeration, or that the local princes, who were forced into retreat by the Mihranids, recovered their former domains, since during the same epoch the Arranshahik Sahl and his son Atrnerseh (who were not from the Siunid dynasty – see below) became masters of the entire region.

62. C. Toumanoff, *Studies, op. cit.*, pp. 216–17, note 250; C. Toumanoff, *Manuel, op. cit.*, pp. 589–90; C. Toumanoff, 'Aransahikides', *op. cit.*, pp. 172 and 174; R. Hewsen, 'The Meliks', *op. cit.*, pp. 309–10.

63. J. Marquart, *op. cit.*, p. 210; A. Ter Ghevondian, *Armenia, op. cit.*, pp. 168 and 183; G. Svazian, *op. cit.*, p. 6; also see M. Daskhurantsi, book II, chapter 19 (Dowsett translation, p. 114) on the marriage of Juansher (Jivanshir) with a Princess of Siunik.

64. M. Daskhurantsi, book III, chapter 23 (Dowsett translation, chapter 22, p. 226); S. Orbelian (Brosset translation), p. 183; B. Ulubabian, *The Principality, op. cit.*, p. 62; C. Toumanoff, *Studies, op. cit.*, p. 216; C. Toumanoff, *Manuel, op. cit.*, p. 231; C. Toumanoff, 'Aransahikides', *op. cit.*, p. 172; R. Hewsen, 'The Meliks', *op. cit.*, part 1, pp. 309–10, part 2, pp. 284 and 286. Several authors treat Atrnerseh as Siunid because they believe that he was the son of Sahak Siuni; see Brosset, *op. cit.*, introduction, p. 24; R. Grousset, *op. cit.*, p. 351; Toumanoff and Hewsen, *ibid.*; M. Hasratian and J. M. Thierry, 'Le couvent de Ganjasar', *Revue des Etudes Arméniennes*, Paris, vol. XV, 1981, p. 292. But, as we shall see in note 65, his father Sahl belonged to the Arranshahik line.

65. Sahl's dynastic line is clearly indicated by M. Daskhurantsi, book III, chapter 20 (Dowsett translation, chapter 19, p. 214) where he calls him 'Lord of the Arran-shahiks'. Nevertheless, some authors believe that he could have been a Bagratid. This is refuted by B. Ulubabian, *The Principality, op. cit.*, pp. 66–9. Several authors believed that Sahl was Siunid or identified himself as Prince Sahak Siuni (Brosset, Toumanoff, Hewsen) because Daskhurantsi (book III, chapter 23; Dowsett, p. 226) presented him as 'Lord of Siunik who took possession by force of the Canton of Guegham'. But, as B. Ulubabian has noted, there is an obvious contradiction since the Canton of Guegham was already in Siunik and, consequently, a lord of this region could not 'take possession of it by force'. The most

plausible explanation (B. Ulubabian, *The Principality, op. cit.*, pp. 71–3) is that Artsakh in this period was sometimes called 'Little Siunik', and one must understand 'lord of Little Siunik' when this expression is applied to Sahl and his descendants such as Grigor-Hamam, 'Prince of Siunik and Albania'. It could also be thought that the extension of Sahl's domain to the south-east banks of Lake Sevan, taken from the Siunids, justified his title Lord of Siunik. In addition, we note that Sahl's movements (first half of the ninth century) essentially unfolded in Artsakh and Cambysen (whose centre was Shake) and not, strictly speaking, in Siunik.

66. A. Mnatsakanian, *op. cit*, pp. 83–4; H. Anasian, 'Une mise au point', *op. cit.* , pp. 317–18; A. Ter Ghevondian, *Armenia, op. cit.*, p. 158; A. Ter Ghevondian, 'Notes sur le Sake-Kambecan (Ier–XIVe s.)', *Revue des Etudes Arméniennes*, Paris, vol. XXI, 1988–1989, p. 325. Z. Buniyatov, *op. cit.*, p. 185, wants to transform Sahl into an Albanian and to present his domains acquired in Siunik (presently the southern portion of the Republic of Armenia) as a part of Albania. This is not accidental. About this author's perspective, H. Anasian has written: 'everything capable of being considered Albanian automatically becomes Azerbaijani'.

67. M. Daskhurantsi, book III, chapters 20 and 21 (Dowsett translation, chapter 19, p. 215 and chapter 20, p. 218).

68. On the Shahdadids of Ganja see V. Minorsky, *Studies in Caucasian History* (London, 1953), chapter 1, 'New Light on the Shaddidads of Ganja (951–1075)', pp. 1–77. On the emirates of Shirvan and Derbend see V. Minorsky, *A History of Sharwan and Darbend in the Tenth–Eleventh Centuries* (Cambridge, 1958). The Shahdadids of Ganja, as well as their Turkish successors, always attempted to expand to the west, toward the Armenian mountains where they progressively dislodged the Princes of Utik, who were obliged to seek refuge elsewhere. One of them, Oshin of Utik, went to Cilicia where he would be one of the founders of the new Armenian state, giving birth to the Hetumian Dynasty. See M. Chamchian, *History of Armenia*, vol. II (Venice, 1785), p. 995; B. Ulubabian, *The Principality, op. cit.*, p. 96; G. Dedeyan, *Les pouvoirs arméniens dans le Proche-Orient méditerranéen (1068–1144)*, doctoral thesis, University of Paris I, 1990, p. 283.

69. For an overview of the Armenian kingdoms of the ninth–eleventh centuries see *Histoire des Arméniens, op. cit.*, chapter 6, pp. 215–68.

70. On this 'Albanian particularism' see Akopian, Muradian and Yuzbashian, *op. cit.*, p. 169; A. Akopian, *op. cit.*, pp. 261–5 and 275. Concerning the tendency of the Princes of Artsakh to seek independence with regard to the Bagratids whose suzerainty extended, in principle, to the Kura, see A. Akopian, *op. cit.*, pp. 269–70.

71. B. Ulubabian, *The Principality, op. cit.*, pp. 63–4 and the genealogical table.

72. B. Ulubabian, *The Principality, op. cit.*, p. 64.

73. C. Toumanoff, *Manuel, op. cit.*, pp. 112–15, 519, and 588.

74. M. Daskhurantsi, book III, chapter 22 (Dowsett translation, chapter 21, pp. 221–2); also S. Orbelian, chapter 55 (Brosset translation, p. 172); B. Ulubabian, *The Principality, op. cit.*, p. 75. Daskhurantsi and the Catholicos John VI Draskhanakertsi reported that Grigor-Hamam also distinguished himself by his action to free the Armenian Catholicos Georg from the Arabs in 895; R. Grousset, *op. cit.*, p. 403.

75. On Grigor-Hamam and his possessions see B. Ulubabian, *The Principality, op. cit.*, pp. 74–8; A. Ter Ghevondian, 'Notes,' *op. cit.*, pp. 324–6. Based on the research of A. Mnatsakanian, H. Anasian, *op. cit.*, p. 318, writes, 'The Kingdom of Albania

reconstituted by Hamam the Oriental was incontestably an Armenian kingdom established on the Armenian lands of Albania.'

76. A. Mnatsakanian, *op. cit.*, pp. 80–1 and 183–204; H. Anasian, *op. cit.*, p. 318 and 324–5; B. Ulubabian, *The Principality, op. cit.*, pp. 74–82 disputes the identification of the two Hamams.

77. A. Ter Ghevondian, 'Notes', *op. cit.*; C. Toumanoff, *Manuel, op. cit.*, pp. 69–70, 587, and 590; B. Ulubabian, *The Principality, op. cit.*, pp. 81 and 84. Chalcedonism was adopted by the son of Atrnerseh, Ishkhanak, under the influence of his mother, the Georgian Princess Dinar.

78. A. Ter Ghevondian, *op. cit.*; however, the author indicates that in 1404 the majority of the population of the region of Shake was still certified as Armenian by the Catholic Archbishop Jean de Gaillefontaine.

79. B. Ulubabian, *The Principality, op. cit.*, pp. 82 and 101. In chapter 44 of his *History of Armenia*, the Catholicos of Armenia John VI Draskhanakertsi reports that at the start of the tenth century, when fleeing the Arabs, he chose refuge 'in the Eastern Province, Aghvank', with the Grand Prince Sahak-Sevada and his brother King Atrnerseh of Cambysen because 'These people are also of our fold, and flocks of our pasture.' See Yovhannes Drasxanakertc'i, *History of Armenia*, translated from classical Armenian by K.H. Maksoudian (Atlanta, 1987), p. 166.

80. According to the historian and Catholicos John VI Draskhanakertsi, chapter 60 (Maksoudian translation, pp. 208–12), for wanting to appropriate the Cantons of Dzorapor and Gardman, newly united with the crown of Armenia, Sahak-Sevada was defeated and blinded by his son-in-law, King Ashot Erkat; R. Grousset, *op. cit.*, pp. 454–5; C. Toumanoff, *Manuel, op. cit.*, p. 236; B. Ulubabian, *The Principality, op. cit.*, pp. 102 and 105–6.

81. M. Daskhurantsi, book III, chapter 23 (Dowsett translation, chapter 22, p. 227); B. Ulubabian, *The Principality, op. cit.*, pp. 90–1; A. Akopian, *op. cit.*, p. 213.

82. According to the historian Stepanos Asoghik Taronetsi, the Kingdom of Parissos ended in 1003; this is repeated by M. Brosset in S. Orbelian, *op. cit.*, Introduction, p. 31; C. Toumanoff, 'Aransahikides', *op. cit.*, p. 174. But B. Ulubabian, *The Principality, op. cit.*, pp. 92–5 calls attention to a final king of Parissos who reigned until about the mid-eleventh century.

83. R. Grousset, *op. cit.*, pp. 401, 451, 455, 518; B. Ulubabian, *The Principality, op. cit.*, pp. 88–9; A. Ter Ghevondian, *Armenia, op. cit.*, pp. 238–9; A. Akopian, *op. cit.*, p. 269.

84. Constantine Porphyrogenitus, *De Cerimoniis aulae byzantinae*, book II, chapter 48 (Corpus Scriptorum Historiae Byzantinae, Constantinus Porphyrogenitus, vol. I [Bonn, 1829], p. 687); A. Ter Ghevondian, *Armenia, op. cit.*, p. 239.

85. M. Brosset in S. Orbelian, *op. cit.*, Introduction, pp. 138–9; B. Ulubabian, *The Principality, op. cit.*, p. 30.

86. V. Minorsky, *Studies, op. cit.*, p. 25 (cites the source on the fall of the Shahdidads of Ganja as Ahmad B. Lutfullah, Jami al-duwal); R. Huseinov, 'La conquête de l'Azerbaïdjan par les Seldjoucides', *Bedi Kartlisa, Revue de Kartvélologie*, Paris, vols 19–20, 1965, p. 108 (promotes the confusion between Arran-Shirvan in Transcaucasia and Azerbaijan south of the Arax in Iran).

87. According to B. Ulubabian, *The Principality, op. cit.*, pp. 107–9, Senekerim was the son of the Grand Prince Sevada, himself the grandson of Sahak-Sevada of Parissos. This relationship derives from the facts presented by S. Orbelian (chapter 59). A different relationship adopted by C. Toumanoff (*Manuel, op. cit.*, p. 588 and 'Aransahikides', *op. cit.*, pp. 169–71 and 175) seems less convincing. It relies on

an unknown branch of the Arranshahiks based on an unidentified genealogy by Matthew of Edessa.

88. S. Orbelian, chapter 59 (Brosset translation, p. 182); R. Grousset, *op. cit.*, pp. 616–17; C. Toumanoff, *Studies, op. cit.*, pp. 216–17; C. Toumanoff, *Manuel, op. cit.*, p. 235; C. Toumanoff, 'Aransahikides', *op. cit.*, pp. 170–1; B. Ulubabian, *The Principality, op. cit.*, p. 108.

89. S. Orbelian, chapter 61 (Brosset translation, p. 191); R. Hewsen, 'The Meliks', *op. cit.*, I, pp. 310–11, II, p. 235, IV, p. 467; C. Toumanoff, *Manuel, op. cit.*, pp. 71–2, 520, 525; C. Toumanoff, 'Aransahikides', *op. cit.*, p. 172. This Hasan is sometimes confused with his homonym, son of Vakhtang I Sakarr of Khachen who retired to the monastery at Dadivank at the end of his life. R. Hewsen, 'The Meliks', *op. cit.*; C. Toumanoff, *Manuel, op. cit.*, p. 238; M. Hasratian and J. M. Thierry, *op. cit.*, p. 293. In fact, S. Orbelian states that Hasan is from the Gerakaretsi family; he is therefore a distant relative of Vakhtang but not his son. See B. Ulubabian, *The Principality, op. cit.*, p. 26: he refutes Alishan's assertion, which seems to be the source of this confusion.

90. N. Garsoian, 'L'indépendence retrouvée', in *Histoire des Arméniens* (G. Dedeyan, *op. cit.*), p. 245; S. Orbelian, *op. cit.* (Brosset translation) p. 192.

91. B. Ulubabian, *The Principality, op. cit.*, pp. 98–9; A. Akopian, *op. cit.*, pp. 216, 223, 240–1. It is assumed that M. Daskhurantsi was none other than the Catholicos of Albania whom he mentions at the end of his text.

92. A. Akopian, *op. cit.*, pp. 261–5, 268–70; Akpopian, Muradian and Yuzbashian, *op. cit.*, p. 170.

93. A. Akopian, *op. cit.*, p. 270. The tenth-century Arab historian Mas'udi indicates that the states north of the Kura were inhabited by a majority of Moslems with the exception of the Kingdom of Shake.

94. *Encyclopedia of Islam*, under 'Arran'; C. Toumanoff, *Studies, op. cit.*, pp. 58–9, writes of the Albanians: 'Armenianized, and in part Georgianized, in the early Middle Ages, they later lost their identity through submersion by Islam.' Several Armenian specialists estimate that the consolidation and union of the Albanian peoples (on the north bank of the Kura) began in the first centuries AD but was halted by Islamization before the process was concluded. For that reason Albanian was a political category and never fully an ethnic category. For the same reason, the Christian peoples of these regions were assimilated by the Armenians. Akopian, Muradian and Yuzbashian, *op. cit.*, pp. 172–3; G. Sarkissian and P. Muradian, 'We Have Not Yet Seen the Last of the Buniyatov Affair', *Lraber*, Yerevan, no. 5, 1988, p. 43.

95. *Encyclopedia of Islam*, under 'Adharbaydjan'.

96. A. Akopian, *op. cit.*, pp. 271–2 and 276; Akopian, Muradian and Yuzbashian, *op. cit.*, p. 174.

97. A. Ter Ghevondian, *Armenia, op. cit.*, p. 158.

98. A. Akopian, *op. cit.*, p. 276; also see the account given by K. Yuzbashian in *Lraber*, Yerevan, no. 10, 1989, p. 85. We note that the twelfth-century Armenian historian Matthew of Edessa, who lived far from these regions, wrote of 'the country of the Aghuans that we call anterior Armenia' and described Partav and Gandzak as Armenian cities even though they were held by Moslems. E. Dulaurier, *op. cit.*, part II, chapters 126 and 131, part III, chapter 227, pp. 193, 199, and 297.

99. Works cited in note 18. Among the refutations published in Armenian academic journals, we cite B. Arutiunian, 'When Scientific Honesty is in Default', *Lraber*, Yerevan, no. 7, 1987, pp. 33–56; Akopian, Muradian and Yuzbashian, *op. cit.*; G. Sarkissian and P. Muradian, *op. cit.*

100. See note 55 for an extremely tendentious interpretation of the events of ecclesiastical history. For a succinct presentation of the controversies between Armenian and Azerbaijani historians over 'the peculiar ethnogenesis of the Azerbaijanis via the Caucasian Albanians', see C. Mouradian, *De Staline à Gorbatchev, Histoire d'une république soviétique: l'Arménie* (Paris, 1990), pp. 422–3 and p. 460, note 20; also N. Dudwick, 'The Case of the Caucasian Albanians: Ethnohistory and Ethnic Politics', *Cahiers du Monde Russe et Soviétique*, Paris, vol. XXXI (2–3), April–September 1990, pp. 377–84. Certain authors give the appearance of objectivity by placing the two parties side by side and claiming that the arguments are equally well founded. One such author is R. Caratini, *Dictionnaire des nationalités et des minorités en URSS* (Paris, 1990), p. 36, who writes that 'the Azeri thesis [according to which 'the first inhabitants of these mountains' were the 'ancestors of the Azeris'] is based on Persian texts' at least as old as the texts invoked by the Armenians. But Caratini never provides specific information on these mysterious 'ancient Persian texts'.

101. The 'Catholicos of Albania', whose seat was at Gandzasar until the nineteenth century, would have been in the best position to speak about the Albanians if they had survived until the modern period, as certain historians from the Baku school try to demonstrate. But we note that in the eighteenth century, when the Catholicos Essayi Hasan-Jalaliants spoke of the 'Aghvans' (Albanians), he mentions a mythic people who had long since disappeared from the Caucasus and become the ancestors of the Afghans: 'there was near Khorasan and Qandahar a nation called Aghovan, indigenous, it is said, to the mountains of the Caucasus and the land of the Alans who still preserved their ancient name. Formerly Christians, they were conquered by Tamerlane ... and forced to leave their country in the number of 25,000 families and settled in their actual home.' See E. Hasan-Dchalaliants, *Histoire de l'Aghovanie* in M.-F. Brosset, *Collections d'Historiens Arméniens* (St Petersburg, 1874–1876), vol. II, pp. 193–220, chapter 4, pp. 205–6. On the contrary, even deprived of political sovereignty, Armenia, for the Patriarch of Gandzasar, was an actual living, human reality in Karabagh, and he clearly spoke of 'the Armenians, our compatriots' (p. 194) and 'our Armenian nation' (p. 195), thus qualifying all the other Armenian historians, including M. Daskhurantsi. Also see note 166 below.

102. Sh. Mkrtichian, *The Historical–Architectural Monuments of Mountainous Karabagh* (Yerevan, 1988), p. 5.

103. D. Akhundov, *The Architecture of Azerbaijan in Antiquity and the Early Middle Ages* (Baku, 1986), chapter 5, pp. 222–36. Refuted by M. Hasratian, 'The Artsakhian School of Armenian Architecture: Facts and Falsifications', *Lraber*, Yerevan, 1989, no. 9, pp. 3–15.

104. D. Akhundov, *op. cit.*, chapters 6 and 7, pp. 236–52. See also the communication by D. and M. Akhundov to the VIth International Symposium on Georgian Art, Tbilissi, 1983. For a strong rebuttal see A. Jakobson, 'The Monastery at Gandzasar and the Khachkars: Facts and Fictions', *Patma-Banasirakan Handes*, Yerevan, 1984, no. 2, pp. 146–52.

105. A recent summary of these questions is found in A. Musheghian, *op. cit*, pp. 16–33. Let us simply recall that, even in the title of the first chapter of his Collection of Laws, Mkhitar Gosh justified his work thus, 'Chapter One contains the response to those who have spoken badly of us, claiming that there is no court of justice in Armenia.' Regarding the eminent thirteenth-century historian Kirakos Gandzaketsi (of Gandzak), in the introduction to his History, he lists all of the

ancient historians of Armenia whose work he wishes to continue, and he mentions
Movses Daskhurantsi (Kaghankatvatsi). In the two pages which this passage
occupies, the historian uses the expression 'our country of Armenia' three times and
'our Armenian people' once.

106. *Histoire des Arméniens* (Dedeyan), *op. cit.*, chapter 8 ('Time of the Crusades'), p.
297.
107. B. Ulubabian, *The Principality, op. cit.*, pp. 113–23.
108. *Histoire des Arméniens, op. cit.*, p. 301, map. On Khachen during this period see
B. Ulubabian, *The Principality, op. cit.*, pp. 124–62.
109. *Histoire des Arméniens, op. cit.*, pp. 299–300.
110. B. Ulubabian, *The Principality, op. cit.*, pp. 130 and 133.
111. B. Ulubabian, *The Principality, op. cit.*, p. 130.
112. The inscription of Hasan of Haterk in the monastery at Dadivank: *Corpus
Inscriptionum Armenicarum*, book V, by S. Barkhudarian, Yerevan, no. 707, 1982,
p. 198.
113. B. Ulubabian, *The Principality, op. cit.*, p. 135.
114. B. Ulubabian, *The Principality, op. cit.*, pp. 137–41.
115. *History of the Armenian People*, vol. III (Armenian Academy of Sciences, Yerevan,
1976), pp. 549–50.
116. B. Ulubabian, *The Principality, op. cit.*, p. 145.
117. Due to the coincidence of dates and names, the Vakhtangians of Haterk and those
of Khokhanaberd have been confused by several authors including S. Orbelian
(Brosset translation), p. 179; I. Orbeli, 'Hasan Jalal, Prince of Khachen' in *Selected
Works* (Yerevan, 1963), pp. 146–7; R. Hewsen, 'The Meliks', *op. cit.*, I, p. 311; II,
pp. 286–7; C. Toumanoff, *Manuel, op. cit.*, pp. 238–9; J. M. Thierry, *Revue des
Etudes Arméniennes*, vol. XV, *op. cit.*, p. 294 (he argues that there was only one
Vakhtang, that of Khokhanaberd, and that he had two wives). However, there are
several indications in the sources, as well as family differences and differences in
the titles, which allow us to distinguish these two families. Thus, Hasan of Khokhanaberd had as his wife 'Takouhi, daughter of the King of Baghk', while Hasan
the Monk of Haterk had married Mama, daughter of King Kyurike of Lorr. Vardan
Vardapet points out that in 1214 'both Vakhtang, reigning Lord (of Haterk) and
the other Vakhtang Sakarriants (Vakhtang-Tangik of Khokhanaberd), son-in-law
of Ivane, Lord of Lower Khachen, died....' Vakhtang of Haterk, 'Primate of
Princes', had as his wife Arzu Khatun Artsruni while Vakhtang-Tangik was married
to Khorishah Zakarian. See the references in B. Ulubabian, *The Principality, op.
cit.*, pp. 138–47 (but the genealogical tables contain errors).
118. See note 112.
119. *Corpus Inscriptionum Armenicarum*, book VI, by S. Avakian and R. Janpoladian
(Yerevan, 1977), pp. 64–5, note 127.
120. *Corpus Inscriptionum Armenicarum*, book V, pp. 198–9, note 708.
121. B. Ulubabian, *The Principality, op. cit.*, p. 148. The author points out errors in the
Dopian genealogy (pp. 153–4).
122. *History of the Armenian People, op. cit.*, pp. 606–10; *Histoire des Arméniens, op. cit.*,
pp. 302–3.
123. B. Ulubabian, *The Principality, op. cit.*, p. 184.
124. *History of the Armenian People, op. cit.*, p. 614.
125. *Corpus Inscriptionum Armenicarum*, book V, pp. 38–40, note 82.
126. B. Ulubabian, *The Principality, op. cit.*, pp. 190–2.
127. I. Orbeli, *op. cit.*, p. 149; B. Ulubabian, *The Principality, op. cit.*, p. 172.

128. Kirakos Gandzaketsi, *History of Armenia*, classical Armenian edition (Yerevan, 1961), chapter 55, p. 358; M.-F. Brosset translation, *Deux historiens arméniens* (St Petersburg, 1870), p. 173 (chapter 55 numbered 56 here). The passage in question is truncated and mentions 'the Grand Prince of Khachen, province of Artsakh, Hasan, familiarly named Dchalal, a devoted and God-fearing person'.

129. B. Ulubabian, *The Principality*, op. cit., pp. 189, 219–20, and 226.

130. I. Orbeli, op. cit., pp. 153–4 and 161; B. Ulubabian, *The Principality*, op. cit., pp. 194–5.

131. I. Orbeli, op. cit., pp. 154–6 and 162; B. Ulubabian, *The Principality*, op. cit., pp. 196 and 203–4.

132. *History of the Armenian People*, op. cit., p. 622; *Histoire des Arméniens*, op. cit., pp. 303–4.

133. B. Ulubabian, *The Principality*, op. cit., pp. 207–8.

134. I. Orbeli, op. cit., pp. 157–8; B. Ulubabian, *The Principality*, op. cit., pp. 211–12. These titles confirm that Hasan was the first prince of all of Khachen (Upper, Lower, and Tsar). The titles 'autocrat' and 'king' indicate that his power was not limited by any authority.

135. B. Ulubabian, *The Principality*, op. cit., pp. 176–7 and 180. On the rapid cultural expansion of Khachen during the thirteenth century, see pages 244–8.

136. The inscriptions at Khachen were collected by S. Barkhudarian, *Corpus Inscriptionum Armenicarum*, book V (Artskah, Yerevan), 1982.

137. Works on the monastery at Gandzasar available in western languages include M. Hasratian and M. Thierry, op. cit., pp. 289–316; J. M. Thierry and P. Donabedian, *Les arts arméniens* (Paris, 1987), p. 526; B. Ulubabian and M. Hasratian, *Gandzassar*, Documenti di Architettura Armena, no. 17 (Milan, 1987); P. Cuneo, *Architettura Armena* (Rome, 1988), pp. 443–5.

138. M. Hasratian, 'The Artsakhian', op. cit., p. 3, note 3, specifies that Gandzasar was mentioned for the first time as the seat of a Catholicossate in 1420. Nevertheless, we know that Catholicos Hovhannes was buried at St James of Mets Arrank, the former residence of the Catholicos, in 1469.

139. *History of the Armenian People*, op. cit., pp. 628–32 and 637–41; *Histoire des Arméniens*, op. cit., pp. 304–5.

140. *History of the Armenian People*, op. cit., pp. 656–68; *Histoire des Arméniens*, op. cit., pp. 305–6.

141. B. Ulubabian, *The Principality*, op. cit., pp. 130–1, 269, and 293.

142. B. Ulubabian, *The Principality*, op. cit., pp. 301–14.

143. B. Ulubabian, *The Principality*, op. cit., p. 305.

144. *History of the Armenian People*, op. cit., vol. IV, p. 39.

145. B. Ulubabian, *The Principality*, op. cit., p. 320.

146. B. Ulubabian, *The Principality*, op. cit., p. 333.

147. *History of the Armenian People*, op. cit., vol. IV, p. 25.

148. On Tamerlane and the Karakoyunlu in Armenia, see *History of the Armenian People*, op. cit., vol. IV, pp. 24–38; *Histoire des Arméniens*, op. cit., pp. 344–7.

149. On the reign of Jihan Shah, see *History of the Armenian People*, op. cit., vol. IV, pp. 39–46; *Histoire des Arméniens*, op. cit., pp. 347–8.

150. *History of the Armenian People*, op. cit., vol. IV, pp. 39–40.

151. R. Hewsen, 'The Meliks', op. cit., I, pp. 297 and 312; also see Hewsen, 'The Meliks, op. cit., IV, p. 467; *Histoire des Arméniens*, p. 381. B. Ulubabian, *The Principality*, op. cit., pp. 417–20, disputes that the melikate was instituted by Jihan Shah in the fifteenth century. According to him, although it had existed since the

beginning of the sixteenth century, this title was officially recognized during the reign of Shah Abbas I at the close of the sixteenth and the beginning of the seventeenth centuries.

152. On the domination of the Akkoyunlu, see *History of the Armenian People, op. cit.*, IV, pp. 47–56; *Histoire des Arméniens, op. cit.*, pp. 348–50.

153. R. Hewsen, 'The Meliks', *op. cit.*, I, pp. 288–9.

154. On the history of the melikates, see R. Hewsen, 'The Meliks', *op. cit.*, I, 1972 and II, 1973–1974; *Histoire des Arméniens, op. cit.*, pp. 377–84; Raffi, *The Melikates of Khamsa* in *Works*, vol. X (Yerevan, 1964).

155. On the genealogy of the meliks, see C. Toumanoff, *Manuel, op. cit.*, pp. 243–59, 302–9, 528–32, and 540–1; R. Hewsen, 'The Meliks', *op. cit.*, in particular I, pp. 308–24; *Histoire des Arméniens, op. cit.*, pp. 380–2.

156. *Histoire des Arméniens, op. cit.*, p. 382.

157. *Ibid.*, p. 358.

158. *History of the Armenian People, op. cit.*, IV, p. 99; *Histoire des Arméniens, op. cit.*, pp. 412–13; B. Ulubabian, *The Principality, op. cit.*, pp. 368–9.

159. *History of the Armenian People, op. cit.*, IV, pp. 85 and 250–1; B. Ulubabian, *op. cit.*, p. 347.

160. R. Hewsen, 'The Meliks', *op. cit.*, I, pp. 297–8.

161. This can be considered the origin of the differentiation between Mountainous and Lower Karabagh.

162. R. Hewsen, 'The Meliks', *op. cit.*, p. 298; *Histoire des Arméniens, op. cit.*, p. 383.

163. G. Libaridian, ed., *The Karabagh File* (Paris, Cambridge, MA and Toronto, 1988), p. 3.

164. On these missions and the liberation movement of the first decades of the eighteenth century see *History of the Armenian People, op. cit.*, IV, pp. 128–75; *Armenian–Russian Relations During the First Third of the Eighteenth Century* (collection of documents), vols I and II (Yerevan, 1964 and 1967); P. Arutiunian, *The Armenian People's Liberation Movement in the First Quarter of the Eighteenth Century* (Moscow, 1954); A. Essefian, 'The Mission of Israel Ori for the Liberation of Armenia' in *Recent Studies in Modern Armenian History* (Cambridge, MA, 1972); G. Ezov, *The Relations of Peter the Great with the Armenian People* (St Petersburg, 1898); A. Johannisjan, *Israel Ori und die armenische Befreiungsidee* (Munich, 1913); Leo, *Works*, vol. III, book 2 (Yerevan, 1973), pp. 29–209; *Histoire des Arméniens, op. cit.*, pp. 421–4.

165. *History of the Armenian People, op. cit.*, IV, pp. 162–3.

166. For the history of the Armenian–Georgian alliance of 1722 following Catholicos Essayi Hasan-Jalaliants' mission to King Vakhtang in Tiflis, see M.-F. Brosset, *Collection d'Historiens Arméniens*, vol. II (E. Hasan-Dchalaliants, *Histoire de l'Aghovanie*), pp. 215–17. The Catholicos wrote: 'I left and organized the princes' troops which were thought able to restore the Armenian principality'; concerning 'the Armenian troops which the meliks had gathered' and their leaders, he specifies, 'With the meliks of Karabagh, they brought together the brave and energetic youth of the House of Aghuania and formed a corps exceeding 12,000 men' (p. 216). To explain the aid of the king of Georgia, the Catholicos adds, 'His manner of treating us was filled with kindness, reflecting, above all, his innate affection for the Armenian nation' (p. 217). We note that in a recent Russian language edition of the work of Catholicos E. H. Jalaliants by the Institute of History of the Academy of Azerbaijan (Baku, 1989), the expressions 'principality of Armenia' and 'Armenian nation' have been replaced by 'Albanian state' (p. 35)

and 'our people' (p. 36). The objective of these changes is, clearly, to lead the reader to believe that the author, Catholicos Essayi, was not Armenian, but Albanian.

167. *Histoire des Arméniens, op. cit.*, p. 423.

168. *History of the Armenian People, op. cit.*, IV, p. 147.

169. *History of the Armenian People, op. cit.*, IV, p. 155.

170. *Histoire des Arméniens, op. cit.*, p. 424. On the battles between the meliks' troops and the Turkish occupation forces during the 1720s, see *History of the Armenian People, op. cit.*, IV, pp. 156–61.

171. *History of the Armenian People, op. cit.*, IV, pp. 185–6.

172. Leo, *Works, op. cit.*, III, 2, p. 263; R. Hewsen, 'The Meliks', *op. cit.*, I, p. 325; *History of the Armenian People, op. cit.*, IV, pp. 194–5.

173. *Mountainous Karabagh: Historical Handbook, op. cit.*, p. 13.

174. Leo, *op. cit.*, pp. 264–5.

175. Leo, *op. cit.*, p. 267; Hewsen, 'The Meliks', *op. cit.*, I, p. 325. On the history of the khanate of Karabagh also see Mirza Adiguezal-Bek, *Karabagh-name* (Baku, 1950); Mirza Jamal Jevanshir Karabakhski, *History of Karabagh* (Baku, 1959); Ahmedbek Javanshir, *The Political Existence of the Khanate of Karabagh (from 1747 to 1805)* (Baku, 1961).

176. Leo, *op. cit.*, pp. 266–71. Independent master of such a vast territory, Panah Khan even coined his own money called the 'panahabar' (Leo, *op. cit.*, p. 271).

177. Leo, *op. cit.*, p. 306.

178. Leo, *op. cit.*, p. 317; *History of the Armenian People, op. cit.*, IV, p. 209; *Histoire des Arméniens, op. cit.*, p. 434.

179. Leo, *op. cit.*, pp. 338, 342–5, 350, and 355; *History of the Armenian People, op. cit.*, IV, pp. 220–4 and 229.

180. Leo, *op. cit.*, pp. 352, 354–5, and 358; *History of the Armenian People, op. cit.*, pp. 229–30.

181. Leo, *op. cit.*, pp. 346 and 354; *History of the Armenian People, op. cit.*, p. 229.

182. Leo, *op. cit.*, pp. 221, 359–61, and 364; *History of the Armenian People, op. cit.*, p. 229.

183. Leo, *op. cit.*, pp. 383 and 385–6; *History of the Armenian People, op. cit.*, pp. 236 and 241.

184. Leo, *op. cit.*, pp. 401–2; *History of the Armenian People, op. cit.*, pp. 240 and 243. This campaign was encouraged, accompanied, and facilitated by Archbishop Arghutian who, in particular, organized the supply of Russian troops by Armenian villagers. But after the precipitate departure of these troops, thousands of Armenians had to flee reprisals from the Moslem population.

185. Leo, *op. cit.*, pp. 404–5, 409–11, and 414.

186. R. Hewsen, 'The Meliks', *op. cit.*, I, pp. 386–7.

187. *Encyclopedia of Islam*, under 'Arran', 'Adharbaydjan', 'Ghuzz', and 'Kara Bagh'.

188. *History of the Armenian People, op. cit.*, IV, p. 69.

189. *Encyclopaedia Universalis* (Paris, 1985), entry for 'Azerbaïdjan'.

190. Minorsky, 'Studies', *op. cit.*, p. 34, note 1; *Mountainous Karabagh, op. cit.*, p. 13.

191. *Mountainous Karabagh, op. cit.*, pp. 16–17. The Russian translation of *Travels in Europe, Asia, and Africa from 1394 to 1427* by Johan Schiltberger, published in Odessa in English in 1866 by P. Bruun, was reissued in Baku in 1984 by academician Z. Buniyatov. We note that in this new edition the passage referring to Karabagh 'situated in Armenia' and 'the Armenian villages' has been removed by the Azerbaijani editor.

192. *Mountainous Karabagh, op. cit.*, pp. 17–18.

193. *Mountainous Karabagh, op. cit.*, p. 18.

194. *Mountainous Karabagh, op. cit.*, pp. 18–19.

195. This applies specifically to Mountainous Karabagh. One could reach different conclusions using population figures for the other areas of the former khanate of Karabagh. Indeed, under Khan Ibrahim, the melikates only constituted five of the 21 districts in the khanate and several of them were populated by turcophone Moslems (Tatars); *History of the Armenian People, op. cit.*, V, p. 15. One must exercise care to avoid confusing Mountainous Karabagh, essentially Armenian, and neighbouring districts with mixed populations. With this in mind, one cannot write, as R. Caratini has done in *Dictionnaire des nationalités, op. cit.*, p. 38, that 'There have been centuries when Mountainous Karabagh has been as much home to Azeris as to Armenians' without specifying that these 'centuries' of Azeri Turkish presence only began in the second half of the eighteenth century and that this Turkish population remained a very small minority.

196. A. Marutian, G. Sarkissian, and Z. Kharatian, 'The Ethno-Cultural Characteristics of Artsakh', *Lraber*, Yerevan, no. 6, 1989, pp. 5–7. The figures cited refer only to territories corresponding to the actual Autonomous Region.

197. I. Aliev, *op. cit.*, pp. 76–8. The author does not hesitate to write, 'On the territory of the actual Autonomous Region of Mountainous Karabagh until the nineteenth century, there was never any Armenian presence which could be considered even remotely important' (p. 78).

198. *History of the Armenian People, op. cit.*, V, pp. 171 and 175; *Histoire des Arméniens, op. cit.*, p. 445. Regarding the transfer of Armenian populations from the Ottoman Empire in 1829–1830, this had no bearing whatsoever on Karabagh. *History of the Armenian People, op. cit.*, V, p. 192; *Histoire des Arméniens, op. cit.*, p. 446.

199. *Mountainous Karabagh, op. cit.*, p. 19.

200. *Mountainous Karabagh, op. cit.*, p. 19.

201. *History of the Armenian People, op. cit.*, V, pp. 113–14, 121, and 134–5; *Histoire des Arméniens, op. cit.*, pp. 443–4. On the Treaty of Gulistan see *Russian Treaties with the East: Political and Economic Treaties*, collected by T. Yuzefovich (St Petersburg, 1869), pp. 208–14; A. Yoannissian, *The Unification of Transcaucasia with Russia and International Relations at the Start of the Nineteenth Century* (Yerevan, 1958).

202. *History of the Armenian People, op. cit.*, V, p. 18; *Mountainous Karabagh, op. cit.*, p. 15.

203. *History of the Armenian People, op. cit.*, V, pp. 136–40.

204. *History of the Armenian People, op. cit.*, V, p. 170; *Histoire des Arméniens, op. cit.*, p. 445.

205. *History of the Armenian People, op. cit.*, V, pp. 202–5 and 210; *Histoire des Arméniens, op. cit.*, pp. 447–8.

206. *History of the Armenian People, op. cit.*, V, pp. 209–10.

207. *History of the Armenian People*, VI (Yerevan, 1981), p. 15.

208. S. Manukian and H. Vahramian, *Gharabagh, Documenti* (Milan, 1988), p. 47.

209. D. Ananun, 'Gharabagh', in *Hayastani Kooperatsia*, August 1920, reissued in *Grakan Tert*, Yerevan, no. 52 (2352) 22 December 1989.

210. M.-F. Brosset, *Collection d'Historiens Arméniens*, II, p. 194, note 2; *History of the Armenian People, op. cit.*, V, p. 214; *Histoire des Arméniens, op. cit.*, p. 448.

211. A. Marutian, G. Sarkissian and Z. Kharatian, *op. cit.*, p. 6.

212. This section is based on several studies mentioned above, notably the articles in

the *Encyclopedia of Islam* and the *Encyclopaedia Universalis* as well as G. Asatrian, 'Concerning the Toponym Azerbaijan, the Azeri Language, and Related Questions', *Grakan Tert*, Yerevan, no. 40 (2360), 29 September 1989. See also R. Enayatollah, *Azerbaijan and Arran (Caucasian Albania)* (Teheran, 1981); R. Caratini, *op. cit.*, pp. 40–1.

213. According to D. McDowall, the Kurdish population in Azerbaijan is 150,000. See *The Kurds*, Minority Rights Group Report no. 23 (London, 1989), p. 26.

214. On the medieval architecture of Artsakh-Khachen see H. Voskian, *The Monasteries of Artsakh* (Vienna, 1953); Sh. Mkrtichian, *op. cit.*; M. Lala Comneno, P. Cuneo and S. Manukian, *Gharabagh*, Documenti di Architettura Armena, no. 19 (Milan, 1988); M. Hasratian, 'The Artsakhian School', *op. cit.*; P. Cuneo, *Architettura*, *op. cit.*, pp. 428–59.

215. Concerning the inscriptions see note 136.

216. On Tsitsernavank see P. Cuneo, 'La basilique de Tsitsernakavank (Cicernakavank) dans le Karabagh', *Revue des Etudes Arméniennes*, Paris, vol. IV, 1967; J. M. Thierry and P. Donabedian, *Les arts arméniens*, *op. cit.*, p. 509.

217. For this monastery see M. Hasratian, 'Le complexe monastique de Dadivank', *Terzo Simposio Internazionale di Arte Armena, 1981, Atti* (Venice, 1984), pp. 275–87; P. Donabedian, *op. cit.*, pp. 511–12; J. M. Thierry and M. Hasratian, 'Dadivank en Arc'ax', *Revue des Etudes Arméniennes*, Paris, vol. XVI, 1982, pp. 259–88; P. Cuneo, *Architettura*, *op. cit.*, pp. 450–5.

218. J. M. Thierry and P. Donabedian, *op. cit.*, p. 521; M. Usseynov, L. Bretanitski and A. Salamzade, *History of the Architecture of Azerbaijan* (Moscow, 1963), pp. 151–6; L. Bretanitski, *Architecture of Azerbaijan from the Twelfth to the Fifteenth Centuries* (Moscow, 1966), pp. 188–95.

219. B. Ulubabian, *The Principality*, *op. cit.*, pp. 45 and 74–5. A yet older *khachkar* existed here but only the base dated 853 remains. It is the oldest dated inscription known in Mountainous Karabagh. See *Corpus Inscriptionum Armenicarum*, *op. cit*, V, inscr. no. 1, p. 12.

220. E. Korkhmazian, I. Drampian and G. Akopian, *La miniature arménienne, XIIIe–XIVe siècles* (Leningrad, 1984), pp. 17–18; H. Hakopian, *The Miniatures of Artsakh and Utik, Thirteenth–Fourteenth Centuries* (Yerevan, 1989).

221. B. Ulubabian, *The Principality*, *op. cit.*, p. 267.

222. Kirakos Gandzaketsi, classical Armenian edition (Yerevan, 1961), chapter XIV, pp. 215–16), mentions altar curtains made by Arzu Khatun and her daughters for the churches at the monasteries of Nor-Getik, Haghpat, Makaravank, and Dadivank (Brosset translation, *Deux historiens*, *op. cit.*, chapter 14 numbered 15, pp. 107–8); K. Gandzaketsi, chapter XXX (1961 edition, p. 268). The author reports that after the death of her husband Vakhtang-Tangik, Khorishah left for Jerusalem where she lived on her 'hand work' (the word *dzeragorts* can also mean embroidery but Brosset, *op. cit.*, chapter 30 numbered 31, p. 132, translates it incorrectly as 'work').

223. L. Der Manuelian and M. L. Eiland, *Weavers, Merchants, and Kings* (Forth Worth, 1984); M. Kazarian (Ghazarian), *Armenian Carpets* (Yerevan, 1985); M. Ghazarian, *Armenian Carpets* (Los Angeles, 1988).

224. This, at least, is what emerges in *Weavers, Merchants and Kings*, *op. cit.*, where over half of the 66 pieces with inscriptions come from Karabagh or are attributed to it. The same is true for A. and J. Gregorian, *Armenian Rugs from the Gregorian Collection*, (Needham, MA, 1987), where over half of the 104 rugs with inscriptions are from Karabagh.

SELECT BIBLIOGRAPHY

Abrahamian, A. *Deciphering Caucasian Albanian Inscriptions.* Yerevan, 1964 (in Russian).

Adjarian, H. *Classification des dialectes arméniens.* Paris, 1909 (in French).

Adonts, N. *Armenia in the Period of Justinian.* Revised translation by N. Garsoian, Lisbon, 1970.

Agathange. *History of the Armenians.* Classical Armenian edition, translated into modern Armenian, Yerevan, 1983; French translation in V. Langlois, *Collection des historiens … de l'Arménie.* Paris, vol. I, 1867.

Akhundov, D. *The Architecture of Azerbaijan in Antiquity and the Early Middle Ages.* Baku, 1986 (in Russian).

(H)Akopian, A. *Albania-Aghuank in Greco-Latin and Ancient Armenian Sources.* Yerevan, 1987 (in Russian).

(H)Akopian, A., P. Muradian and K. Yuzbashian. 'A Contribution to the Study of the History of Caucasian Albania', *Patma-Banasirakan Handes* (Review of History and Philology of the Armenian Academy of Sciences). Yerevan, no. 3, 1987 (in Russian).

Aliev, I. *Mountainous Karabagh: History, Facts, and Events.* Baku, 1989 (in Russian).

Aliev, K. *Caucasian Albania from the First Century BC to the First Century AD.* Baku, 1974 (in Russian).

Alishan, Gh. 'Artsakh', *Bazmavep,* Venice (St Lazzaro), vols CXLVI and CXLVII, 1988 and 1989 (in Armenian).

Ananun, D. 'Gharabagh', *Hayastani Kooperatsia,* August 1920, republished in *Grakan Tert,* Yerevan, no. 52, 22 December 1989 (in Armenian).

Anasian, H. 'Une mise au point relative à l'Albanie caucasienne (Aluank)', *Revue des Etudes Arméniennes,* Paris, vol. VI, 1969.

Armenian-Russian Relations during the First Third of the Eighteenth Century (collection of documents). Yerevan, vols I and II, 1964 and 1967 (in Russian).

(H)Arutiunian, B. 'When Scientific Honesty Is in Default', *Lraber,* Yerevan, no. 7, 1987 (in Russian).

(H)Arutiunian, N. *Biainili (Urartu).* Yerevan, 1970 (in Russian).

(H)Arutiunian, P. *The Armenian People's Liberation Movement in the First Quarter of the Eighteenth Century.* Moscow, 1954 (in Russian).

Asatrian, G. 'Concerning the Toponym Azerbaijan, the Azeri Language, and Related Questions', *Grakan Tert,* Yerevan, no. 40, 29 September 1989 (in Armenian).

Ashkharatsuïts (Armenian World Atlas), see under *Géographie de Moïse de Corène,* and Eremian.

Avagian, S. *History of the Press in Karabagh (1828–1920).* Yerevan, 1989 (in Armenian).

Barkhudariants, M. *The Country of the Aghuans and Its Neighbours.* Tiflis, 1893 (in Armenian).

Barkhudariants, M. *Artsakh.* Baku, 1895 (in Armenian).

Bournoutian, G. *A History of Qarabagh: An Annotated Translation of Mirza Jamal Javanshir Qarabaghi's* Tarikhe-e Qarabagh. Costa Mesa, CA, 1994.

Brosset, M.-F. *Histoire de la Siounie,* by S. Orbelian, translated by M. Brosset. St Petersburg, 1864, Introduction, 1866.

Brosset, M.-F. *Collection d'Historiens Arméniens.* St Petersburg, 2 vols, 1874–1876.

Buniyatov, Z. *Azerbaijan from the Seventh to the Ninth Centuries.* Baku, 1965 (in Russian).

Caratini, R. *Dictionnaire des nationalités et des minorités en URSS.* Paris, 1990.

Chamchian, M. *History of Armenia.* Venice, vol. II, 1785 (in Armenian).

Constantine Porphyrogenitus. *De Cerimoniis aulae byzantinae.* Book II, chapter 48 (Corpus Scriptorum Historiae Byzantinae. Constantinus Porphyrogenitus, vol. I), Bonn, 1829.

Corpus Inscriptionum Armenicarum. Book V, Artsakh by S. Barkhudarian, Yerevan, 1982; book VI, Ijevan District by S. Avakian and R. Janpoladian, Yerevan, 1977 (in Armenian).

Cuneo, P. *Architettura armena.* Rome, 1988.

Cuneo, P. 'La basilique de Tsitsernakavank (Cicernakavank) dans le Karabagh', *Revue des Etudes Arméniennes,* Paris, vol. IV, 1967.

Danielian, E. 'The Date of the Partition of Armenia: 387 or 385?', *Patma-Banasirakan Handes,* Yerevan, no. 1, 1980 (in Armenian).

Dedeyan, G. *Les pouvoirs arméniens dans le Proche-Orient méditerranéen (1068–1144).* Doctoral thesis, University of Paris I, 1990.

Der Manuelian, L. and M.L. Eiland. *Weavers, Merchants, and Kings.* Fort Worth, Kimbell Art Museum, 1984.

Dion Cassius. *Roman History.* Book XXXVI, English translation by E. Cary, coll. Loeb, vol. III, London, 1969.

Donabedian, P. 'Une nouvelle mise au point sur l'Albanie du Caucase', *Revue des Etudes Arméniennes,* Paris, vol. XXI, 1988–1989.

Donabedian, P. and C. Mutafian. *Le Karabagh: Une terre arménienne en Azerbaïdjan.* Paris, 1989.

Dudwick, N. 'The Case of the Caucasian Albanians: Ethnohistory and Ethnic Politics', *Cahiers du Monde Russe et Soviétique,* Paris, vol. XXXI (2–3), April–September 1990.

Dumezil, G. 'Une chrétienté disparue, les Albaniens du Caucase', *Mélanges Asiatiques,* Paris, part I, 1940–1941.

Eghishe. *On Vardan and the Armenian War.* Classical Armenian edition with modern Armenian translation, Yerevan, 1989. English translation by R. Thomson. Elishe, *History of Vardan and the Armenian War.* Cambridge (MA), London, 1982.

Enayatollah, R. *Azerbaijan and Arran* (Caucasian Albania). Teheran, 1981 (in Persian).

Encyclopedia of Islam. New edition. Leiden, 1978, 1979, 1983.

Eremian, S. *Armenia According to Ashkharhatsuïts.* Yerevan, 1963 (in Armenian).

Essefian, A. 'The Mission of Israel Ori for the Liberation of Armenia', in *Recent Studies in Modern Armenian History.* Cambridge (MA), 1972.

Ezov. G. *The Relations of Peter the Great with the Armenian People.* St Petersburg, 1898 (in Russian).

Géographie de Moïse de Corène. Translated by A. Soukry, Venice, 1881 (in classical Armenian and French).

Georgian Chronicle (1207–1318). Armenian translation by P. Muradian, Yerevan, 1971.

Geyushev, R. *Christianity in Caucasian Albania.* Baku, 1984 (in Russian).

Ghazarian (Kazarian), M. *Armenian Carpets.* Los Angeles, 1988 (in Armenian and English).

Ghaziyan, A. *Artsakh.* Armenian Ethnography and Folklore, vol. XV, Yerevan, 1983 (in Armenian).

Grousset, R. *Histoire de l'Arménie.* Paris, 1947.

Hakopian, H. *The Medieval Art of Artsakh.* Yerevan, 1991 (in Armenian).

Hakopian, H. *The Miniatures of Artsakh and Utik, Thirteenth–Fourteenth Centuries.* Yerevan, 1989 (in Armenian).

Hakopian, T. *Historical Geography of Armenia.* 2nd edition, Yerevan, 1968 (in Armenian).

Hamd Allah Mustawfi of Qazwin. *The Geographical Part of the Nuzhat al-Qulub.* Translated by G. Le Strange, Leiden, 1919.

Harutiunian, B. 'The Administrative and Political Situation in the Northeast Regions of the Kingdom of Greater Armenia, 387–451', *Banber Erevani Hamalsarani,* Yerevan, no. 2, 1976 (in Armenian).

Hasan-Dchalaliants, E. *Histoire de l'Aghovanie* in M.-F. Brosset, *Collection d'Historiens Arméniens.* St Petersburg, vol. II, 1874–1876.

Hasratian, M. 'The Artsakhian School of Armenian Architecture: Facts and Falsifications', *Lraber,* Yerevan, no. 9, 1989 (in Russian).

Hasratian, M. 'Le complexe monastique de Dadivank', *Terzo Simposio Internazionale di Arte Armena,* 1981, *Atti.* Venice, 1984.

Hasratian, M. 'L'ensemble architectural d'Amarass', *Revue des Etudes Arméniennes,* Paris, vol. XII, 1977.

Hasratian, M. 'La tétraconque à niches d'angle de Moxrenis', *Revue des Etudes Arméniennes,* Paris, vol. XXI, 1988–1989.

Hasratian, M. and M. Thierry. 'Le couvent de Ganjasar', *Revue des Etudes Arméniennes,* Paris, vol. XV, 1981.

Hewsen, R. 'The Meliks of Eastern Armenia', *Revue des Etudes Arméniennes,* Paris, part I, vol. IX, 1972; part II, vol. X, 1973–1974; part IV, vol. XIV, 1980.

Hewsen, R. 'On the Alphabet of the Caucasian Albanians', *Revue des Etudes Arméniennes,* Paris, vol. I, 1964.

Histoire des Arméniens. Under the direction of G. Dedeyan, Toulouse, 1982.

History of the Armenian People. Yerevan, Armenian Academy of Sciences, vols I–VI, 1971–1984 (in Armenian).

Hovhannes Draskhanakertsi (John VI Catholicos). *History of Armenia.* Tiflis, 1912 (classical Armenian). English translation by Rev. K.H. Maksoudian, Yovhannes Drasxanakertc'i, *History of Armenia.* Atlanta, 1987.

Hübschmann, H. *Die altarmenischen Ortsnamen.* Strasbourg, 1904.

Huseinov, R. 'La conquête de l'Azerbaïdjan par les Seldjoucides', *Bedi Kartlisa, revue de Kartvélologie,* Paris, vols 19–20, 1965.

Jakobson, A. 'The Monastery at Gandzasar and the Khachkars: Facts and Fictions', *Patma-Banasirakan Handes,* Yerevan, no. 2, 1984 (in Russian).

Javanshir, Ahmedbek. *The Political Existence of the Khanate of Karabagh (from 1747 to 1805).* Baku, 1961 (in Russian).

Johannisjan, A. *Israel Ori und die armenische Befreiungsidee.* Munich, 1913.

Kapantsian (Ghapantsian), G. *Chetto-Armeniaca.* Yerevan, 1931 (in Russian).

Kartlis Tskhovreba (History of Georgia). Tbilissi, vol. II, 1959 (in Georgian).

Kazarian (Ghazarian), M. *Armenian Carpets.* Yerevan, 1985 (in Russian and English).

Khatchatrian, A. *The Armenian Army in the Eighteenth Century.* Yerevan, 1968 (in Russian).

Kirakos Gandzaketsi. *History of Armenia.* Yerevan, 1961 (classical Armenian); French translation by M.-F. Brosset, *Deux historiens arméniens.* St Petersburg, 1870.

Korkhmazian, E., I. Drampian and G. Akopian. *La miniature arménienne, XIIIe-XIVe siècles.* Leningrad, 1984.

Krkyasharian, S. *Essays on the History of Cities in Armenia and Ancient Asia Minor.* Yerevan, 1970 (in Armenian).

Kurdian, H. 'The Newly Discovered Alphabet of Caucasian Albanians', *Journal of the Royal Asiatic Society,* 1956.

Lala Comneno, M., P. Cuneo, and S. Manukian. *Gharabagh.* Documenti di Architettura Armena, no. 19, Milan, 1988.

Langlois, V. *Collection des historiens anciens et modernes de l'Arménie.* Paris, vols I and II, 1867 and 1869.

Laurent, J. *L'Arménie entre Byzance et l'Islam.* Revised edition by M. Canard, Lisbon, 1980.

Leo. *Works.* Yerevan, vol. III, book 2, 1973 (in Armenian).

Libaridian, G. *The Karabagh File.* Cambridge, MA, Paris, Toronto, The Zoryan Institute, 1988. French edition *Le Dossier Karabagh.*

Lisitsian, S. *The Armenians of Mountainous Karabagh, Ethnographic Essay.* (Armenian Ethnography and Folklore, XII), Yerevan, 1981 (in Armenian).

Mamedova, F. *Political History and Historical Geography of Caucasian Albania.* Baku, 1986 (in Russian).

Mamedova, F. 'Le problème de l'ethnos albano-caucasien', *Cahiers du Monde Russe et Soviétique,* Paris, vol. XXXI (2–3), April–September 1990.

Manukian, S. and H. Vahramian. *Gharabagh, Documenti.* Milan, 1988.

Marquart, J. *Eransahr nach der Geographie des Ps. Moses Chorenaci.* Berlin, 1901.

Marutian, A., G. Sarkissian and Z. Kharatian. 'The Ethno-Cultural Characteristics of Artsakh', *Lraber,* Yerevan, no. 6, 1989 (in Russian).

Matthew of Edessa (Matteos Urhayetsi). *Chronicle.* Vagharchapat, 1898 (classical Armenian); French translation by E. Dulaurier. *Chronique de Matthieu d'Edesse.* Paris, 1858.

Mecerian, J. *Histoire et institutions de l'Eglise arménienne.* Beirut, 1965.

Melikishvili, G. *Urartian Cuneiform Inscriptions.* Moscow, 1960 (in Russian).

Mikaelian, V. and L. Khurshudian. 'Historical Questions Relative to Mountainous Karabagh', *Lraber,* Yerevan, no. 4, 1988 (in Russian).

Minorsky, V. *A History of Sharwan and Darband in the Tenth–Eleventh Centuries.* Cambridge, 1958).

Minorsky, V. *Studies in Caucasian History.* London, 1953.

Mirza Adiguezal-Bek. *Karabagh-namé.* Baku, 1950 (in Russian).

Mirza Jamal Jevanshir Karabakhski. *History of Karabagh.* Baku, 1959 (in Russian).

Mkrtichian, Sh. *The Historical–Architectural Monuments of Mountainous Karabagh.* Yerevan, 1st edition, 1980, 2nd edition, 1985 (in Armenian), 3rd edition, 1988 (in Russian).

Mnatsakanian, A. *On the Literature of the Country of Aghvank.* Yerevan, 1966 (in Armenian) and 1969 (in Russian).

Mountainous Karabagh: Historical Handbook. Under the direction of G. Galoyan, Yerevan, Armenian Academy of Sciences, 1988 (in Russian). English and Armenian translations, Athens, 1988.

Movses Daskhurantsi (or Kaghankatvatsi). *History of Albania* (Aghuank). Yerevan, 1983 (classical Armenian). English translation by C. Dowsett: *Movses Dasxuranc'i, The History of the Caucasian Albanians.* London, 1961. Russian translation with commentaries by C. Smbatian: *Movses Kalankatuatsi, History of the Country of Aluank.* Yerevan, 1983.

Movses Khorenatsi (Moses of Khoren). *History of the Armenians.* Tiflis, 1913 (classical Armenian). English translation by R. Thomson, Cambridge, MA, London, 1978.

Muradian, P. *History Is the Memory of the Generations: Problems of History in Mountainous Karabagh.* Yerevan, 1990 (in Russian).

Muraviev, S. 'La forme interne de l'alphabet albanais caucasien et la phonologie de l'oudien', *Le Museon,* Louvain, vol. 93, nos 3–4, 1980.

Muraviev, S. 'Three Studies in Caucasian Albanian Literature', *Annual of Ibero-Caucasian Linguistics,* Tbilissi, vol. VIII, 1981 (in Russian).

Musheghian, A. 'Pseudo-Albanian Literature and Its Apologists', *Lraber,* Yerevan, no. 8, 1989 (in Russian).

Muyldermans, J. *La domination arabe en Arménie, extrait de l'Histoire Universelle de Vardan.* Louvain-Paris, 1927.

Novoseltsev, A. 'Regarding the Political Frontier Between Armenia and Albania in Ancient Times', *Kavkaz i Vizantiya,* Yerevan, I, 1979 (in Russian).

Orbeli, I. *Selected Works.* Yerevan, 1963 (in Russian).

Ormanian, M. *L'Eglise arménienne.* 2nd edition, Antelias, Lebanon, 1954.

P'awstos Buzand. *History of Armenia.* Yerevan, 1987 (classical and modern Armenian). French translation in V. Langlois, *Collection des historiens...de l'Arménie.* vol. I (Faustus de Byzance, *Bibliotheque historique*), Paris, 1867. English translation by N. Garsoian, *The Epic Histories Attributed to P'awstos Buzand.* Cambridge, MA, 1989.

Pliny the Elder. *Natural History.* Book VI, translated by A. de Grandsagne, vol. V, Paris, 1830.

Plutarch. *Lives.* Vol. VIII, Pompey, coll. G. Bude, Paris, 1973.

Popular Armenian Tales. Yerevan, vol. 5 (Artsakh), 1966, vol. 6 (Artsakh-Utik), 1973, vol. 7 (Artsakh–Zangezur), 1979 (in Armenian).

Ptolemy. *Geography.* Book V, edited by C. Muller, vol. I, Paris, 1901.

Raffi. *The Melikates of Khamsa.* Vienna, 1906 (in Armenian); reissued in *Works,* Yerevan, vol. X, 1964 (in Armenian).

Russian Treaties with the East: Political and Economic Treaties. Collected by T. Yuzefovich, St Petersburg, 1869 (in Russian).

Sarkissian, G. and P. Muradian. 'We Have Not Yet Seen the Last of the Buniyatov Affair', *Lraber,* Yerevan, no. 5, 1988 (in Russian).

Schiltberger, J. *Reisen in Europa, Asia, und Afrika von 1396–1427.* Edited by C. Neumann, Munich, 1859. Russian translation by F. Bruun, Odessa, 1866. English translation by J. Tefler, London, 1879.

Sebeos. *History.* Yerevan, 1979 (classical Armenian); French translation by Fr. Macler, *Histoire d'Héraclius par l'évêque Sebêos.* Paris, 1904.

Shanidze, A. *The Language and Writing of Caucasian Albania.* Tbilissi, 1960 (in Russian).

Smbatian, Sh. *Movses Kalankatuatsi, History of the Country of Aluank.* Russian translation with commentaries. Yerevan, 1983.

Smbatian, Sh. 'The Southern Frontier of Caucasian Albania Reconsidered', *Lraber,* Yerevan, no. 10, 1989 (in Russian).

Stepanos Orbelian. *History of Siunik.* Paris, 1859 (classical Armenian); French translation by M.-F. Brosset, St Petersburg, 1864.

Stepanos Taronetsi Asoghik (Stephen Asoghik of Taron). *Universal History.* St Petersburg, 1885 (classical Armenian); French translation, part I, E. Dulaurier, Paris, 1883, part II, F. Macler, Paris, 1917.

Strabo. *Geography.* book XI, text compiled and translated by F. Lasserre, coll. G. Bude, vol. VIII,

Paris, 1975.

Svazian, G. 'Artsakh in Historical Sources', *Lraber*, Yerevan, no. 11, 1989 (in Russian).

Svazian, H. 'Aghvank and the Mihranian Line', *Lraber*, Yerevan, no. 9, 1980 (in Armenian).

Ter Ghevondian, A. *Armenia and the Arab Caliphate.* Yerevan, 1977 (in Russian).

Ter Levondyan (Ghevondian), A. 'Notes sur le Sake-Kambecan (Ier-XIVe s.)', *Revue des Etudes Arméniennes*, vol. XXI, Paris, 1988–1989.

Thierry, J. M.. *Eglises et courants du Karabagh.* Antelias, Lebanon, 1991 (in French).

Thierry, J. M. and P. Donabedian. *Les arts arméniens.* Paris, 1987; English translation, *Armenian Art.* New York, 1989.

Thierry, J. M. and M. Hasratian. 'Dadivank en Arc'ax', *Revue des Etudes Arméniennes*, Paris, vol. XVI, 1982.

Toumanoff, C. 'Aransahikides ou Haykides? Derniers rois de Siounie', *Handes Amsorya*, Vienna, 1976.

Toumanoff, C. *Manuel de généalogie et de chronologie pour l'histoire de la Caucasie chrétienne.* Rome, 1976.

Toumanoff, C. *Studies in Christian Caucasian History.* Washington, 1963.

Trever, C. *Studies in the History and Culture of Caucasian Albania.* Moscow-Leningrad, 1959 (in Russian).

Ulubabian, B. 'Concerning the Administrative and Political Situation in Northeast Armenia before the Marzpanate', *Banber Erevani Hamalsarani*, Yerevan, no. 2, 1975 (in Armenian).

Ulubabian, B. *Gandzasar.* Yerevan, 1981 (in Armenian).

Ulubabian, B. *The Principality of Khachen between the Tenth and Sixteenth Centuries.* Yerevan, 1975 (in Armenian).

Ulubabian, B. *Studies in the History of the Eastern Province of Armenia, Fifth–Seventh Centuries.* Yerevan, 1981 (in Armenian).

Ulubabian, B. and M. Hasratian. *Gandzassar.* Milan, Documenti di Architettura Armena, no. 17, Milan, 1987.

The Unification of Eastern Armenia with Russia. Yerevan, Collection of documents, vol. I (1801–1813) and II (1814–1830), 1972 and 1978 (in Russian).

Voroshil, G. 'De l'histoire de l'Albanie caucasienne et de l'écriture albanaise', *Bedi Kartlisa, revue de Kartvélologie*, Paris, vol. XXXII, 1974.

Voskian, H. *The Monasteries of Artsakh.* Vienna, 1953 (in Armenian).

Yoannissian, A. *The Unification of Transcaucasia with Russia and International Relations at the Start of the Nineteenth Century.* Yerevan, 1958 (in Russian).

Yuzbashian, K. 'Review of *Mountainous Karabagh: Historical Handbook*', *Lraber*, Yerevan, no. 10, 1989 (in Russian).

4

KARABAGH IN THE TWENTIETH CENTURY

Claude Mutafian

Russian Transcaucasia

The nineteenth century south of the Caucasus is marked by a series of Russian victories over Persia and the Ottoman Empire. The 'Vice-Royalty of the Caucasus' in 1880 incorporated Transcaucasia from west to east, nearly all of Georgia, the eastern part of Armenia – western Armenia remained within the Ottoman Empire – and the northern section of Azerbaijan, with Persia retaining the major part of this region in the area of Tabriz.

This Transcaucasia presented a veritable mosaic of peoples. If the Georgians were concentrated in the west, the Armenians lived more or less throughout the region together with Turkic Moslems, essentially Shiites, whom the Russians classified under the heading 'Tatars of the Caucasus'. This was particularly the case in the three districts located between the lower reaches of the Arax and Kura Rivers: Nakhichevan, Zangezur, and Karabagh, respectively portions of the ancient Armenian provinces of Vaspurakan, Siunik, and Artsakh-Utik. The eastern portion of Karabagh is flat and populated mostly by Tatars, nomadic herders who would migrate with their herds in the summer to the higher elevations where the majority of the population were Armenian: this Mountainous Karabagh constituted a sort of advanced citadel protecting Armenia from the Turkish east.

A glance at the map reveals that the geographic situation of Armenia, on both sides of the Russian–Ottoman frontier, represented a break in the continuity of Islam from the Bosphorus to Central Asia; that is one of the reasons for the eagerness and fury of the Turks, in the east as in the west, to liquidate the Armenian presence.[1] With the turn of the century, we also see the development of ideas of pan-Turkism (also referred to as pan-Turanism), as much in the Ottoman Empire as in Azerbaijan: an ideology of Turkish 'racial purity' bolstered by the parallel growth of pan-Islam. The Turkish General Khalil Pasha stated it explicitly to Armenian leaders in 1918: 'We wish to re-establish our ties with our ancient territory, Turan; for that, we wish a unified route between our two territories, free of all foreign jurisdiction.'[2] The route in question is formed by the three regions mentioned above, in particular Karabagh, which explains the intense struggle and furious resistance which would unfold in this small mountain complex.

In such a context, relations between Armenians and Tatars could scarcely be good, despite the long coexistence between the two peoples in the same regions, even in the same towns. The historic metropolis, Tiflis (Tbilissi) in Georgia, had, at the time, an Armenian majority. The other great urban centre, on the shores of the Caspian, Baku, owed its spectacular rise to petroleum and attracted an important Armenian minority which held considerable economic power. Far behind these two centres, a small number of cities exceeded 20,000 in population by the beginning of the twentieth century. Yerevan and Alexandropol were for the most part Armenian, and Elisavetpol for the most part Tatar.[3]

It is in fact in Mountainous Karabagh that we find the third largest city in Transcaucasia, Shushi, with nearly 40,000 inhabitants, a majority of them Armenians.[4] A large minority of Tatars occupied the lower city, while the upper city, Armenian, was like a fortress.[5]

In 1865 the Russian traveller Vereshagin compared Shushi favourably with other cities in Transcaucasia.

> Shushi is a city unlike the others. Her homes are well laid out, large, and beautiful. The many windows make for bright, well-lit interiors.... The streets are wide and paved with cobblestones.... From the outside it is difficult to distinguish the home of an Armenian from that of a Tatar. The exteriors of the houses reveal no difference, but the layout of the interiors is totally different.[6]

Further on, when Vereshagin speaks of the three communities in Shushi (Russian, Tatar, and Armenian), he remarks, 'In this city, rich and commercial, communal life is unknown. Interests are divided and each race [sic] keeps to itself.'[7] Leaving Shushi, he noted that most villages in the district were Armenian.[8]

Later, in 1890, the anthropologist Mme Chantre visited Karabagh. 'The city of Shushi is a natural fortress and practically impregnable. It rises on a plateau at an altitude of 1,100 metres.'[9] She also noted that the homes 'are all solidly built' and attractively decorated.[10] 'You sense that Shushi is an important city when you see the wonderful activity which reigns in the markets.'[11] Further on she reports that the 'Moslem population of Shushi is known throughout Transcaucasia for its fanaticism'.[12]

At this time Shushi was a flourishing cultural centre without equal outside of Tiflis and Baku.[13] Its revival dates from 1821, when Protestant missionaries from Basle received authorization from the czar to establish a base in Transcaucasia, and they chose Shushi. There they opened schools and founded a press which went into operation in 1827, long before there was a press in Baku.[14] An active theatrical life developed after 1865, crowned by the construction of a large theatre complex in 1891. A periodical press was put into operation in 1874, and the printing presses published first editions of several authors, including the great historian Leo who was born in Shushi in 1860.[15] By 1900, we find that Shushi ranked third, just behind Constantinople and Tiflis, in the number of Armenian students it sent abroad to complete their studies. On the eve of the Russian Revolution, Shushi was home to 21 newspapers and magazines, of which 19 were in Armenian and 2 in Russian.[16]

The Turn of the Century

This period of robust Armenian cultural development could not endure, because of the evolution of czarist politics in the last decades of the nineteenth century. From 1867, an artificial administrative reorganization of Transcaucasia created governmental districts which divided eastern Armenia into three. The province of Yerevan, with an Armenian majority, included Nakhichevan but was cut off from Zangezur and Karabagh. These latter two areas formed two of the five departments of the province of Elisavetpol (the city of that name had been the old Armenian centre of Gandzak until 1804, was renamed in 1918, renamed again in 1935 by the Soviets as Kirovabad, and most recently Turkified as Ganja in 1989). At this time the Tatars were a majority in this province overall, but the Armenians constituted 70 per cent of the population in the mountain areas.[17]

In 1881, with the advent of Alexander III, Russia turned increasingly toward the Far East. Its interest in Transcaucasia declined, and its new policies sought to avoid all problems with the Ottoman Empire, however decadent, and naturally favoured the Caucasian Tatars over the Armenians. As early as 1882 the title 'Viceroy' was replaced by 'Governor-General'. In 1896 Nicholas II conferred the post upon one of his close associates. Prince Golitsyn was a narrow-minded man, lacking in finesse, cruel, and exceedingly anti-Armenian. Golitsyn decided to Russify everything by force. Having closed Armenian schools, he decreed, in June 1903, the confiscation of Armenian church properties, provoking a popular upsurge, notably in Shushi.

For Armenians, the need to organize for self-defence became increasingly clear, especially after the 1895 massacres in the Ottoman Empire. Political parties were formed. The key role was taken by the Armenian Revolutionary Federation (Dashnaktsutiun, abbreviated as Dashnak). Founded in Tiflis in 1890, it employed all means of action including terrorism.

Golitsyn was relieved of his duties in January 1905, but the seeds of conflict had been sown in that year marked by the First Russian Revolution. What we customarily call the Armeno-Tatar War would last a year and a half, and Karabagh would be one of its principal theatres.

The Armeno-Tatar War

It was in effect with the acquiescence, in truth with the complicity, of the czarist authorities that several days of riots broke out in Baku in February 1905. At the start the Tatars had complete freedom to massacre. But soon the Armenian response, organized by the Dashnaks, was in full force, and the body count yielded several hundred dead on both sides. From Baku the riots spread to Nakhichevan, a border district with the Ottoman Empire, with a large land-owning Tatar population. The unarmed Armenians were decimated there in May 1905.

Soon, Karabagh itself was engulfed.[18] Encouraged by the impunity of their earlier crimes, the Tatars, in July, attacked a bus on an important road between Shushi and Evlakh, a station on the railroad line linking Batum and Baku. In August the number of incidents multiplied on this strategic route and in Shushi. The district capital was attacked and set ablaze. Nearly four hundred Armenian homes were burned to the ground, but the Armenians held the main road and their high position. These, as well as their effective preparations, gave them the advantage during five days of battle. This First Battle of Shushi ended at the close of August with a Dashnak victory. Further offensives against Armenian villages followed in September, but the Tatars were defeated. The violence then advanced to the neighbouring district of Zangezur, where a large part of the Turkish population fled; and then to Yerevan, at that time half Armenian and half Tatar.

Earlier, Baku had been the scene of new confrontations, the most spectacular and bloody in September.[19] Furious at the new developments in Shushi, the Moslem population blamed the local Armenians. For several days, the carnage raged amidst flames rising from oil fields set afire throughout the district. For the most part the wells belonged to Armenians. Material damage was considerable, and of 600 victims, two-thirds were Tatars. The end of 1905 saw a third pogrom in Baku while the Armeno-Tatar War reached Tiflis and Elisavetpol: there the better organized Armenians suffered far fewer casualties than the Tatars.

The year 1905 marked the peak of Dashnak Party power in this period, and the party would soon affiliate with the Second International. In an attempt to oppose its power, czarist authorities ordered the reopening of schools and the return of church properties in August 1905.[20]

In 1906 a new outbreak of violence shook Karabagh. In the summer the Tatar nomads took their herds up to Armenian Mountainous Karabagh. This time the nomads were armed and provided with precise instructions. They cut roads, isolated Shushi, and systematically began to liquidate surrounding Armenian villages populated by unarmed Armenians. At the same time, from the Tatar village of Aghdam, along the strategic Shushi–Evlakh route, they prepared an attack on Shushi, part of which was Tatar. The Armenians avoided direct confrontations. Yet despite the pro-Tatar attitudes of the Russian authorities and their own inferiority in manpower and weapons, the Armenians held their ground in this 'Second Battle of Shushi' which, 'with a few intervals, lasted nine days and turned the city into a veritable battlefield'.[21] The fighting ended on 22 July 1906.

From 1906 to 1918

While in Russian Armenia, and particularly in Mountainous Karabagh, the Armenians successfully resisted Turkish attacks, the 'final solution' was being readied in Ottoman Armenia. Indeed, in this region, the Turks held power and were planning to put into action the ideology of pan-Turkism well summarized in 1918 by Vehib Pasha, Commander of the Turkish Army on the Eastern Front:

> We left the Balkans, we also left Africa, so we must expand to the east, it is there that we find our blood, our faith, and our language.[22]

Two Turkish parties were going to play the leading role in the execution of this plan. In the Ottoman Empire, the Ittihad, or Committee of Union and Progress, took power in Constantinople in 1908; in Russian Transcaucasia, the Tatars organized themselves under the nationalist and pan-Islamic ideology of the Musavat (Equality) Party, founded in 1912. Its ties with the Ittihad often made it a kind of Turkish fifth column in Russia, squeezing Armenia and, in particular, the three contested regions of Nakhichevan, Zangezur, and Karabagh.

On the eve of the First World War, the three dominant parties in Transcaucasia were the Mensheviks among the Georgians, the Dashnaks among the Armenians, and the Musavats among the Tatars. The Bolshevik following was weak, its work concentrated in Tiflis and, above all, in Baku which would become its stronghold. One of its leading figures was the Armenian Stepan Shahumian, loyal companion of Lenin. But his popularity was greatly overshadowed by the legendary Armenian hero Andranik (or Antranig), a former Dashnak (he had quit the party in 1907) and remarkable guerrilla organizer. The activities of this 'Turkish terrorizer' extended along both sides of the Russian–Ottoman frontier.

Until 1918 Transcaucasia remained outside the major war zones of the First World War, in which the two great powers which divided Armenia found themselves on opposite sides. Starting in 1915 the Ittihad took advantage of the situation to put in hand the genocide of Ottoman Armenians. In 1917 the Russian revolutions broke out. First there was the February Revolution, warmly welcomed by the Armenians, especially since the provisional government recognized several contested Transcaucasian territories, in particular Karabagh, as Armenian. Then came the October Revolution which would completely upset all the givens in the region, leading to the rout of the Russian army and, for the Ottoman leadership, opening bright new vistas of filling the vacuum and advancing the pan-Turkish agenda. This is why, contrary to the advice of their German allies, the Ottomans moved some of their troops from the Palestinian front to the Caucasian front.[23]

The three peoples of Transcaucasia appeared unified, though this had no basis in fact, when they signed an armistice with Turkey at the end of 1917. Since October, Karabagh had been *de facto* independent. An astonishing alliance developed between Tatars and Armenians at the Council of Commissars. Three joint congresses were held in Shushi and a precarious peace held until the summer of 1918.[24] To be sure, there were sporadic incidents between Tatars and Armenians. Looking ahead, the Armenians organized an Armenian Union of Karabagh-Zangezur, headed by the historian Leo. Its task was to tighten links between the two mountainous regions, because no one entertained illusions about this period of peaceful co-existence.[25] With the Ottoman invasion in the summer of 1918, everything fell to pieces.

In March of 1918, when Russia accepted German peace terms at Brest-Litovsk, the Turkish army moved east across the 1914 borders. The Ottoman Minister of War, Enver Pasha, sent his half-brother Nuri Pasha to Elisavetpol (re-named Ganja) to help the Musavatists and to establish the 'Army of Islam'.[26]

Mountainous Karabagh was isolated from the rest of Azerbaijan, where Armenian villages were pillaged and the people massacred. The objective was to force the people to recognize Musavat authority. At the same time, the Ottoman army advanced inexorably despite the creation in Alexandropol in April of the First Armenian Attack Division under Andranik's command. The Ottomans seized the port of Batum where negotiations began in May between an intransigent Turkish delegation and a Transcaucasian delegation whose three components had nothing in common. The visit by the Ottoman Minister of the Navy, Ittihadist Jemal Pasha, on 22 May was revealing. He treated the Tatars as brothers who the Turks had come to rescue, acted positively and deferentially toward the Georgians, but made it clear to the Armenians that relations with them were governed by hatred.[27] Everything was now in place for the rupture of the Transcaucasian state.[28]

On 26 May Georgia declared its independence under a German protectorate.

The next day Azerbaijan did the same in connivance with Turkey. This represented the birth of a totally artificial state whose name did not correspond to any prior historical entity and whose diverse population (Tatar, Russian, Armenian) could not lay claim to the concept of a nation.

The *Encyclopedia of Islam* explains the 'name of Azarbaydjan … in view of the similarity of its Turkish speaking population with the Turkish speaking population of the Persian province of Adharbayjan'.[29] The Tatar population, now in the majority, would take its time to create this notion of 'Azerbaijani' or 'Azeri' which would, step by step, shift from the character of 'inhabitant of Azerbaijan' to that of 'Moslem inhabitant of Azerbaijan', rendering the numerous ancient Christian minorities alien populations in their own lands. They would then be told to go elsewhere where their communities were in the majority. The capital of this Azerbaijani state was, for the moment, Ganja, for Baku was then in the hands of the Communists, a 'Bolshevik isle' known as the Baku Commune and directed by the 28 Commissars, one of whom was Shahumian. The Tatar attempts to encircle and then destroy this power failed. The 'Days of March' ended in a massacre of Moslems in Baku carried out by the odd alliance of Bolshevik and Dashnak Armenians.

Encircled by two independent republics, the Armenians had little choice and declared independence on 28 May. Several days before, at the point of desperation, the Armenians had stopped the Turkish advance at Sardarapat, a victory which entered national legend. But the situation remained critical, and the young Armenian Republic immediately opened negotiations with Ottoman Turkey. By the Treaty of Batum (4 June), the western frontier was set well to the east, ceding even Alexandropol and the majority of Nakhichevan to the Ottoman Empire.

The border between the republics of Armenia and Azerbaijan was still in dispute, in particular Zangezur and Karabagh. It was there that Andranik would concentrate his efforts. He rejected the Treaty of Batum and disavowed the Republic which had signed it, to count on the only two anti-Turkish forces available to him: the Baku Soviet and the British, then moving in from Iran. He would soon be disappointed: the first fell in September 1918 and the second quickly set in motion policies favourable to Azerbaijan.*

The Rescue of Armenian Karabagh

Mountainous Karabagh, the Armenian fortress inaccessible to the Tatars, was *de facto* independent.[30] It had been declared independent at the First Congress

---

* From this point on dates are provided according to the Gregorian calendar, even though Armenia officially employed the Julian calendar, which runs 14 days behind, until early 1919.

of Karabagh Armenians, convened in Shushi on 5 August 1918. Representatives from all the villages had named a National Council which rejected Musavat authority and stopped the Ottoman army from subduing Karabagh on its way to Baku to smash the Baku Commune. The region was in the process of establishing a truly independent government headed by seven persons.[31] Pursuing their strategy of isolation, the Moslems tried to cut Karabagh off from Zangezur. On 26 August 1918 they launched a long-term offensive against Armenian villages linking the two districts, destroying them one by one. The important village of Karakeshlagh (formerly Berdadzor), lying between Shushi and Goris, was razed in September.[32] At the other end of Karabagh, north of the Kura, Armenian villages met the same fate.[33]

During the same period, a naïve Armenian delegation from the Armenian Republic was in Constantinople, where it was overmatched by experienced Ottoman politicians. When Khatisian protested to Minister of the Interior Talaat against Turkish preparations for an attack on Karabagh, Talaat telephoned War Minister Enver. It must have amused the two principal organizers of the 1915 genocide of Ottoman Armenians to reassure the Armenian representative of their 'peaceful intentions' *vis-à-vis* Karabagh![34] More realistically, the Karabagh Armenians counted on Andranik who had just entered Nakhichevan with his First Attack Division in June 1918.[35] There, near the secular Armenian cultural centre of Abrakulis (nearly destroyed), he received an envoy from the Karabagh National Council.[36] He left Nakhichevan, which would soon be occupied by the Turks,[37] entered Zangezur and struggled successfully to deny the region to the Ottomans, who would have received help from the local Tatars.[38] Thus he created an Armenian outpost protecting Karabagh from the west.[39] This was a difficult task because Musavat propaganda was inciting rebellion in the Tatar villages in Zangezur.[40] That is why, despite urgent appeals by the Karabagh Armenians, he delayed his entry into this region, which was being closed in on by Turkish–Tatar forces, especially after Baku fell to the Ottoman army on 15 September.[41]

This is the context in which the Armenians of Karabagh convened their Second Congress on 20 September 1918. They once again refused to submit to the Azerbaijani authorities.[42] The Armenians protested in vain to the Turks and even sent a delegation to the commander of the Second Ottoman Division based in Aghdam, the eastern key to Karabagh, always in the hands of the enemy.[43] The response was predictably negative with a call for unilateral disarmament and submission in order for the Turkish army to march on Shushi.[44] This was debated by the Third Congress of Karabagh Armenians which convened in a special session on 1 October 1918. Two days later the Ottoman commander Nuri Pasha arrived at Aghdam and issued a 24-hour ultimatum.[45] Despite the determination of the rural population, which was ready to fight without regard to the inferiority of its forces, the Armenian National Council of Karabagh gave in to the defeatist attitude of the urban dwellers,[46] negotiated with the Turkish forces in Aghdam[47] and ended by accepting the presence of the Ottoman army in Shushi in return for certain concessions which were never honoured.[48] On 6 October 1918, without waiting for the arrival of emissaries in Aghdam, Turkish troops, over 5,000 men armed with cannons, rushed into the Karkar Valley. Their advance on Shushi was slowed by the resistance of all the Armenian villages,[49] but these were destroyed one by one, and on 9 October 1918, with the aid of the Moslem population in the lower town, the Ottoman army entered Shushi to arrest, pillage, and massacre.[50]

Mountainous Karabagh was not reduced to the level of its capital, however, and the thousands of Turkish troops occupying Shushi were not assured of control of the entire district. The Armenians knew that with defeat the fate which befell their compatriots in the Ottoman Empire in 1915 awaited them: the objective of the invaders was to Turkify the district and permanently attach it to Azerbaijan. It is useful to compare two Karabagh delegations which visited Andranik one after the other in Zangezur. On 25 October the official envoys from Shushi presented a plan for submission to Azerbaijan, while ten days later delegates from the southern village of Khijaberd pledged to the general the determination of the entire region to struggle against the invasion in spite of the fall of Shushi.[51]

Ferocious resistance foiled Turkish plans.[52] The Turks attacked first at the northern city of Martakert which controlled northern access to Karabagh. After three fruitless assaults, the Turkish forces retreated to the north, venting their frustrations by massacring villagers in Chailu. The Turkish commander in Shushi then turned his attentions to the districts of Varanda and Dizak in the east and south-east. On the evening of 31 October, troops accompanied by heavy artillery left the capital with the intention of joining with Tatar reinforcements from the Karabagh Plain to the east. This was undertaken without proper consideration of the determination of the Armenians and the remarkable military organization installed by a thirty-year-old hero, Aslan Muradkhanian in the villages on both banks of the Varanda River. On 2 November the Turks fell into an ambush between Shushi and Martuni and were decimated at the Battle of Msmena.[53] Scarcely eighty of them were able to escape, leaving behind considerable spoils. Several days later a larger force was dispatched from Shushi to Varanda, but it made a quick retreat when it found all access closed.[54] At this time Constantinople surrendered to the Allies, and by mid-November the Ottoman armies finally evacuated Mountainous Karabagh.[55]

These two months of September and October 1918 were decisive for Mountainous Karabagh. The two victories at Martakert and Varanda saved Armenian Karabagh from annexation by Azerbaijan, and from total destruction. The Bolsheviks, who were following developments in Transcaucasia closely, were worried – as a letter of 12 October to Lenin from his close friend Orjonikidze illustrates:

> In the occupied regions, the Turks have massacred half the population of Karabagh. They have invaded the districts of Shushi and Zangezur. The population manifests steadfast resistance. Andranik was killed by treachery in Karabagh.[56]

This last piece of news was false, but it illustrates the reputation of the Armenian *fedayee* leader even among the Bolsheviks. The letter added: 'The Armenian population awaits the aid of Soviet Russia.' In reality, the hour of Soviet Russia in Transcaucasia had not arrived. The new factor in the autumn of 1918 was Great Britain, whose cynical diplomacy would again prove to be disastrous to the Armenians.

Great Britain against Karabagh

Turkish ambitions concerning Baku and its strategic oil resources, as well as the formation of this Turkish–Tatar 'Army of Islam', disturbed the British, and they ordered a detachment of troops from Baghdad to the north of Iran in early 1918 under the command of Dunsterville.[57] Gradually, however, the reasons for the British presence in eastern Transcaucasia would be modified: coming to stop the Turkish advance, the British would work, basically, in response to the threat of the Bolsheviks who were fighting Denikin's White army in the north.[58] Moreover, accommodating the pan-Russian tendencies of the latter was one reason, among others, that the Allies withheld diplomatic recognition from the three Transcaucasian republics. Against the advice of Shahumian, the Baku Soviet, facing the Turkish threat, invited the British to enter the city, but they were quick to leave it in mid-September when the situation worsened. The taking of Baku by the Ottoman Turks was accompanied by the traditional massacre of thousands of Armenians.[59] Shahumian and the commissars were executed with the complicity of the British, and Baku became the new capital of Azerbaijan.

The autumn of 1918 also marks the end of the First World War and the defeat of the Central Powers, including the Ottoman Empire which signed the armistice at Mudros on 30 October. According to more or less tacit agreements among the Allies, the Caucasus was a British sphere. British objectives had two foci, at times contradictory, but both dictated by anti-Bolshevism: to assist the White armies of Denikin in the north and to foster a strong and pro-British Azerbaijan in the south.[60] Many of the British officers had served in India and had developed strong pro-Moslem sentiments. It should not be forgotten that by virtue of its many colonies in Africa and Asia, the British Empire was a major Moslem power. General Thomson entered Baku on 17 November,[61] and he quickly disappointed the Armenians who had been hopeful in the light of the armistice.[62] With over 30,000 soldiers in Transcaucasia,[63] the British commander began demanding that the Armenians in Karabagh submit to the Azerbaijani authorities following the withdrawal of Ottoman forces. This was unequivocally rejected. Karabagh Armenians impatiently awaited the arrival of the great hero of Zangezur.

October brought urgent requests. Andranik himself recalled his emotions when faced with an elderly Armenian man who had not hesitated to cross Turkish lines into Kornidzor in Zangezur to tell him that the armed population awaited his arrival to liberate the region.[64] This fitted well with Andranik's plans: going as far as Baku to liberate the city.[65] He wanted to be sure that he was called there, however, and he sent a messenger to Shushi. Another reason for caution was that certain leaders did not look favourably upon Andranik's arrival and preferred to wait for the outcome of futile negotiations with the Moslems.[66] This was particularly the case with the head of the central district of Varanda, who asked Andranik to wait ten days. Was this an ambitious figure who wanted the role of liberator for himself, or a traitor?[67] Precious time was lost. Andranik did not begin his march until the end of November. It took three days for him to break through but only at the price of bloody confrontations with numerous Tatar villages and the troops of Nuri Pasha, who were still operating in the region around the Hagaru River which separates Zangezur and Karabagh.[68] On 2 December 1918 the road to Shushi was finally opened and Andranik planned on entering the capital of Armenian Karabagh the next day. This day was to play a critical role in the region's destiny. Perhaps influenced or bought by the Musavats, Thomson telegraphed Shushi from Baku, and the messages were delivered to Andranik who received them on entering Karabagh on 2 December.[69] In a dry tone,[70] the British commander ordered Andranik to halt and await the arrival of messengers who would provide details. Andranik doubted the authenticity of these telegrams, and his soldiers, many of whom were from Karabagh, urged him to disregard the order and create a *fait accompli.* In the north, was Nuri Pasha having second thoughts about attacking Armenian villages? The next day an automobile arrived displaying a white flag. Two soldiers, one British and one French, delivered a letter to Andranik from Thomson.[71] With veiled threats which strongly irritated the general, the Allied representative from Baku reported that Germany had surrendered, and ordered that all operations cease in light of peace negotiations which would resolve pending issues. Confident in the Allies, and hoping, even, that they would liberate western Armenia, Andranik agreed.[72] He would bitterly regret his decision.[73] His return to Goris threw the Karabagh Armenians into dismay and encouraged the Tatars to take advantage of British indifference to liquidate the remaining Armenian villages between Karabagh and Zangezur. Through London's intervention, the historic opportunity definitively to unite Armenian Karabagh with the Republic of Armenia was lost.[74]

Furthermore, the British commitments were merely a further lure. In mid-December the British mission representing the Allies arrived in Shushi from Baku.[75] Major Gibbon was in charge, among other things, of the settlement of refugees.[76] The mission tried, in vain, to re-open communications between Evlakh, on the one hand, and Goris, on the other. The Azerbaijani attack on the Armenian village of Dolanlar, in south-western Karabagh,[77] angered Andranik who, from Goris, accused the British of deceit.[78] At the same time the British mission conducted its inquiry on the state of Karabagh, getting information from the naïve district governors.[79] The objective was clear: the annexation of Zangezur and Karabagh to Azerbaijan.[80] The Karabagh Armenians refused to obey but their protests had no more effect than those of the Armenian Republic. On the contrary, British diplomacy was about to take a third anti-Armenian step: at Baku on 15 January 1919 it supported the appointment of Khosrov bey Sultanov as the Governor-General of Karabagh and neighbouring districts, including Zangezur. This wealthy Kurdish landowner, a prominent Musavat figure in Karabagh, born of pan-Turkism and Armenophobia, had actively participated in massacres of Armenians during the destruction of the Baku Commune.[81] If his authority over Zangezur, where the Armenians had been in control since the return of Andranik, was at best theoretical, that was not the case in Shushi: there he assumed his duties on 10 February 1919 with a strong commitment to solving 'finally' the problem of Karabagh where power was still in the hands of the Armenian National Council.[82] Yerevan's objections had no effect on Britain's decisions,[83] nor on the continuous attacks on Armenian villages.[84]

In this perilous situation, the Fourth Congress of Karabagh Armenians convened in Shushi on 12 February. The Armenians continued to refuse to submit to Baku, and they protested against the appointment of Sultanov:[85] 'Karabagh has never recognized the authority of an Azerbaijani government within its borders and never will.'[86] The National Council elaborated several projects for the provisional administration of Karabagh: anything but submission to Azerbaijan.[87] A delegation was sent to Baku to see Thomson and denounce the deployment of Azerbaijani troops.[88]

At the same time Sultanov clearly presented his plans in an Azerbaijani governmental note (no. 165) of 25 February:

Sow discord between the poor Armenian populace and its leadership.... Employ English intermediaries to arrest and deport the leadership.... By these means, without any aggressive measures, we can resolve the question of Karabagh.[89]

The British hardened in their pro-Azerbaijani attitudes. They stationed 400 of their soldiers in the Armenian section of Shushi[90] under the orders of Major Monck-Mason, an Armenophile carrying out Turcophile British policy.[91] The response of the National Council to Thomson's 21 February telegram confirmed the decision of the Fourth Congress.[92] Faced with the hostility of the authorities since the beginning of the year, the Karabagh Armenians once again turned to Andranik, who had been following the developments from Goris, in neighbouring Zangezur, all the while refusing to follow British orders to transfer the province to the authorities in Baku.[93] His presence in the neighbouring province posed a permanent threat to the plans of Sultanov, who was propped up by the British and the Musavats. In the spring of 1919, these 'allies' sent delegations to Goris to meet Andranik.[94] Many of his closest associates had already left the province. On poor terms with the Dashnak authorities in Yerevan, whom he continued to think of as traitors ready to come to terms with the Turks,[95] disgusted with the duplicity of the British 'allies',[96] Andranik, more a warrior than a diplomat, also decided to leave. Only the Catholicos retained respect in his eyes. In order to journey to Etchmiadzin, the British proposed his travelling to Tiflis by way of the route from Shushi to Evlakh and from there to Shamkhor through open Tatar territory. In all likelihood this was an Anglo-Tatar trap designed to rid themselves once and for all of the respected warrior. In any case, the Karabagh Armenians warned Andranik, and he rejected the British proposal.[97] On 2 April he started for Etchmiadzin by way of the Armenian mountains, having turned Zangezur over to the authorities in Yerevan.[98] The defence against the Turks would soon be turned over to another celebrated Armenian partisan fighter, Nzhdeh.[99]

During this period the struggle in Karabagh continued. A delegation convened in Baku on 26 March 1919 heard Colonel Shuttleworth, soon to be Thomson's successor, threaten that, 'We have the power to subdue you by force.'[100] The mayor of Shushi again responded that Karabagh would never accept domination by Azerbaijan. This was confirmed by the Fifth Congress of Karabagh Armenians meeting in Shushi on 23 April 1919, where Shuttleworth and Sultanov appeared in person to demand that the Armenian National Council submit to Baku,[101] once again in vain.[102]

Azerbaijan has always been and remains today an accomplice and ally of the Turks and of all the cruelties committed by the Turks against the Armenians in general and Karabagh Armenians in particular.[103]

The government of Armenia also rejected Azerbaijani authority over Zangezur and Armenian Karabagh.[104]

The Azerbaijanis were always able to rely on British support, which was offered by Shuttleworth once again on 3 April.[105] This was clearly expressed on 18 May in a telegram from the Azerbaijani ambassador to Yerevan.[106] Feeling secure, Sultanov decided on exceptional methods: terror and famine. On 20 May he cut all access routes to the Karabagh Plain.[107] All trade with Armenians was punishable by death. Gradually the blockade sowed famine in Mountainous Karabagh.[108] The British advised Sultanov to seize arms caches in the Armenian quarter of Shushi.[109] The city was surrounded and placed under siege.[110] On 4 June 1919 systematic shelling began. Less well-armed, the Armenians nevertheless fought back for three days, after which the British separated the two camps.[111] Sultanov was to take revenge on the villages. He took his inspiration from the Ottoman 'Red Sultan' Abdul Hamid and organized irregular bands of Kurds to spread terror. Two of these brigades were commanded by his brothers.[112] Once again Armenian villages disappeared from the map.[113] The most ghastly was the case of Ghaibalikend. Six hundred out of seven hundred inhabitants were massacred on 5 June.[114] The village was in the process of evacuating when it was destroyed. The church, built in 1844, which served as a stable, was also destroyed. Ghaibalikend remains a symbol of Anglo-Tatar collusion which was clearly defined by Shuttleworth when he told the Karabagh Armenians, 'Your roads are cut, you will not receive bread and you will die of famine; we will bring you no aid whatsoever as long as you do not recognize the authority of Musavat Azerbaijan.'[115] Other villages met an analogous fate: Kerkjan, Pahlu, Jamillu.[116] Elsewhere, in the Varanda District, villages resisted sucessfully.[117]

Soon after, the British representatives left Karabagh, giving Sultanov a totally free hand.[118] Vigorous protests from Etchmiadzin, Yerevan, and Tiflis had no effect.[119] To be sure, the British sent an inquiry commission, and its report clearly brought out the premeditation of the massacres and the responsibility of Sultanov, concluding that he ought to be brought to justice.[120] Sultanov was called to Baku, but he quickly returned to Shushi where he increased the repression.[121] Armenian leaders were forced into exile under orders from the British or arrested;[122] many, though, had already gone under-ground. The military encirclement of Karabagh accelerated.[123] Sultanov himself convened the Sixth Congress of Karabagh Armenians.[124] It met on 28 June at Shosh, a little east of Shushi. The discussions were heated and the principle of a provisional agreement with the Musavat authorities was accepted despite strong opposition from the villages, in particular from the central district of Varanda.[125] A delegation of three Armenians was sent to Baku with full negotiating power. One of them, who was travelling alone, was killed, supposedly by bandits.[126] The other two entered discussions with the Azer-baijanis. The latter cleverly took advantage of the fact that one of the Armenian delegates was more favourable to their plans, and he was placed in charge of calling a new Congress to consider Azerbaijani counter-proposals.[127] He returned to Shushi accompanied by Sultanov, who had been called back to Baku and had not attended the Sixth Congress.[128] Moreover, for him the Karabagh matter was settled, and he had his sights set on Zangezur.[129] Sultanov took up residence in the Armenian quarter of Shushi and was astonishingly friendly to the Armenians, going so far as to re-open the Shushi–Evlakh road.[130] This was a ruse, of course, which concealed intense military preparations.[131] At the same time dissension among the Armenians grew. The villagers, in particular, were opposed to any compromise with the Azerbaijanis, and they distrusted the city dwellers, who were more inclined to an agreement.[132]

On 12 August the Seventh Congress opened at Shosh, minus two delegates from the north who were killed *en route* by Azerbaijani militiamen. Sultanov tried to have the Congress moved to Shushi and went so far as to use Bishop Vahan, but he was not successful.[133] Furious, he sought to break the 'hard line followers' and, on the 14th, issued a 48-hour ultimatum for the ratification of the 'Baku agreements'. His 'military persuaders' had been carefully prepared and proved all the more persuasive now that there was no hope of outside assistance from the Armenian Republic.[134] On 15 August the Congress provisionally – that is to say, until the conclusion of the Paris peace negotiations – recognized the authority of the Azerbaijani government while preserving its leadership institutions, in particular the Armenian National Council. The accord was celebrated in Shushi amid great pomp on 22 August.[135] It was a victory for Sultanov, to be sure, but one that failed to satisfy him, due to the persistence of Armenian leadership and institutions. While waiting, he was able to disarm Armenian villages thanks to money and the assistance of inevitable Armenian 'collaborators'.[136]

It is important to be aware of the exact wording of the accord[137] because Azerbaijani propaganda employs it to argue that Karabagh was already subordinated to Musavat Azerbaijan, and, therefore, that its incorporation into Soviet Azerbaijan was merely the continuation of a pre-existing situation.[138] But Article I begins with the words, 'The contractual parties accept this provisional accord while awaiting the decision taken at the Paris Peace Conference, a decision which the two parties agree to respect.' Does this constitute an annexation?

In any case, this was the consummation of pernicious British policy.[139] After having sown all the seeds of future conflicts, London was able to carry out its own plans, decided upon several months earlier. At the end of August 1919, British troops withdrew from Karabagh, leaving it in a deplorable economic and moral state,[140] and began to withdraw gradually from the Caucasus altogether.[141] This was at a time when Denikin's White armies in the north were in luck and made no secret of their plans to annex Transcaucasia.

The anti-Armenian policies of Great Britain in Karabagh, openly allied with the Musavats of Azerbaijan, kept pace with new French policies in Cilicia, where they drew nearer to the Kemalist Turks. In both cases, the 'allies' contributed to clearing these areas of their Armenian populations. For reasons which are clear enough, this goal was attained in Cilicia but not in Karabagh where, despite the total lack of outside assistance, the population resisted all initiatives. It is not an exaggeration, however, to say that the present problems in Karabagh are due in large part to the diplomacy of London during the first months of 1919: that is what prevented the permanent reunification of Mountainous Karabagh with Armenia. At the end of August1919, the British military attaché in Yerevan said:

> Attaching Karabagh to Azerbaijan was, I think, the bitterest blow of all ... being the cradle of their race, and their traditional last sanctuary when their country has been invaded. It is Armenian in every particular....[142]

The Destruction of Shushi

Given the grave problems faced by the Armenian Republic during this period, she could scarcely assist her compatriots in Karabagh. The Ottoman surrender provided an unhoped-for opportunity to extend Armenian territories which had been reduced to Yerevan and the Lake Sevan region. At the end of 1918 another famous Dashnak military commander, Dro, recovered Alexandropol (Leninakan) in the north-west and then moved against the Georgians in the northern region of Lori. Concerning the district of Kars, which the Treaty of Brest-Litovsk had ceded to the Ottoman Empire, and Nakhichevan, under dispute with Azerbaijan, the British this time did not oppose the Armenian Republic, which recovered these areas in 1919[143] despite the efforts of the Azerbaijani ambassador in Yerevan, who exerted pressure for an intervention in Nakhichevan.[144] Thomson had first offered these territories to the Armenians on the condition that they cede Zangezur and Karabagh to Azerbaijan.[145] These gains were all relative. The Allies had not yet recognized the Trans-caucasian republics, and the Paris Conference was not moving quickly on territorial questions. In addition, Armenia was brought face to face with significant Turkish–Tatar populations in these territories.[146] As for the Ottoman Empire, its defeat did not prevent it from signing a mutual assistance pact with Azerbaijan on 29 October 1919 which contained several articles with a scarcely veiled anti-Armenian tenor.[147]

The end of 1919 brought new anti-Armenian violence to Karabagh.[148] In neighbouring Zangezur, Anglo-Azeri efforts to force a settlement analogous to the 15 August agreement in Karabagh failed. Azerbaijan tried to impose a military solution, but its forces were pushed back, and Azerbaijan was forced to sign an accord in the presence of the Allies.[149] At the end of 1919 Nzhdeh arrived from Yerevan, and his partisans quickly overcame Turkish resistance and destroyed their villages.[150]

In November the Karabagh Armenians rejected proposals for further submission presented by an Azerbaijani governmental delegation which demonstrated the weakness of the August accords. They relayed their decision to Thomson who sent British officers on assignment. Their report was issued in a week and expressed scepticism concerning the possibility of annexation by Azerbaijan.[151] On 23 November, a new accord was signed by the parties under the aegis of the American Haskell, representative of the Allied High Commission. The agreement was doomed. Moreover, Haskell was shown to be an opportunist who was selling the Azerbaijanis Western aid which had been provided for the Armenians, while doing all he could to stimulate Baku's ambitions concerning Karabagh.[152] At the beginning of 1920 Sultanov renewed his threats, first verbally in Shushi, and then in a letter to the Armenian National Council where he even spoke of razing Karabagh![153] A peace delegation sent to Baku on 20 February was returned to Shushi by the Musavats.

At this time the international context was changing dramatically. The rout of Denikin's White armies certainly strengthened Soviet Russia and her Red Army, which was already at the doorstep of Transcaucasia. In addition, an alliance was gradually taking shape between the two rising powers in the region: Russian Bolshevism and Turkish Kemalism. The Allied powers realized – quite late – that they had to come to terms with the Transcaucasian republics. They were finally accorded *de facto* recognition in January 1920.[154] In point of fact, this recognition brought no benefits to Armenia whatsoever. As for Azerbaijan, the new political situation condemned the Musavat government to a brief term.

Before its fall, this government would leave a terrible legacy of its passage to power: the destruction of Armenian Shushi. Sultanov had prepared for this by providing abundant weapons to the Moslem population and sending major Azerbaijani troop reinforcements to Karabagh.[155] For him, the word 'provisional' in the 22 August accord was to disappear.

The only outside assistance Karabagh could expect was from Zangezur, where the military command had been turned over to General Dro by the Republic of Armenia. Dro had been stationed in Goris since mid-December 1919.[156] While he was pursuing the fight against Turks there, Dro remained aware of the danger threatening Karabagh, and he alerted the authorities in Yerevan. Sultanov made little attempt to conceal his plans. In early February he told his Armenian friends: 'The problem of Zangezur and Karabagh will be resolved in 10–12 days.'[157] He knew he could count on Armenian spies, the Bolsheviks, and a goodly portion of the city dwellers. On 19 February, once the region was thoroughly surrounded, he presented an ultimatum to the Armenian National Council: unconditional unification of the region with Azerbaijan given that the 'territory is indissolubly linked to the latter economically'.[158] This false claim would be taken up later by Soviet Azerbaijan.

To strengthen his position, Sultanov took control of the Karkar Valley while massacring the Armenian population of several villages on 22 February, including Khankend (present-day Stepanakert).[159] In the countryside, the Armenians stocked food and munitions in preparation for self-defence. Rather than immediately avenging the massacres as the villagers demanded, the Central Body for the Self-Defence of Karabagh preferred to wait for the Eighth Congress. Convened to debate a response to Sultanov, this Congress openly split into two factions, and there were, in fact, two distinct assemblies.[160] In Shushi, a minority of 40 to 50 representatives (mostly city dwellers and Bolsheviks) accepted Sultanov's terms.[161] But the villagers, who had no trust in Sultanov, refused to gather in Shushi and met, instead, in Shosh. The northern delegates arrived armed and in secret because they had to break through the Shushi–Evlakh line controlled by the Azerbaijanis.[162] The 96 participants in the Shosh Congress (22 February –4 March) rejected Sultanov's ultimatum and accused him of breaking the 22 August accords: 'Never has the Armenian population been subjected to so many ravages, murders, and economic sanctions as they have since the signing of the accord.'[163] They affirmed that the Armenians of Karabagh would meet all eventualities by suitable means.[164] From that point on Sultanov increased his military preparations and in early March he left no doubt that the assault on Armenian Karabagh was imminent. In an effort to cut communications with Zangezur, the order was given to 'raze to the ground Khtsaberd, Tum, and Hin Thaghlar',[165] three well-armed Armenian villages in south-western Karabagh. The Turkish generals Nuri Pasha and Khalil Pasha, former Ittihadists turned Kemalists, arrived to assist in the assault.[166] The journal *Mshak*, in Tiflis, wrote on 29 February 1920:

> The Armenian government has officially announced that Nuri Pasha has gone to Shushi with the objective of invading Karabagh and Zangezur.... He has called on the Armenians of Karabagh to surrender; otherwise they should call Adana to mind, which is to say the massacre of 30,000 Armenians. [In 1909 Adana, in Cilicia, was the scene of the first anti-Armenian massacres organized by the Ittihadists in Asia Minor].

The month of March was punctuated by blockaded roads, massacred Armenians, and Turkish, Tatar, and Kurdish troop reinforcements.[167] The Armenians decided to take the initiative and organize an uprising during the night of 22–23 March 1920, the Moslem New Year. But the capital was saturated with Turkish-Tatar soldiers. On 23 March Armenian Shushi was put to fire and sword,[168] thousands of homes were reduced to cinders and the majority of the populace were massacred. For several days the Armenians were able to cut themselves off from the rest of the region where battles raged.[169] But on 3 April the enemy broke through the battle lines and entered Shushi the next day. Sultanov ordered the decapitation of Rubeni, the founder of the Karabagh Communist Party. His head was placed on a pike and paraded through the region. Bishop Vahan and other dignitaries met a similar fate. The Georgian Communist leader Orjonikidze commented, 'I shudder to recall the images we saw in Shushi in May, 1920. The beautiful Armenian city was ruined, destroyed.'[170] One of the principal members of the Armenian government, Simon Vratsian, later wrote that, 'the facts show that the organizers of the rebellion lacked experience. The consequences would have been worse if Dro and his troops had not arrived on April 13th.'[171] It was, in fact, only in mid-April that the Republic of Armenia was able to aid Armenian Karabagh by sending its two most talented military leaders. Dro advanced from Yerevan to the Varanda District (which included Shushi) while Nzhdeh, then the military commander in Zangezur, led his troops from Ghapan (Kapan) toward the southern district of Dizak.[172] Their military intervention along with pressure by the Entente powers from Tiflis brought the massacres to an end.[173]

Since March 1920, Shushi, one of the beacons of Armenian culture, has been a Turkish bastion in Armenian Karabagh.

Soviet Azerbaijan

The Turkification of Shushi was the swan song of Musavatism. Taking advantage of the fact that the largest portion of the Azerbaijani army was engaged in massacring Armenians in Karabagh, the 11th Red Army entered Baku on 27 April and, without a great deal of resistance, Azerbaijan became the first Soviet republic in Transcaucasia.[174] Concerning the Armenian Republic and Karabagh, the Bolshevik Azerbaijani leadership faithfully followed the line of its predecessors, backing their demands with utterly false assertions to the effect that these regions had previously been under Musavat authority! As early as 29 April, Huseinov, the Minister of Foreign Affairs of Soviet Azerbaijan, presented the Armenian government with a three-day ultimatum to 'recall its forces from Zangezur and Karabagh, to withdraw within its borders, and to put a halt to inter-ethnic massacres'.[175]

Baku had the field to itself *vis-à-vis* Moscow, since it was already Sovietized and Armenia would not be until December. It is, therefore, not surprising to find, the next day, a similar ultimatum issued by the commander of the 11th Red Army and several Bolshevik leaders, including Orjonikidze and Kirov.[176] Was this not the same Kirov who had written to Lenin on 3 June 1919, prior to the Sovietization of Azerbaijan, that Karabagh and Zangezur were 'Armenian territories?'[177] Certainly, several of them would quickly change their perspectives, but it was only Chicherin, Commissar of Foreign Affairs, who always remained convinced of Armenian rights. On 26 June 1920 he told Orjonikidze that these territories 'should be occupied by Russian and not Azerbaijani troops ... until a politically favourable situation is created. We hope that you can prevent comrades in Baku from infringing on the politics of the Central Committee.'[178] Other Bolsheviks, such as Stalin, to the contrary, followed Narimanov, strongman of Soviet Azerbaijan.[179]

Meanwhile in Karabagh Dro devoted himself to recreating an army in the southern districts of Varanda and Dizak, the only two under his control at the time. There, in the village of Taghavard, the Ninth Congress of Karabagh Armenians convened on 23 April and decided to unite with Armenia. They declared the 22 August agreement null. It was already void in the light of the massacres of March–April.[180] The other districts of Karabagh approved of this decision.[181] They took measures to notify Moscow by means of a telegram addressed to Chicherin.[182] Karabagh was provisionally governed by Dro. Since the initiative of Andranik in December 1918, the union of Karabagh with Armenia had never seemed so close. Once sabotaged by the British, this time it would be blocked by the Bolsheviks. On 12 May Yerevan had categorically rejected the ultimatums from Baku and denounced its collusion with Turkey.[183] However, the permanent Azerbaijani threat was increased by pressure from the 11th Red Army whose 32nd Division had left Evlakh for Karabagh to Sovietize the province. What should Dro do? The local assemblies refused to submit to the 11th Red Army, just as they had always rejected the authority of Azerbaijan.[184] The situation was made more difficult by a Bolshevik insurrection which broke out on 1 May in Armenia. Dro refused to obey the Bolsheviks, who ordered him to move back to Zangezur.[185] The Red Army slowly infiltrated from the north and found a measure of support for this 'new element'. Given this state of affairs, without orders from the Armenian government and faced with the weariness of their troops, Dro and Nzhdeh decided on 24 May to leave Karabagh to the Bolsheviks.[186] This would leave the people to hope for the lesser of two evils: namely, that 'the local Bolsheviks could save the situation by taking power and declaring Karabagh a part of Soviet Russia and not Azerbaijan'.[187] Even this minimal hope would be disappointed, however. While Dro left Karabagh for Zangezur on 26 May with his troops, the Tenth Congress met in Taghavard to ratify the Sovietization of Karabagh which was finalized by the entry of the 11th Red Army. From there it would await the opportune moment to pass into Zangezur, defended by General Nzhdeh.

Meanwhile, an Armenian delegation, the Shant Mission, was in Moscow[188] to normalize relations between Moscow and Yerevan and to defend itself against Turkey where the Kemalists, by all appearances, were fortifying themselves and reclaiming the Brest-Litovsk borders which included the district of Kars. Narimanov moved to counter these negotiations. In a telegram addressed to Lenin and Chicherin, he dismissed negotiations as useless and presented strategic arguments for annexing the three contested territories to Azerbaijan; specifically, this would create a direct link between the Bolsheviks and Kemalist Turkey.[189] This telegram was co-signed by Anastas Mikoyan who, like many of his peers, was a communist before he was an Armenian, while Narimanov was first and foremost an Azerbaijani and then a communist.[190]

At the start of the negotiations Chicherin proposed granting Zangezur and Nakhichevan to Armenia and organizing a referendum for Mountainous Karabagh. At the end of June a second proposal was made: Nakhichevan to Armenia, Karabagh to Azerbaijan, and the status of Zangezur to be decided by a special Soviet envoy, Legran.[191] Armenia, obsessed by the Paris Conference from which it awaited miracles, delayed its response and then made an odd proposal, demanding not only Mountainous Karabagh but also Lower Karabagh, the plains occupied by Tatars which, to this point, had never been an issue. Once again, in Paris, Yerevan, and Moscow, Armenian diplomacy floundered; at the same time the Soviet capital welcomed shrewd Turkish diplomats to strengthen Kemalist–Bolshevik ties with an eye to a promising future.[192]

Meanwhile Soviet Azerbaijan examined every means of permanently annexing the three territories. Initial steps to convince the Bolshevik 'suzerains' proved inconclusive. When Lenin asked on 22 June 1920 if it 'wasn't possible to reach an agreement with Narimanov', Chicherin responded, 'Karabagh is an authentically Armenian territory.'[193] One week later he warned Lenin against the aggressive plans of Orjonikidze and Narimanov for the Sovietization of Armenia and Georgia and, above all, against the exorbitant expansionist demands of Narimanov at the expense of Armenia.[194] Moscow did not have a clear position on the matter. Thus Chicherin, while he was in Moscow presenting his proposals to the Shant Mission, wrote to Orjonikidze on 19 June 1920 that the territories 'must not be reunited with Armenia or Azerbaijan but must be placed under the authority of Russian occupation troops and put at the disposal of the local Soviets'.[195] That is why the 7 July 1920 meeting of the Political Bureau of the Russian Communist Party, with Lenin presiding, decided that Russian troops should occupy the three territories instead of attaching them to Soviet Azerbaijan whose leader, Narimanov, was accused by Chicherin of 'connivance with Moslem tendencies'.[196]

These policies were put into effect at the beginning of July 1920. The 11th Red Army, already well established in Karabagh, invaded Zangezur where it was opposed by the Armenian army under the command of Dro. Neither reunification with Yerevan nor occupation by the Red Army could be expected to satisfy Narimanov, however, who did not conceal his displeasure from Chicherin and sought other means, certain of the aid of Stalin whose position at the time was clear: 'We must clearly side with one of the two parties, and in the present case it must be Azerbaijan and, at the same time, Turkey.'[197] Narimanov's activities did not deceive all of his colleagues: Legran, for example, accused Azerbaijan of 'torpedoing our work'.[198]

First of all, little by little, Narimanov secretly placed Azerbaijanis in command of positions in Soviet institutions in Karabagh,[199] taking advantage of the naïveté of his Armenian colleagues who placed internationalism – and careerism – above all else. At the same time, he tried to 'incite the people of these areas to come out in favour of union with Azerbaijan'.[200] By what means? They were explained in the correspondence, until now kept secret in the Party archives in Moscow, addressed to his counterparts in Zangezur by Karaiev, President of the Revolutionary Committee of Karabagh, a member of the Bolshevik leadership of Azerbaijan and close to Narimanov. On 19 July 1920 he wrote:

> We know that our troops retreated in defeat, but today instead of the army our money works.... The government has decided to allocate two hundred million roubles for the reunification of Karabagh and Zangezur with Azerbaijan.

Two days later there was a still more explicit letter which merits being quoted at length. The postscript would not have been disavowed by Talaat Pasha and the other organizers of the 1915 genocide.[201]

Top Secret. Shushi, 21 July 1920
The Provincial Revolutionary
Committee of Karabagh to the
Regional Revolutionary Committee at Goris

Comrades,

Comrades who have recently arrived tell us that up to now 90 per cent of the villages in Zangezur are not yet disarmed. This is unfortunate. But what is even more unfortunate is that the Armenian population of Zangezur has not yet been decapitated [i.e., deprived of its leaders]. Its intelligentsia and military chiefs remain in the villages. Tomorrow, if there is an uprising, they will take charge and expel our forces from Zangezur. I repeat again and forever: we must seize the moment. Work day and night. Take steps to ensure that all the important Armenians are arrested. Deportations and pillages are not a serious matter. Time will pass, situations will change, and they will return to their country. Put human sentiments to one side. It is not with these sentiments that one builds a state: conquer countries and live in peace. Our comrades here are displeased with the members of the Revolutionary Committee of Geroussi (Goris). Try to force new elections to the Committee and allow only Moslems and Russians we know to pass. Armenak Karageuzian should be arriving in Geroussi soon. He is late because he has not received his money. As long as he has not received his twenty-two million roubles, he will not leave. It is a good opportunity for him to enrich himself, and why should he not take advantage of it? After all, let him profit from what our government gives him. He promises to re-unite Zangezur with Azerbaijan in seven days. We have no doubt that you will soon make us very happy by announcing the reunification of Ghapan. If your forces are insufficient, resort to money. Why hold back the reunification of this district in revolt because of a certain Ajda (Nzhdeh)? Use blessed and time-honoured methods. What Armenian, when we will give three million roubles, would not bring in his head? If you need money, telegraph us and we will send it.

Salutations, Asad Karaiev

PS In order to weaken the Armenians in areas where the guerrillas are active, kill a Russian soldier and accuse the Armenians of the crime. You know well what the Russians will do to them. Leave no honest man alive in Zangezur and no wealth in order that this accursed tribe [the Armenians] can never stand on their feet again....

Asad Karaiev

The Fall of the Armenian Republic

The solution advocated by Chicherin was confirmed during the following months. Without the strength to resist the 11th Red Army, Armenia had to resign itself to the Bolshevik occupation of the three regions and signed the Tiflis Agreement on 10 August, with Legran representing Soviet Russia. Thus the latter would occupy Karabagh, Zangezur, and Nakhichevan in order to create favourable conditions for an equitable solution for the territories contested by Armenia and Azerbaijan.[202] These 'conditions' were probably tied, in the spirit of the Bolsheviks, to the Sovietization of Armenia which could no longer be postponed. In an irony of history, this same 10 August 1920 finally saw the signing of the Treaty of Sèvres which opened tremendous possibilities for Armenia. The treaty would become a dead letter in the light of new betrayals by the Western powers following their policy of appeasing the Kemalists and drawing them away from the Bolshevik alliance, which had been strengthened at the Congress of Peoples of the East, held in Baku during this same summer of 1920.[203] The 'secret report' of this Congress, dated 17 September 1920, openly advocated aid to Kemalism and a joint attack on Armenia without further delay.[204]

Another irony is provided by the British government. Whereas the British did all they could, as we have seen, to neutralize Armenian rights in the three areas, the Foreign Office vigorously condemned the Tiflis Agreement, accusing the Armenians of betraying Great Britain, which had done so much to help them![205] Power relations had changed. Bolshevism had been fortunate in southern Russia and Transcaucasia, as Kemalism had been in Asia Minor. The three regions formed a bridge between these two enemies of London – which realized, a little too late, that supporting Armenia might have been preferable.

As one would expect, the 'provisional' occupation of the contested territories was accompanied by Bolshevization policies which were not part of the Tiflis Agreement, but protests by the Armenian government to Legran were in vain. Several Dashnak leaders were executed in Karabagh, and entire villages were razed in Zangezur. It was in the west, however, that the mortal danger lay.

For several months the commander of Kemalist troops on the eastern front, Karabekir, waited impatiently, dreaming of wiping Armenia off the map. Kemal also had this solution in mind in order to overcome the only obstacle between himself and his Bolshevik allies, especially in Azerbaijan. Always politically astute, however, he waited for the most favourable moment, conscious of the sensitivity of his allies and their unease over Turkish ambitions concerning Baku. He also had to disregard the conditions set by Chicherin, once again the lone Bolshevik concerned about the Armenians. When Chicherin raised the issue of Turkish Armenia as a condition for the Soviet–Kemalist entente, Karabekir responded, 'In Turkey, there has never been an Armenia or a territory inhabited by Armenians....'[206]

The green light was given in September 1920 when Kemal was finally sure that Soviet Russia would not aid Armenia, 'ally of the Entente'.[207] Armenia once again waited in vain for aid from this 'Entente'. Even worse, Great Britain strongly advised Armenia against any accord with the Soviets or the Kemalists at the very moment when something could have been saved. She advised against it but provided no assistance. Karabekir's offensive was dazzling and pitiless. Kars fell on 30 October and Alexandropol on 7 November. Once more abandoned and alone, Armenia signed a truce on 18 November.

The Turkish victory was unsettling to Moscow, which decided to keep this Armenia alive as a buffer between Turkey and Baku: alive, but Soviet. The Red Army entered Armenia from the north at the end of November. The Dro–Legran Accords on 2 December sealed the Sovietization of Armenia (including Zangezur). But what Armenia was this? It is on the western front that we find the answer. During the night of 2–3 December, Karabekir, uncompromising, forced the Dashnaks to sign the Treaty of Alexandropol, returning Armenia roughly to the borders defined by the Treaty of Batum.[208] Armenia lost the districts of Kars, Nakhichevan and Zangezur and became, in fact, a protectorate of Turkey. Paradoxically, this treaty was signed by the ex-government of Armenia, which had become Sovietized in the meantime![209]

Soviet Armenia

The Sovietization of Armenia (or what remained of it) opened a new chapter in the history of the three regions now contested by two Soviet republics. As early as 9 November Stalin had said that Zangezur and Karabagh 'could not be handed to Armenia under the Dashnaks'[210] without excluding the possibility of a return to a future Soviet Armenia. On 30 November, the day after the entry of the Red Army into Armenia, Narimanov, President of the Revolutionary Committee of Azerbaijan, sent his Armenian counterpart an astonishing telegram explicitly stating in a 'burst of enthusiasm':

> From this day on, the old borders between Armenia and Azerbaijan are declared null and void. Mountainous Karabagh, Zangezur, and Nakhichevan are recognized as integral parts of the Socialist Republic of Armenia.[211]

The next day Narimanov confirmed his words in an address before the Baku Soviet. Orjonikidze was there and enthusiastically described it as 'an historic document without parallel in the history of humanity'.[212] On 2 December he informed Lenin and Stalin that 'Azerbaijan has already declared the reunification of Nakhichevan, Zangezur, and Karabagh with Soviet Armenia'. The declaration was published in *Pravda* on 4 December 1920. In this same issue, Stalin also provided confirmation in enthusiastic terms.

> Soviet Azerbaijan has officially renounced the contested provinces.... The age-old conflict between Armenia and her Moslem neighbors has been resolved in a single blow.[213]

The surprise was so general that several Azerbaijani leaders disavowed Narimanov.[214]

How can we explain this about-face by someone who had always fought for the opposite goals? It was a tactical stratagem which fooled the Bolsheviks and the Armenians. One detail should already have raised suspicion. The text of Narimanov's speech published in the Baku press differed, on a single point, from the speech heard and reported (without contradiction) by Orjonikidze.[215] On the subject of Mountainous Karabagh, it said that there should be the right to self-determination.[216] True to himself, Narimanov envisioned a rigged referendum if necessary.

In any case, by the end of 1920 the situation in the three contested zones was quite complex. Zangezur presented the Bolsheviks with many problems. Their repressive policies provoked a revolt at the end of 1920. The leader was the prestigious Dashnak Nzhdeh, who had successfully fought the Tatars since November 1919. On 25 December 1920, Zangezur declared itself independent. After the Dashnak uprising, which seized Yerevan on 18 February 1921, was crushed on 2 April, Zangezur was, for several months, the last bastion of anti-Bolshevism. There Nzhdeh proclaimed the 'Independent Republic of

Mountainous Armenia'. It was crushed in July with the aid of Red Army detachments from Karabagh. But it is undeniable that if Zangezur has since been an integral part of Soviet Armenia, it was Nzhdeh who made it possible. Following Andranik, he successfully implemented a 're-Armenianization' of the region, rendering even more tenuous the claims of Baku.

Nakhichevan would not enjoy the same fate, despite the promises of Narimanov. Penetration by the Turkish army, stationed nearby, provided good reason to look to Ankara. In front of Lenin, Narimanov cleverly dangled the prospect of an alliance with Turkey against England which could be sealed by satisfying Turkish ambitions with regard to Armenia. In February 1921 he wrote to Lenin, 'If Moscow, because of the Armenian Question, rejects the Ankarians [Kemalists], then they will be thrown, in desperation, into the arms of England.'[217] It was classic blackmail. Chicherin was denounced. 'He is too interested in the Armenian Question.' The February anti-Bolshevik insurrection in Armenia came just at the right time. On 21 February Narimanov wrote to Lenin:

> You already know that Soviet power has been cast aside in Armenia. In the light of this fact, I propose that the Armenian Question play no role whatsoever in negotiations with the Turkish delegation.[218]

At the Soviet-Turkish conference in Moscow (February–March 1921), the Armenian delegate, Bekzatian, was swept aside. There were Azerbaijani–Turkish negotiations,[219] and Stalin took a pro-Turkish position:

> You have already resolved the Armenian Question. If anything else remains which has not been resolved, resolve it, only inform us of the moment when you do it.[220]

We have many examples of gratitude from the Turks for such an ally.[221]

In these circumstances the question of Nakhichevan was resolved by the Turks and the Soviets without the Armenians. By the Soviet–Turkish Treaty of Moscow (16 March 1921), ratified by the Treaty of Kars (13 October 1921) between Turkey and the three Soviet Transcaucasian republics, Nakhichevan was declared autonomous 'under the protection of Azerbaijan' with the additional qualification that 'this protection could never be transferred to another state'.[222] This was a flagrant case of Turkish interference, since it was under pressure from Ankara that the decision was ratified to transfer to a Turkish Soviet republic a region which was Armenian by history and population, even though the territory was geographically separated from Azerbaijan.

The Separation of Karabagh from Armenia

Failure in Zangezur, success in Nakhichevan. It was now time for Narimanov to go after the 'third parcel'. Disowning his declarations of December, he now demanded Karabagh for Azerbaijan. At that time, Karabagh was in full revolt under the direction of a partisan leader from the south of the province, Tevan Stepanian. At the head of his own brigade, Stepanian led a struggle against the Turks, claiming to act under orders from Dro. In January 1920, news of his attack on a Turkish village reached Shushi.[223] Shortly thereafter, he demobilized at the moment of the Soviet takeover of Karabagh. He was quickly arrested by the Bolsheviks, but fled to take up arms again. Nzhdeh, whom he had met in Ghapan, supplied him with money and men. He commanded a force of 1,800 and captured the southern districts, where a traditional administration was re-installed. Soon the Red Army took up the attack, and Stepanian fought a retreat into Zangezur and passed into Iran in May 1921. The following year, he secretly returned to his village of Tum. The authorities urged him to join them, but he felt he was being closely watched and fled again to Iran. The rest of his life is obscure. This independent rebel, without party affiliation, would be labelled as an 'enemy of the people', but his memory lives on in numerous legends.[224]

In 1921 the Azerbaijanis worked hard to create a climate of tension and insecurity in Karabagh that would encourage the emigration of Armenians, especially the intelligentsia.[225] This was the policy they would follow for seventy years: Baku's demands were, moreover, a total contradiction of the accord signed on 12 May 1921 between the representative of Soviet Armenia and the Red Army, which confirmed the Armenian character of Zangezur and Mountainous Karabagh. The matter was taken up by the Caucasian Bureau of the Communist Party on 3 June 1921. In the presence of Narimanov himself, it decided that Mountainous Karabagh belonged to Armenia.[226] Several days later, the decree of the Armenian government was published in Yerevan and Baku.[227] It clearly stated that 'Mountainous Karabagh is henceforth an integral part of the Soviet Socialist Republic of Armenia.' Narimanov threatened that he would allow 'anti-Soviet groups to resurface in Azerbaijan'.[228] The spectre of nationalist agitation in Azerbaijan began to concern the Caucasian Bureau, which created a special commission on 2 May to draw the borders. Aside from the president, Kirov, it consisted of two Georgians, four Azerbaijanis, and a lone Armenian, Bekzatian.[229] The situation had begun to change! They decided to send a commission to Karabagh on 25 June composed of an Armenian, Mravian, and an Azerbaijani who was none other than Karaiev, author of the sordid letter cited above. When the train arrived in Evlakh, Karaiev tried to persuade Mravian to go to Baku to settle the issue. Sensing a trap, Mravian refused and cabled Orjonikidze from Karabagh, insisting on the urgency of the situation.[230] Orjonikidze, with Kirov, warned Narimanov and insisted that he follow 'the principle that no Armenian village be attached to Azerbaijan while not even the smallest Moslem village be given to Armenia'.[231] The overwhelming number of villages in Mountainous Karabagh were

Armenian. In total disregard of this reality, the Political Bureau of the Communist Party of Azerbaijan on 27 June refused to restore Mountainous Karabagh to Armenia on the pretext that the economy of Mountainous Karabagh was tied to a greater degree to Azerbaijan.[232] With no further reason for its existence, the 'Commission on Frontiers' was disbanded, and Narimanov was more active than ever.[233]

The Caucasian Bureau decided to meet in Tiflis in early July 1921 in a final attempt to resolve border problems in Transcaucasia. At the Tiflis sessions Narimanov and Miasnikian were seated and voted in the presence of Stalin (who did not vote) along with five of the six members of the Bureau, including Orjonikidze, Kirov, and an Armenian, Nazaretian, who would consistently take a pro-Azerbaijani position. Two surreal sessions sealed the fate of Mountainous Karabagh. On 4 July the Bureau decided to reunify Mountainous Karabagh with Armenia, subject to a referendum.[234] Kirov and Orjonikidze had voted in favour. A furious Narimanov demanded that the question be taken to Moscow and placed before the Central Committee.[235] What followed defies all logic. The Bureau accepted Narimanov's proposal but re-convened the next day and there, on 5 July, accepted, without a vote or debate, a decision diametrically opposed to the one taken the day before.

> Considering the necessity of peace between Moslems and Christians, considering the economic link between Mountainous and Lower Karabagh and their ties with Azerbaijan, Mountainous Karabagh is left within the borders of Azerbaijan with the city of Shushi as the centre of this Autonomous Region.[236]

The proposition was presented at the start of the session by Orjonikidze and Nazaretian, two non-Azerbaijanis who had voted the opposite way only the day before! The fact that they were the closest to Stalin suggests that he was probably pushed by Narimanov to 'work' them during the night of the 4th and 5th. As for Miasnikian, he did not even insist, at least, that the question be reverted to Moscow, which was the pretext for reconsidering the decision of the 4th.

In addition, the term 'left' is odd, given that 'During the short lived Muslim Republic of Adharbaydjan (1918–20), Karabagh enjoyed freedom from foreign control.'[237]

In a single day what had been the standard for a year was reversed. It is clear that Mountainous Karabagh, with its 94 per cent Armenian majority, had to be united with Armenia, even if Tatar massacres had cut it off from neighbouring Zangezur by a narrow strip of land which had been emptied of Armenians. After all, Nakhichevan was united with Azerbaijan even though it was cut off from it by Armenian Zangezur. As for the economic argument, it is indefensible, and even if it possessed merit, it would work against Nakhichevan for the same reasons of total separation. Why was there this *volte-face* by the

Soviet authorities?[238] First of all, we must understand that the more time passed, the more the relationship of forces worked to the disadvantage of Armenia. As long as Georgia was not Sovietized (February 1921), the Dashnak insurrection in Armenia was not suppressed, and Zangezur was in revolt, that is to say, as long as Soviet power was not well established, it was advisable to court the Armenians. By the summer of 1921 this was no longer the case. The rebellion had been put down, and perhaps the desire to punish the Armenians also played a role in the decision. To that must be added the economic and demographic weight of Azerbaijan, the relations between the higher authorities of Moscow and Turkey, the desire to please the Moslem East, Narimanov's threats ('If Armenia reclaims Karabagh, we will cut off their petroleum'),[239] the unfortunate attitude among certain Armenian Bolsheviks motivated by 'internationalism' and a hatred of the Dashnaks, and the weight of Stalin. Lenin, who was ill by this time,[240] spoke later of the problems of 'autonomization' and said, 'I think that the haste and excess administrative zeal of Stalin has played a fatal role.'[241] We could add the visceral Armenophobia of the future 'Little Father of Peoples' who demanded of Lenin that they rid themselves of the 'imperialist penchants' of the Armenian people! Stalin's opposition to the pro-Armenian demands of Chicherin is clear in the Turkish sources and explicit in Stalin's correspondence with Lenin.[242] What then can be said of the following phrases taken from an official brochure published in Moscow in 1988 to legitimize the 5 July 1921 decision? Concerning Narimanov, 'He was one of the great figures in the history of Azerbaijan' and, further on, 'Stalin had a true internationalist position, just and, therefore, Socialist....'[243]

The Autonomous Region of Mountainous Karabagh

Mountainous Karabagh was unified with Azerbaijan by means of this surprising decision of 5 July. On the 16th the Central Committee of the Armenian Communist Party expressed its disagreement – a little late to change the course of events.[244] At the very least, the 5 July document spoke of 'wide regional autonomy'. The authorities in Baku tried to disregard this provision. First of all, on 26 September a majority of the Azerbaijani Political Bureau demanded that the Caucasian Bureau reconsider the autonomy clause[245] (which was, in any case, more symbolic than real). The year 1922 was marked by meetings of Azerbaijani commissions concerned with the matter. Meanwhile, Baku continued to drag its feet on the question of autonomy.

But the overwhelming Armenian majority protested. Through the Regional Party Committees in Shushi on 3 July 1922, they demanded the administrative unity and autonomous status they had been promised. Several months before, the three republics had been joined in the Federated Soviet Socialist Republic of Transcaucasia (disbanded in 1936). Unrest in Mountainous Karabagh continued. A report was presented on 15 February 1923 to the Regional Committee of Transcaucasia which examined the issue in June 1923. A reasonable suggestion was made in Tiflis to the Transcaucasian authorities by an Armenian delegate from Mountainous Karabagh. He suggested that the region be administered directly by the Transcaucasian Federation, by-passing Azerbaijan, but without result.[246] It should be mentioned in passing that this prefigured the idea of direct administration by Moscow suggested at the end of the Soviet period, which, if it had been accepted, could have led to a solution to the problem.

Finally, it was not until 1 July 1923 that Baku resigned itself to autonomous status for Karabagh, which was promulgated on 7 July.[247] The first point says: 'To create an autonomous region in the Armenian portion of Mountainous Karabagh which will be an integral part of the Azerbaijan SSR, with its centre in the locality of Khankend.'[248] This formulation would merit detailed analysis. Moreover, at this time, the plenipotentiary in Karabagh was none other than Karaiev, whom we have cited above for his anti-Armenian remarks.

The borders were to be drawn before 15 August by a mixed commission made up of representatives from Mountainous and Lower Karabagh, Kurdistan[249] and Azerbaijan, but without the participation of either Yerevan or Moscow. All would be presided over by Karaiev. Under such circumstances, the Armenians could expect to be grossly disappointed. On the one hand, as should have been expected, they excluded, on the west, the 'corridor' made up of Lachin, Kelbajar, and Kedabek which had been carefully emptied of its Armenian population to separate Mountainous Karabagh from Armenian Zangezur. On the other hand, in the north, without any justification, they removed the districts 'of Shamkhor, Khanlar, Dashkesan and Shahumian (formerly Gulistan) where the Armenian population was predominant (about 90 per cent)', as was recalled in a 1963 petition from Armenians in Mountainous Karabagh to Khrushchev.[250] Events in recent years have shown the reasoning behind these exclusions. From Shamkhor in the north to Shahumian in the south, Armenian villages in these districts have been systematically emptied of their secular populations. Mountainous Karabagh delimited in this way is only a portion of what had always been Armenian Karabagh, which itself is only a part of what was included in the ancient Armenian provinces of Artsakh and Utik.

The historians in Baku have recently found a new 'justification': in 1923 a referendum had been organized in Mountainous Karabagh (then 95 per cent Armenian) and a majority had chosen Azerbaijan. No details are provided, and for good reason. It seems that local Armenian Bolsheviks were organized to pass the petitions, which were signed by their peers but not by the people.[251] Moreover, this operation was directed by the same Karaiev.

It was a sombre summer for Armenians. A little earlier, on 24 July 1923, the Allies had accepted Turkey's terms by signing the Treaty of Lausanne, from which even the name of Armenia is absent. Western Armenia was put to death while eastern Armenia was being pitilessly mutilated.

On 1 August 1923 the capital of Mountainous Karabagh was moved from Shushi, Turkified since March 1920, to Khankend, the former Armenian Vararakn, then a small town (whose location was more open than Shushi). Ten kilometres from Shushi, it was re-named Stepanakert on 20 September in honour of the Bolshevik hero Stepan Shahumian. The first administrative reorganization of the district corresponded roughly to four of the five 'melikates'. The districts were Jraberd in the north (with the celebrated monastery at Gandzasar), Khachen in the centre, Varanda in the east (with the ancient monastery of Amaras), and Dizak in the south.[252] Soon thereafter Khachen was divided in two to create one Armenian district (now called Askeran) at Stepanakert and a Turkish one at Shushi. The three other districts, like Shushi, were re-named for their district capitals: Martakert in the north, Martuni in the east, and Hadrut in the south.

In early November 1923, the First Congress of the Soviets of the Autonomous Region of Mountainous Karabagh opened with 116 Armenian delegates and 16 Azerbaijanis.[253] The president of the Revolutionary Committee, Karageuzian, did not hesitate to praise the Armenian defeat.

> The Armenian peasant worker must receive his autonomy not from imperialism or its Dashnak or Musavat lackeys but only from the proletariat of Baku and the revolutionary peasantry of neighbouring Azerbaijan.[254]

These mocking words would echo tragically throughout the region from 1923 to 1988.

Meanwhile, the Presidium of the Central Committee of the Communist Party of Azerbaijan confirmed all the decisions on 23 June 1924. It considered that a solid foundation had been laid for 'the best possible neighbourly inter-ethnic relations in Karabagh'.[255] On 3 July it adopted the Constitution for the Autonomous Region, and it was published on 26 November. A chapter was closed and a new one was opened.

Azerbaijani Politics

In all official Soviet publications, the northern section of the former Atropatena is presented as the Azerbaijan SSR, or simply as Azerbaijan, with a rich history, while the real Azerbaijan, south of the Persian frontier, is called

'Iranian Azerbaijan'. The roles are actually reversed! The historians in Baku labour to create an 'Azeri past' by appealing to the Albanians just as the Turks in Ankara appeal to the Hittites in order to give themselves an Anatolian past. In such a context, the political objective is to define the country as the motherland of the Azerbaijanis, referring to the Moslem majority. During the 1980s we find the following in the official government brochure on Azerbaijan:

> The 6 million inhabitants of the republic are not only the Azerbaijanis but also the Russians, Armenians, Georgians, Lezghians, Jews ... in a word representatives of over 70 nations and ethnic groups.[256]

The territory's *de facto* status has thus shifted from a multinational republic to a Turkish republic. The Armenians, who had been on the land for centuries and had made up 10 per cent of the total, were not even Azerbaijanis but a people reduced to one among a constellation of minorities.

In order to complete the process, Baku had to rid itself of these two 'autonomous Armenian' wounds, Nakhichevan and Karabagh. For Nakhichevan, the task has been completed. The region, between Iran on one side and Soviet Armenia on the other, was given the title 'Autonomous Soviet Socialist Republic' on 9 February 1924, united with Azerbaijan. Of the 50,000 Armenians who lived there in 1917 and made up 40 per cent of the population, only a fifth remained by 1926, and 3,400 or 1.4 per cent by the time of the 1979 census.[257] In 1987, on the eve of the 'Karabagh Movement', two Armenian villages remained, as opposed to 44 in 1917, and since 1988 there have been none. The same holds true for Armenian monuments, which were formerly numerous in this cradle of the Armenian people.[258] Ankara made no secret of its intentions, carrying out an exchange of territory with Iran in order to obtain several kilometres of border with Nakhichevan, which has become a Turkish-populated region.[259]

The spectre of 'Nakhichevanization' haunts the Autonomous Region of Mountainous Karabagh, which had 125,000 inhabitants in 1926 who were 89 per cent Armenian.[260] This region has become an 'enclave' since the 'cleansing' of the Hagaru Valley in order to separate Karabagh from Zangezur by a narrow strip emptied of Armenians. The strip runs from Mt Hinal in the north to the approaches of the Arax River. In the middle lies the city of Lachin which cuts the road from Goris to Stepanakert.

Red Kurdistan

This 'Lachin Strip', which had been emptied of Armenians before Sovietization, was not populated by Turks but largely by Kurds, who themselves had autonomous status for a brief period in the 1920s. This is recalled in a letter by Soviet Kurdish intellectuals to the leaders of the USSR in early 1988 demanding, in another dimension of the Karabagh conflict, that the strip be united with Armenia.

> In 1923, in Azerbaijan, the district of Kurdistan was created with its capital at Lachin. This district included Kelbajar, Kubatla, Kurdaji, Muradkhanli, and Karakeshlagh: areas populated by Moslem Kurds.... A technical school and other cultural institutions opened at Shusha.... But this lasted only for a short time.... In 1929 the Kurdish District was abolished. Later the majority of Kurds were deported by force to Kazakhstan and Turkmenistan.... After the death of Stalin, in 1957 the garrisons were suppressed and the Kurds were allowed to return to their native territories, but it was impossible to revive the district.... Pan-Turkism, re-born during the Stalin epoch, was working secretly, and hiding behind the banner of Marxism-Leninism.

Faring much better in Armenia than in Azerbaijan, where no rights, even cultural, were granted to them, the Kurds demanded that:

> The territory between Mountainous Karabagh and Armenia, the former District of Kurdistan, be united with the Armenian SSR to be rescued from the white genocide ordered by the Azeri authorities in 1929 and practised to this day.[261]

The 'white genocide' is irrefutable. While the 1926 census listed 41,200 Kurds in Azerbaijan, 'Kurd' has since disappeared as a statistical category.[262] Officially, there are no longer any Kurds living in Azerbaijan.

Around 1940 in the *Larousse du XXe siècle*, H. Froidevaux had this to report on Kurdistan: 'Regarding Transcaucasian Kurdistan, there are about 50,000 inhabitants (capital Abdaljar) and it comes under Azerbaijan' (Abdaljar or Avdalar designates Lachin). Is it a coincidence that 'Red Kurdistan' disappeared at the same time that Republican Turkey was massacring Kurds on a grand scale on the other side of the frontier?

The Exodus of Armenians from Karabagh

Due to incessant conflicts, the population of Mountainous Karabagh declined between 1913 and 1923. From 1923 to the Khrushchev era, and thanks to Stalinism, there is only sporadic data on the evolution of the situation. Even census figures are quite imprecise.

The city of Shushi, formerly the third largest city in Transcaucasia, saw its Armenian population decimated by the massacre of March 1920. There were

40,000 inhabitants at the turn of the century but only 5,000 in 1929.[263] It became a city with no Armenians (though this has not been the case since Karabagh Armenian forces occupied the city in 1992). A totally Turkish city in an Armenian environment, Shushi, along with Lachin in the west and Aghdam in the east, comprised the trio of anti-Armenian bastions which control Mountainous Karabagh. It is 10 km to the north, in the Karkar Valley, that we find the new Armenian capital, Stepanakert, whose architecture was originally designed by Alexander Tamanian, who had drawn the plans for Yerevan. In 1929 its population did not exceed 3,000.[264] By 1990 it exceeded 60,000.

It is interesting to compare official texts on the 'cultural and economic development' of Armenian Karabagh under the Soviet regime from 1923 to 1988 with the ominous picture often drawn by the same authors after the start of the Karabagh Movement in late 1987, when the truth could finally be told.

On the one hand we have the opening of the Maxim Gorky Library in Stepanakert, which now houses a collection of over 160,000 volumes in three languages (Armenian, Russian, and Turkish). In 1932 the national theatre of the same name was established. Later, in 1945, the Azerbaijani Academy of Sciences opened an affiliate in Stepanakert specializing in agricultural research. Concerning the media, the newspaper *The Karabagh Peasant*, in Armenian, was founded in Shushi in June 1923. The title was soon changed to *Soviet Karabagh*, and it was edited in Stepanakert. It became a daily in 1967. Each district has its own paper in Armenian, except Shushi, where it is in Turkish. The year 1934 saw the launching of a weekly, *Young Bolshevik*, which lasted until 1941, and a monthly, *Attack*, which had only one issue. Earlier, the monthly *Spark* put out five issues in 1929.[265]

On the other side of the ledger, it is sufficient to cite Arkady Volsky, who headed the district in early 1989 for a brief, unsuccessful period of direct administration by Moscow: 'During my travels throughout the country (USSR), I have never been confronted with such a state of abandonment, such scorn for the destiny of people as in Mountainous Karabagh.'[266] It is not surprising that from 1920 to 1987 we find a spectacular decline in the Armenian population. Until the Second World War, the exodus was more or less compensated for by a high birth rate.[267] The war took a heavy toll. Of the 45,000 who were conscripted, nearly half were casualties. After the war the process of de-Armenianization accelerated due to Armenian migration and Turkish settlement in Karabagh. Between 1926 and 1980, 85 Armenian villages, or 30 per cent of the total, disappeared, while no Azerbaijani village met the same fate.[268] The figures on the proportion of Armenians in the total population speak eloquently of this process.[269]

1921	1926	1939	1959	1970	1979
94.4%	89.1%	88.1%	84.4%	80.6%	75.9%

The 1959 census records approximately 120,000 Armenians out of a population of 160,000. Since 1970 the Turkish population has increased 36.3 per cent and the Armenian 1.7 per cent. Since 1926 the figures are 200 per cent and 10.2 per cent respectively. During the same period 1926–1979, Armenians in Zangezur, who are not nearly so well off, saw their population multiply 2.2 times, which represents an increase of 120 per cent. In 1979, only one Armenian in 10 born in Mountainous Karabagh remained there, and since 1926 an average of 2,000 Armenians have left annually.[270] The situation in the northern districts, which were excluded from the boundaries of the Autonomous Region, was obviously worse. The population of these areas was 90 per cent Armenian.[271] Yet Armenian villages have disappeared one by one, a process which has accelerated since 1988 when the Azerbaijanis employed military means to expel Armenians (Azat, Kamo, Getashen, Shahumian....)

This exodus was not fortuitous and is clearly related to the persistent policies of Baku which has sought the 'Nakhichevanization' of the territory: first, cultural de-Armenianization, followed by physical exodus. This project has been facilitated by the fact that the Azerbaijani government named the leaders of the Autonomous Region. It has been sufficient for them to draw upon Armenian 'collabos' (collaborators), Turkified or Russified, who have efficiently carried out the anti-Armenian policies of Baku. Armenian schools were dependent on the Azerbaijani Ministry of Education, where no one spoke Armenian. The history of the Armenian people was not taught and books from Armenia were not used in the schools. Television was only available in Turkish or Russian, and only after the demonstrations in 1988 could the territory receive television broadcasts from Armenia. Obstacles to Armenian cultural development could easily be multiplied. Special attention should be given to Armenian monuments: is their number and richness not the most eloquent statement on the Armenian character of Karabagh? While Azerbaijani historians labour to 'prove' that these monuments are not Armenian but 'Albanian, and hence Azerbaijani', they let the monuments decay, sometimes to the point of destruction. This is particularly the case with numerous *khachkars* or 'stone crosses', so typical of Armenian art. Of course, these architectural treasures are systematically absent from tourist guides to Azerbaijan, where one only finds reference to Islamic or revolutionary monuments. In a certain sense, partly by inertia and also by virtue of the desire not to 'create problems', Armenia has been complicit in this Azerbaijani policy. It was not until 1980 that a small book appeared in Armenian on the monuments of Karabagh. Only 1,500 copies were printed, and it quickly sold out. As an example of change, Shahen Mkrtichian, the author, was allowed to publish a much longer second edition in a print run of 10,000 in 1985. In 1988 there was a Russian edition, with professional quality illustrations, published in 25,000 copies.

To a great degree, this explains the birth of the 'Karabagh Movement' in

1987; it would soon have been too late. This movement did not, however, spring up without any precedent, though the precedents were less spectacular for reasons one can easily imagine.

Finally, it should be stressed that Armenian emigration from the territory was not caused by poverty. Certainly, Karabagh conveys the image of under-development due to a deliberate policy of pauperization which was periodically denounced. But the soil is rich (the name means 'black garden'),[272] and this fertility contrasts with the rocky and arid soil of Armenia where only the Ararat Plain can nourish the population. Armenia and Karabagh complement each other economically as well as culturally.[273]

Early Attempts at Reunification with Armenia

During the 1920s there was already an organization 'Karabagh to Armenia', underground of course, with branches as far as Ganja. Its members were drawn from the remains of the various political parties.

Early in 1927, seven Armenians from Karabagh fled to Iran. From Enzeli, on the shores of the Caspian, one of them sent an interesting letter to the Armenian daily in Paris, *Haratch*. It spoke, already, of the 'difficult times' their compatriots lived in due to the dual yoke of Bolshevism and Turkish leader-ship. 'The Armenian people there cannot get used to the idea that their leaders are Azerbaijani Turks.' The handful of Armenian Bolshevik leaders in Stepanakert were said to be browbeaten, on the Baku payroll, and cut off from the people. In November 1926, 'Karabagh to Armenia' inundated Karabagh with leaflets. Numerous arrests followed, above all among the Communists. Another distribution of literature took place at the end of that month. The text would prove to be as relevant to the situation in 1988 as it was at the time:

> If the current leaders of Armenia have abandoned a hundred thousand Armenians in Karabagh ... then who do they serve, what is their purpose, sitting as lackeys on the banks of the Hrazdan?

It ends with a call to unity of all the people, whether from Karabagh or not, who support reunification – a unity which had already been achieved in Karabagh itself.[274]

The organization was liquidated in 1927. At the same time certain local Communists in the Armenian districts north of the Autonomous Region signed petitions to extend the region's boundaries to the Kura River, including the Armenian portion of Gandzak on the right bank.[275] Soon after, in 1929, pan-Turkic movements were reported in Azerbaijan,[276] and hence new demands for the reunification of Karabagh with Armenia. In 1936 the new Soviet constitution disbanded the Transcaucasian Federation and separated the three Soviet republics without altering any of the borders. This increased Karabagh's level of dependence on Baku. In Armenia the weak and timid national sentiments of First Party Secretary Khanjian did include the problem of Karabagh. He raised the issue on the occasion of the disbanding of the Transcaucasian Federation, and his initiative was not welcomed by Stalin.[277] This was, perhaps, one of the reasons for his assassination in July 1936 on orders from Beria. His successor, Harutiunian, made two efforts but with no results. The first was in 1945. In a letter to Stalin he explained why Mountainous Karabagh ought to be united with Armenia, and he argued that Shushi ought to be the capital.[278] Malenkov sought the advice of Bagirov, First Secretary of the Communist Party of Azerbaijan, who proposed to exchange the districts, other than Shushi, for border areas in Armenia inhabited by Azerbaijanis.[279] The issue was raised a second time in 1949 on the occasion of the 'repatriation' of diasporan Armenians to Soviet Armenia.[280]

After years of Stalinist terror, we arrive at the era of the Khrushchev thaw. In 1960, on the fortieth anniversary of the Sovietization of Armenia, people began to dream again – in vain – of the redress of grievances. The circumstances were all the more propitious because the new First Secretary Zarobian was more favourable to Armenian demands, but he did not survive the fall of Khrushchev. In any case, in 1963 the question was posed publicly. On 19 May a petition with 2,500 signatures of Armenians from the Autonomous Region and the northern districts was sent to Khrushchev. The lengthy text contained a detailed denunciation of Azerbaijan's 'chauvinist politics' designed to 'weaken the economy of the Armenian population and, finally, to force them to leave'.[281] One of their methods consisted of 'subordinating institutions and enterprises in Mountainous Karabagh to enterprises situated 40–60 kilometres away' in centres such as Aghdam or Barda'a which are outside the Autonomous Region. In addition, 'in forty years not a single kilometre of road has been constructed to link the villages to the regional centre' and 'there has been no attempt to investigate possibilities for developing agriculture in the region'. This was without even considering that 'culture and education are in decline'. The situation was even worse in the northern districts which were not included in the Autonomous Region. The petition ended with a demand for unification with either Armenia or Russia. Khrushchev turned a blind eye,[282] and the Azerbaijanis responded by assassinating 18 Armenians in Karabagh.

After this petition, efforts multiplied. On 24 April 1965, the fiftieth anniversary of the genocide of Armenians in Turkey, there was a spectacular demonstration in Yerevan, amid shouts of 'Our Lands!' which applied equally to Armenian regions in Turkey and Azerbaijan. For Moscow, the first demand was easier to satisfy (erect a monument, etc.) than the second, which required opening internal political questions. Having said that, it would be erroneous to believe that a modification of borders inside the USSR was utopian. From 1930 to 1970 there were 30 decisions on border modifications;[283] the most spectacular was the transfer of the Crimea from Russia to the Ukraine in 1954.[284]

In June of this same year, 1965, a new petition was sent to Moscow, addressed to high-level party and government bodies.[285] The appeal demanded the unification of Karabagh with Armenia and was signed by 13 prominent personalities from Karabagh including Bagrat Ulubabian, novelist and historian and head of the Karabagh Writers' Union since 1949. By the end of the year, the signatories had been threatened. Among the authors of this text was a young deputy, Arkady Manucharov. He would be forced into exile in Armenia, only to return in 1977 to direct the Krunk Committee, linked to the Karabagh Committee. He would also be arrested in December 1988 and held until 29 May 1990. This 'Letter of the 13' was signed by 45,000 people throughout the Region. At this time in Yerevan, the Party of National Unity was formed. Its objective was independence, but it was also very much concerned with the problems of Nakhichevan and Karabagh.

In 1966, the demand for unification came from Yerevan: in vain, of course. In Karabagh the situation continued to deteriorate. The Azerbaijanis decided to repay the Armenians for their timid protests of the past few years. The Karabagh Armenians addressed their request of 19 September 1967 to the authorities in Yerevan. They described illegal imprisonments, unpunished murders, and official threats.[286] 'Our situation is worse than it has ever been, even under the tyrannical rule of the Khans and the Musavats.... Our honour is soiled, our dignity and our rights are flouted.' At this time many Armenian intellectuals, including Ulubabian, had no choice but to enter exile in Armenia under threat of death. In 1968 Stepanakert was the scene of confrontations between Armenians and Azerbaijanis.

Little information filtered out during the next few years, though the continuing deterioration of the situation of Karabagh Armenians was denounced in underground writings. Protests could not prevent the 1973 celebration of the fiftieth anniversary of the creation of the Autonomous Region. In his speech First Secretary Aliev of Azerbaijan described the creation as 'a great stimulus to the renaissance and socialist blossoming of Mountainous Karabagh and Azerbaijan of which it is an integral part'.[287] Mountainous Karabagh continued to be governed by the same 'lackeys of Baku' who had been denounced earlier. The leading example was Boris Gevorgov, the only Armenian member of the Central Committee of the Communist Party of Azerbaijan. In 1973 he had been named the First Secretary of the Regional Committee of Mountainous Karabagh of the Communist Party of Azerbaijan. During his 15 years as head of the Autonomous Region, he played the role of 'collabo' to perfection. Gevorgov's hard-line position immediately gave rise to another futile protest to Moscow on the part of 58 well-known Armenians in Karabagh. His lengthy monologue on 21 March 1975 at the plenary session of the Regional

Committee is a model of obscurantism.[288] The entire intellectual community of Mountainous Karabagh was accused: writers, poets, journalists, (including the editor of the daily *Soviet Karabagh*) and historians (with Ulubabian, of course, attacked, along with others, as a 'retrograde nationalist'). Shahen Mkrtichian saw his study of Armenian monuments in Karabagh dismissed as 'nationalist vanity'. Gevorgov would later order the destruction of a monument to victims of the Second World War on the pretext that the eagle displayed there was an Armenian 'nationalist symbol'. This was an attitude shared by many of the Armenian political and economic leaders in Karabagh. In this situation it is not surprising that the 1975 plenary session of the Regional Committee, although it contained a large Armenian majority, refused the notion of reunification with Armenia, a demand labelled as 'Dashnak propaganda' which brought with it automatic arrest and deportation.[289] An article published in 1977 in the well-known Soviet magazine *Problems of Peace and Socialism* echoed the same themes.

This state of affairs was denounced by the popular writer Sero Khanzadian, a native of Zangezur. In his famous letter addressed to Brezhnev on 15 October 1977, the author attacks the leadership of Karabagh, the defamatory articles in the Soviet press, and the false statements of officials.... He concludes that the only solution is reunification. His letter yielded no concrete results, but it did add to the ongoing history of struggle.[290] The same was true of a long series of articles which appeared in the Boston newspaper *Baikar* (*Struggle*) in early 1979 under the enigmatic name Kevorkian. The style, the references, and the gingerly treatment of Lenin leave no doubt that Kevorkian is the pseudonym of a Soviet Armenian historian.

The Era of Perestroika

After the period we know as the 'Brezhnev stagnation', it was natural that the arrival of Gorbachev in 1985 would once again awaken hopes of reunification, just as the coming of Khrushchev had done after the Stalinist terror. The concepts of *perestroika* and *glasnost* opened promising horizons for all sorts of long-latent demands in the USSR, including cultural, territorial, and even secessionist demands.

On 5 March 1987, it was a geologist and Party member, Suren Aivazian, who posed the problem of the unification of Karabagh and Nakhichevan with Armenia in a long letter addressed to Gorbachev.[291] He highlighted, among other things, the anti-Armenian role played by Gaidar Aliev, an Azerbaijani native of Nakhichevan and long-time First Secretary of the Communist Party of Azerbaijan, who had moved quickly up the Soviet hierarchy due to his servility to Brezhnev.

Several months later, a new step was taken. The Armenian Academy of Sciences put together a petition with several hundred thousand signatures and sent it to Gorbachev in August.[292] It stressed that 'Azerbaijan is a Turkish fifth column within the USSR' and insisted on the fact that this republic sought to rid itself not only of Armenians but also of Russians. This was followed by declarations by Armenians who were well known in the upper echelons of Soviet society. In September 1987, the writer Zori Balayan, a native of Karabagh, asked his colleagues, 'Must we remain silent?'[293] The next month the historian Sergei Mikoyan publicly took a stand.[294] In November the issue was taken up by the celebrated economist Abel Aganbegyan, personal adviser to Gorbachev. While in Paris, he declared:

I would like to hear that Karabagh has been returned to Armenia. As an economist, I think there are greater links with Armenia than with Azerbaijan. I have made a proposal along these lines, and I hope that the problems will be resolved in the context of *perestroika* and democracy.[295]

Along with these developments, individual and collective appeals and letters had been flooding the leadership in Moscow since 1985.[296] Even legal actions were taken by individuals. In October 1987 six Armenians from the two contested regions accused the authorities in Baku of having 'perpetrated a genocide against the Armenian population from 1920 to 1987'.[297] Azerbaijani strongman Aliev himself was accused of 'violations of national and racial equality' in a letter sent to the Prosecutor General of the USSR by two Armenians, one of whom was a young economist from Baku, Igor Muradian, who would soon be thrown into the limelight.[298]

At the end of 1987, events in the Armenian village of Chardakhlu, in the district of Shamkhor in the north-west of Mountainous Karabagh (but outside the border of the Autonomous Region), had far-reaching repercussions given the prestige of this area, home of two decorated Soviet Armenian generals, Babajanian and Baghramian.[299] The First Secretary of the district, Asadov, had been trying to drive out the Armenian population for several months. The Armenians had sent a protest delegation to Moscow but it had returned empty-handed. On 30 November Asadov arrived at the village with his militia and dismissed the Armenian director of the *sovkhoz*. For their resistance, the peasants were beaten for three hours. On 2 December Asadov tried to force the villagers to participate in a commemorative ceremony he had organized on the occasion of the ninetieth anniversary of Baghramian's birth, but the people rejected this 'concession'. Harassment of the village was pursued by other means such as a blockade. By this time the Azerbaijanis had lost their most reliable pillar, Aliev, who was compromised by his ties to Brezhnev and relieved of his duties. This did not prevent him, however, from drawing on his many contacts. Tensions steadily mounted in Yerevan.[300] The demonstrations there were increasingly led by well-known public figures, the poetesses Silva Kaputikian and Maro Markarian, and the president of the Academy of Sciences, Victor Hambartsumian.

1988 – An Historic Year

For Armenians everywhere 1988 will remain an *année folle*, the year when everything was possible ... up until the horrendous earthquake in December. Delegations from Karabagh and telegrams descended on Moscow.[301] There were popular meetings in the Autonomous Region along with anti-Armenian violence. At the end of February an Armenian radio announcer said, 'Mountainous Karabagh literally finds itself in a state of siege.' For their part, Azerbaijani leaders held to their intransigent position expressed by their front man, Boris Gevorgov: 'We will die but we will not give up Karabagh.'[302] Spoken by this Armenian, the word 'we' signifies 'We Azerbaijanis....'

This position was not shared by the deputies of the regional Soviet of Karabagh. These elected representatives of the system took an historic step there on 20 February 1988. In special session, this Soviet adopted a resolution demanding that the Soviets of Azerbaijan and Armenia do their utmost to bring about 'a positive decision concerning the transfer of the region from the Azerbaijani SSR to the Armenian SSR'. This was a true bombshell, all the more so because the First Secretary of the Azerbaijani Communist Party, Bagirov, was present,[303] and could not prevent a vote on this resolution which provided a legal basis, in the Soviet context, for the Armenian demands. Of 140 deputies, the 110 Armenians voted in favour.[304]

This news was warmly greeted in Yerevan. An initial Karabagh Committee was constituted and led by some fifteen members including Silva Kaputikian, Victor Hambartsumian, Igor Muradian, Vazgen Manukian and others who would slowly become the beacons of political life in Yerevan. Progressively other acute problems were added to the demand for Karabagh's reunification: language, pollution, democratization, and official recognition of 24 April to commemorate the genocide of 1915 and 28 May to celebrate the birth of the independent Armenian Republic in 1918 (denied up until then because of its association with the Dashnaks). The week of 20–27 February brought with it massive demonstrations around the Opera House in Yerevan, fuelled by negative responses by the First Secretary of the Armenian Communist Party, Demirchian, on the 22nd (the changes demanded 'go against the interests of the workers of the Armenian and Azerbaijani SSRs')[305] and the Central Committee of the Communist Party of the Soviet Union (CPSU) on the 23rd (same terminology accompanied by threats against 'irresponsible extremists'). The people pinned their hopes and aspirations on Gorbachev, whose portrait was displayed everywhere. The Supreme Armenian Patriarch Vazgen I wrote to Gorbachev on the 25th and asked him to respect the resolution of the 20th.[306] Strikes in Armenia, violence in Karabagh: Silva Kaputikian and Zori Balayan went to Moscow to speak with the head of the Kremlin. Gorbachev asked for a one-month moratorium on protests to prepare 'a new renaissance for Karabagh'.[307] It was decided to suspend demonstrations for a month and to reconvene on 26 March. In the meantime, the head of the Communist Party of Karabagh, Gevorgov, was recalled on 23 February and replaced by Henrik Poghosian, who soon became one of the most courageous and popular Armenian political leaders.[308]

And then, at the end of February, there was Sumgait. For three days, this dormitory city outside Baku became the scene of massacres, an 'Armenian hunt' with a licence to kill which recalled the attitude of the Russian authorities during the pogroms of 1905. The official death toll of 32 was a derisory understatement, and the testimonies overwhelming. In a long open letter Silva Kaputikian wrote on 5 April:

> This carnage, which all indicators reveal was carefully planned ... encountered no resistance on the part of the local authorities in charge of maintaining order. This carnage disgraces not only Azerbaijan but the entire USSR.[309]

In a parody of law, the trial, held discreetly in November, scarcely punished any responsible party and did nothing to establish the facts. Sumgait horrified the world and sent shockwaves throughout all Armenian communities by reviving memories of 1915. A human sea of several hundred thousand Armenians converged on the genocide monument in Yerevan on 8 March to pay homage to the victims of this newest pogrom. Above all, Sumgait marked the first step in the liquidation of an Armenian presence in Azerbaijan outside of Karabagh.

Barring reunification with Armenia, Mountainous Karabagh demanded, at a minimum, its unification with the Russian Federation: anywhere but Azerbaijan. Karabagh also called attention to the Armenian SSR itself, since it did not react with sufficient firmness. Igor Muradian implicated the Soviet media as 'clearly helpless when faced with this situation'. He also attacked Azerbaijani leaders who encouraged the massacres while Armenia had suspended its demonstrations, and 'a group of leaders of the Central Committee of the Communist Party of the Soviet Union' for 'their refusal to recognize the existence of national problems in the Soviet Union and to resolve them in time'.[310]

During the month of March, while they waited, the atmosphere in Yerevan grew tense as troops were dispatched to occupy the city. On 17 March the Regional Committee of Karabagh in Stepanakert confirmed the decision taken by the Soviet on 20 February. By a vote of 84 out of 92 members, they demanded that the Politburo of the CPSU 'positively resolve the problem of reunification for the Autonomous Region of Mountainous Karabagh with the Armenian SSR, to correct the error committed during the 1920s'.[311] But the signs did not point to a positive decision from the Kremlin. The Institute of Oriental Studies in Moscow, charged by the Communist Party of the Soviet Union with studying the question, reached a chilling set of conclusions which may just as well have come from Baku.

> The Commission considered the question at length. The reunification of Karabagh with Armenia is not desirable. It is important to calm the population with concessions in the cultural–social domain and in the realm of daily life, getting rid of a portion of the leadership, if necessary, and certainly finding some guilty at secondary levels of power. However, Mountainous Karabagh must not be reattached to Armenia. It is now necessary to create the impression of pervasive *glasnost* in contrast with the preceding period, and to highlight, as much as possible, the slightest confrontations which should be blamed on the Armenians. One must infiltrate the Armenian ranks as much as possible, using overall the Kurds, who, among those living on Armenian territory, are the most favourably disposed towards them, and try, at the same time, to destroy these friendly relations.[312]

On 21 March, *Pravda* published an article recognizing that the administration of Karabagh had been deficient – and labelling Gevorgov as the scapegoat – but also attacking 'nationalist demonstrations' and speaking of manipulations which 'would not compromise the friendship of the Azerbaijani and Armenian peoples'. One of the three 'authors' – Arakelian, the *Pravda* correspondent in Armenia – criticized and repudiated this article, and denounced the entire manoeuvre as 'essential to the Central Committee of the Communist Party of the Soviet Union'.[313] He was suspended several days later.[314]

Although expected, the decision of the Presidium of the Supreme Soviet of the USSR fell like a cleaver on 23 March 1988: a 'no' without appeal which spoke of 'inadmissible pressures', threats of legal proceedings, and opposition to 'all nationalist and extremist demonstrations'.[315] Several economic and cultural measures were recommended the next day, but they could not conceal the overall impact.[316] There was dismay among the Armenians, who quickly put the 'Gorbachev myth' to rest. There was also a change in leadership whereby Silva Kaputikian turned the leading role over to Igor Muradian without any illusions concerning 'the other side'. Yerevan carried out a one-day 'dead city' protest, while surrounded by the army. The independence leader, Paruyr Hairikian, who had already spent 15 years in prison, was arrested on 25 March. Several days later troops were pulled out of the city.

On 24 April, the day on which the 1915 genocide is commemorated, students from the university installed a traditional *khachkar* sculpture in memory of Sumgait at the side of the genocide monument located on a hilltop overlooking the city. Strikes and demonstrations continued. On 21 May, Moscow announced the simultaneous dismissals of the First Secretaries of the Azerbaijani and Armenian Communist Parties and their replacement by Vezirov and Suren Harutiunian. But one other commemorative date neared, 28 May, the seventieth anniversary of the founding of the Republic of Armenia, with its tricolour red-blue-orange flag, an occasion which had been considered – incorrectly – as 'Dashnak', and, therefore, damned. This year it was impossible to prevent the people from celebrating this day, and even to stop them displaying the flag which the authorities had rejected for so long. The flags changed, and the photographs in public places also changed: Andranik replaced Gorbachev.

Beginning in June, the Karabagh Committee, officially called the Armenian Committee for the Karabagh Movement, took shape in the form of 11 intellectuals, scientists, and writers aged 35–45 (except for one who was older).[317] Igor Muradian was replaced by this collective body within which there was a compatibility of roles and sensibilities. Slowly this Committee, which enjoyed the support of the overwhelming majority of the population, found itself in the position of a *de facto* alternative power organizing political life before huge crowds at the Opera Square. The month of June was marked by demonstrations in Baku where tanks intervened and where, on 13 June, the Soviet rejected the 20 February decision as 'unacceptable'.[318] Azerbaijani attacks on Armenian supply convoys headed for Karabagh intensified and the road through Lachin became ever more dangerous. It was slowly abandoned in favour of the longer northern route, patrolled by the army.

On 15 June the Armenian Supreme Soviet came out unanimously in favour of reunification.[319] This decision was neutralized two days later by a contrary vote in the Supreme Soviet of Azerbaijan.[320] Legally, its approval was also necessary. On the 21st, there were new protests from the Karabagh Soviet.[321] A second setback, following that of 23 March, came on 28 June. At the Nineteenth Congress of the Communist Party in Moscow, Gorbachev dismissed all possibility of border modifications. Armenia responded with a general strike and the occupation of the Zvartnots International Airport in Yerevan on 5 July. The army savagely repressed the demonstrators, claiming one victim, whose burial gave rise to a spectacular demonstration.[322]

A third demonstration approached. The Karabagh question was to be considered again by the Presidium of the Supreme Soviet in Moscow on 18 July. Beforehand, on 12 July, the Soviet of Mountainous Karabagh unilaterally voted in favour of secession from Baku – a decision without precedent in Soviet annals.[323] Several days later, the Karabagh Committee asked the people to suspend their strike while waiting for a decision from Moscow.[324] The Armenians were disappointed a third time. Reunification was rejected again.[325] In addition, the Presidium demanded a normalization of the situation. It was now clear that nothing further could be expected from Moscow. Paruyr Hairikian was released from prison and expelled from the Soviet Union. His independence group continued to agitate in Armenia, but its following was dwarfed by that of the Committee, which proved remarkably adept at operating within legal limits and avoiding being outmanoeuvred. The public meetings were models of democracy and education. In the meantime, there were constant clashes in Azerbaijan and, above all, in Karabagh. The Autonomous Region was paralysed by a strike and soon patrolled by the army, which also made its appearance in Yerevan for a few days at the end of September. In the fall popular interest in public meetings grew. The 11 Committee members were officially recognized as partners of the Party and the government, and their mandate now extended to all that concerned Armenia. Meanwhile, the authorities in Yerevan fell far behind the mood of the people, going so far, on 23 September, as to accept Moscow's resolution of 18 July.[326]

November proved to be a critical point for the movement. On 7 November, the anniversary of the October Revolution, a 'dual power' system emerged in Lenin Square in Yerevan during the official ceremonies, when the Armenian leadership spoke from the rostrum and the Committee members from below. During the course of this extraordinary demonstration, with the tricolour flag displayed everywhere, the crowd made its preferences clear. It was probably at that moment that the authorities realized that they had to strike quickly if they were to maintain their power. On 22 November the Supreme Soviet convened with two new members: Ashot Manucharian, a member of the Committee, and Khachik Stamboltsian, an individual with close ties to the Committee. Fearing an 'osmotic effect' which threatened to sway some members of parliament, the authorities suspended the session indefinitely at the end of a day marked by several spectacular speeches. Events then moved quickly. Two days later, the Committee brought together a legal quorum of the Soviet at the Opera. Its platform was adopted. The government responded by imposing a state of emergency while the session was in progress and declaring the session 'illegal' the next day.

At this time, in Azerbaijan, a new tragedy was unfolding in Kirovabad, formerly Gandzak, the second-largest city in the Republic. The approximately 40,000 Armenians who lived there were descendants of a very old community. The majority lived in a specific city district. Few details of this 'new Sumgait', launched on 21 November, are available to us because this time the Armenian authorities censored all information. Times had changed and the Armenian refugees who poured out of Azerbaijan (close to 200,000 of them) were the victims.

Azerbaijan still contained a large Armenian minority. Aside from the 'bastion' of the Autonomous Region of Mountainous Karabagh, Armenians were numerous in Baku and in the region north of the Autonomous Region, up to Shamkhor where the Armenian villages had been deliberately left outside the frontiers drawn in 1923 and, thereby, subjected to direct Azerbaijani authority. From north to south, these areas had already largely been 'swept clean', with the exception of the area of Shahumian, the northern gateway to the Autonomous Region. The Azerbaijani plan was clearly described in the declaration by the Karabagh Committee on 2 December 1988:

Exploiting the anarchic situation, the Azerbaijani authorities are about to unleash a monstrous programme: to expel Armenians from their several millennia old homes in Gandzak and the areas north of Artsakh, in preparation for an invasion of Mountainous Karabagh. Already about 120,000 Armenians have left Azerbaijan, and 50,000 have sought refuge in Armenia and the others in the North Caucasus and Central Asia. Frightened by this displacement of Armenians and by the Azerbaijani authorities who throw oil on fire, Azerbaijanis in Armenia have begun a massive exodus of their own; already 80,000 of them have crossed the border. ('They Stand Accused', photocopied documents collection, Yerevan, January 1989)

While these developments were a direct consequence of the 18 July decision by Moscow, the central government obligingly looked the other way.

The state of emergency could not stop the extremely popular Committee members. It was Nature, the appalling earthquake of 7 December, which would deliver the Committee to the Party. The Committee was facing the enormous problems of earthquake relief, and it acted quickly to supplant the impotent authorities. Gorbachev, who visited the sites, found nothing better to say than this:

The theme of Karabagh is exploited by dishonest people, political demagogues, adventurers, and worse yet, by corrupted people....We are about to deliver a blow to this riffraff.[327]

The tone was set. In three waves (10 and 24 December and 7 January), the 11 Committee members were arrested along with Igor Muradian, Khachik Stamboltsian and Arkady Manucharov. They were held in isolation in Moscow for six months. On 31 May 1989, with the exception of Manucharov, they were released. Their arrest and release failed to conform to known standards of justice. As for Manucharov, he was to be released in June 1990.

The Impasse

Contrary to the hopes of the authorities, the popularity of the Committee members increased even further with their imprisonment. In November 1989 these ex-prisoners were able to convene officially, in the presence of these same authorities, the constitutive congress of the Armenian National Movement. The Karabagh Committee joined with other organizations – ecological, humanitarian, cultural – and the ANM began to move forward as the established leader of the Armenian struggle.

Meanwhile, on 12 January 1989, a decision was finally made on the status of Karabagh. The Supreme Soviet of the USSR provisionally granted the Autonomous Region a 'special form of administration'. It would remain within Azerbaijan but be administered directly from Moscow which named a sort of 'viceroy', Arkady Volsky, for the region. The advantage was to be the liberation of the Armenians from the arbitrary administration of Baku. But in this new context, the Armenians had practically no voice in the administration of the territory. There was no longer a regional Soviet, only a Council, more or less formal, where the nationalities were well mixed and power was diluted. The popular Poghosian was no more than a deputy in the Supreme Soviet. After three months an evaluation of this new administration was forwarded to Gorbachev by all of the Party leaders and District Committee executives in Karabagh. It was quite disappointing.

> We are obliged to state that the hopes and aspirations of the Armenian population of the Autonomous Region of Mountainous Karabagh have not been confirmed.... Even the installation of a special system of administration has not protected the region against gross interference and impudence on the part of Azerbaijan. In addition, it is our impression that the Special Administrative Commission has taken the position of aiding the leaders of the republic in increasing the pace of Azerbaijanization in the region.... They have laboured to ... accelerate the establishment of Azerbaijani villages.... In Armenian villages no projects are undertaken.... The people of Mountainous Karabagh are indignant in the light of provocative statements by Vezirov and the care and concern shown by the Central Committee of the Communist Party of the Soviet Union toward the heads of the Republic.... The sounder and more just solution has been and remains reunification ... with Armenia.

The situation remained tense and the strikes continued. A year earlier, when Moscow could impose its will on Baku, this solution would have been welcomed, but 'direct administration' was doomed to failure in the deteriorating climate of 1989. It was officially abolished on 28 November and soon replaced by a military regime. The administration was directed by General Safonov, who did little to conceal his objective – to return the Autonomous Region to the lap of Azerbaijan. The Azerbaijani flag was hoisted over the Regional Committee building, and arrests and harassment multiplied. The Armenians responded with boycotts, strikes, and economic paralysis. After the founding of the 'Popular Front of Azerbaijan' in July 1990, the Region was subjected to a blockade by the Azeris.

In a regional context, several factors came into play in early 1990. After Sumgait and Kirovabad, Baku was the scene of a violent anti-Armenian pogrom, unleashed on 13 January. At the same time, Armenian villages in the Khanlar and Shahumian districts, north of the Autonomous Region, were systematically attacked and isolated. The Armenians resisted militarily under highly unfavourable conditions until the army came to 'temporarily' resettle the population 'for its own safety'. Armenia itself was subjected to Azerbaijani attacks and a periodic economic blockade. But on the question of Karabagh, Yerevan totally reversed its politics and supported demands for reunification. On 20 February Yerevan went so far as to declare the 5 July 1921 decision null and void.

The situation had polarized. The borders drawn in 1923 were now more and more ethnic borders between an Armenia largely emptied of its 180,000 Azerbaijanis and an Azerbaijan where the Armenian presence would henceforth be concentrated in Mountainous Karabagh after a massive exodus of 250,000 people. The Armenians there constituted 80 per cent of the population and could not envisage continuing Azerbaijani authority in the light of the pogroms and other trials. Azerbaijan held the upper hand. The little authority still exercised by Moscow was in Azerbaijan's favour, and there was an important current which now openly demanded an independent Azerbaijan. This was a luxury Armenia could not entertain as long as the matter of Karabagh remained unresolved. In such a context, it was difficult to see why Baku would accept a change.

This impasse was a challenge for the new government of Armenia. On 4 August 1990, in an historic parliamentary vote, with the full participation of deputies from Mountainous Karabagh, the former prisoners of the Karabagh Committee were elected heads of the state of the Republic of Armenia (without the words 'Soviet Socialist'). The following day Gorbachev personally telephoned the new President, the well-known historian and linguist Levon Ter Petrosian, whom he had included among the 'riffraff' only a short time before. Would such a profound change in Armenia be followed by a change in the status of Karabagh?

NOTES

1. R. Hovannisian, *The Republic of Armenia*, vol. II (Los Angeles, 1982), p. 168.
2. G. Libaridian, *The Karabagh File* (Cambridge, MA, 1988), p. 8.
3. B. Vereshagin, 'Voyage dans les provinces du Caucase. Seconde partie: la Transcaucasie', in *Le Tour du Monde*, vol. 19, no. 1, 1869, p. 253.
4. Ed. G. Galoyan, *Mountainous Karabagh: Historical Handbook* (Yerevan, Armenian Academy of Sciences, 1988), p. 53.
5. J. Mourier, *Guide au Caucase* (Paris, 1894), p. 179; K. Baedeker, *La Russie* (Leipzig, 1902), p. 410; Mme. Chantre, *A travers l'Arménie russe* (Paris, 1893), pp. 45 and 48.
6. B. Vereshagin, *op. cit.*, p. 279.
7. *Ibid.*, p. 288.
8. *Ibid.*, p. 293.
9. Mme. Chantre, *op. cit.*, p. 45.
10. *Ibid.*, p. 48.
11. *Ibid.*, p. 63.
12. *Ibid.*, p. 65.
13. R. Tavtian, 'Shushi Remembered', *Haratch*, Paris, 2 April 1988; A. Ghazian, 'Shushi', *Haireniki Dzain*, Yerevan, 6 November 1988.
14. S. Avagian, *Pages from the History of the Cultural Life in Mountainous Karabagh* (Yerevan, 1982), pp. 18 ff.
15. *Ibid.*, p. 67.
16. *Mountainous Karabagh, op. cit.*, p. 53; Ch. Harutiunian, *A Brief Chronology of the History of the Armenian People, 1801–1917* (Yerevan, 1955), p. 230.
17. R. Hovannisian, *The Republic of Armenia*, vol. I (Los Angeles, 1971), p. 79.
18. M. Varandian, *History of the Armenian Revolutionary Federation*, vol. I (Paris, 1932), pp. 389 and 404 ff.; L. Villari, *Fire and Sword in the Caucasus* (London, 1906), pp. 198–9.
19. C. Walker, *Armenia: The Survival of a Nation* (London, 1980), p. 78; M. Varandian, *op. cit.*, pp. 421, 430; L. Villari, *op. cit.*, pp. 203 and 328 ff.
20. A. Ter Minassian, 'Particularités de la révolution de 1905 en Transcaucasie', in *1905: La première révolution russe* (Paris, 1986), p. 329.
21. M. Varandian, *op. cit.*, p. 399.
22. V. Sevian, 'On Mountain Paths in the Homeland', *Haratch*, Paris, 18 March 1988; A. Khatisian, *The Birth and Development of the Armenian Republic* (Athens, 1930), p. 70; S. Kevorkian, 'Concerning the Problem of the Creation of the Autonomous Region of Mountainous Karabagh', *Baikar*, Boston, 21 February 1979.
23. A. Nassibian, *Britain and the Armenian Question (1915–1923)* (London, 1984), p. 100.
24. R. Hovannisian, I, *op. cit.*, p. 83; L. Mkrtchian, *Artsakh-Karabagh: Its Past and Present* (Athens, 1988), pp. 29 ff.; *Kavkazskoïe Slovo (Voice of the Caucasus)*, Tiflis, 27 July 1918.
25. Z. Messerlian, *On the Armenian Question* (Beirut, 1978), p. 32.
26. R. Hovannisian, I, *op. cit.*, p. 83; E. Ishkhanian, 'Events in Mountainous Karabagh: Details and Comments', *Hairenik*, Boston, November 1933, p. 86.
27. A. Khatisian, *op. cit.*, pp. 59 ff.
28. A. Astvatsaturian, 'Azerbaijan and Armenia on the Eve of and During Independence', *Hairenik*, Boston, August 1957, p. 50.

29. *Encyclopedia of Islam*, new edition (Leiden, 1979), p. 191.
30. *Kavkazskoïe Slovo, op. cit.*, 27 July 1918.
31. B. Ulubabian, 'Mountainous Karabagh: An Historical-Geographical Survey', *Haireniki Dzain*, Yerevan, 8 June 1988 *passim*; Z. Messerlian, *op. cit.*, p. 132; R. Hovannisian, 'The Armeno-Azerbaijani Conflict over Mountainous Karabagh, 1918–1919', *The Armenian Review*, Boston, 24, summer 1971, p. 9; *Central Historical Archives of the Armenian SSR*, fonds 200, inv. 1, d. 244, f. 38–44; *Mshak* (Culture), Tiflis, 25 July 1918; L. Mkrtichian, *op. cit.*, p. 30; L. Khurshudian, 'The Only Criterion in the Science of History is Truth', *Erekoyan Yerevan*, Yerevan, 23 August 1989.
32. E. Ishkhanian, *op. cit.*, p. 87.
33. *Central Historical Archives of the Armenian SSR*, fonds 276, inv. 1, d. 12, f. 225.
34. A. Khatisian, *op. cit.*, p. 91.
35. A. Mikaelian, 'The Latest Events in Karabagh', *Hairenik*, Boston, May 1923, p. 161.
36. A. Chelebian, *General Antranig and the Armenian Revolutionary Movement*, 2nd edition (Beirut, 1986), p. 515; A. Aivazian, *The Monuments of Nakhichevan* (Yerevan, 1987), pp. 68 ff.
37. *Central Historical Archives of the Armenian SSR*, fonds 200, inv. 1, d. 12, f. 131.
38. A. Chelebian, *op. cit.*, pp. 516 ff.; A. Mikaelian, *op. cit.*, p. 162; A. Astvatsaturian, October 1957, *op. cit.*, p. 47.
39. R. Hovannisian, I, *op. cit.*, p. 83; G. Gharibjanian, 'Antranig in Zangezur and Artsakh', *Sovetakan Haiastan*, Yerevan, December 1988.
40. Z. Messerlian, *op. cit.*, p. 132; R. Hovannisian, I, *op. cit.*, p. 85; G. Hovhannissian, 'The Battle of Msmena', *Banber*, Yerevan, March 1968, p. 150; H. Abrahamian, 'General Antranig and the Artsakh Armenians', *Haireniki Dzain*, Yerevan, 28 February 1990; H. Abrahamian, 'The Struggle for Survival in Mountainous Karabagh, 1917–1923', *Haireniki Dzain*, Yerevan, 2 November 1988.
41. H. Abrahamian, 'General Antranig', *op. cit.*; A. Mikaelian, *op. cit.*, pp. 161–2; E. Ishkhanian, *op. cit.*, December 1933, p. 111.
42. K. Hovhannissian, 'One of the Heroic Battles in Mountainous Karabagh', *Haratch*, Paris, 27 April 1988; E. Ishkhanian, *op. cit.*, November 1933, p. 89.
43. G. Hovhannissian, *op. cit.*, p. 150; E. Ishkhanian, *op. cit.*, November 1933, p. 89.
44. G. Hovhannissian, *op. cit.*, p. 151.
45. *Ibid.*, p. 151; E. Ishkhanian, *op. cit.*, November 1933, p. 89.
46. A. Astvatsaturian, *op. cit.*, September 1957, p. 50.
47. *Kavkazskoïe Slovo, op. cit.*, 22 October 1918; H. Abrahamian, 'The Struggle', *op. cit.*; K. Hovhannissian, *op. cit.*
48. *Mshak, op. cit.*, 27 February 1919.
49. G. Hovhannissian, *op. cit.*, p. 151.
50. A. Ghazian, *op. cit.*, 6 November 1988; K. Hovhannissian, *op. cit.*; Z. Messerlian, *op. cit.*, pp. 132 ff.; S. Vratsian, *The Republic of Armenia* (Paris, 1928), p. 281; *Kavkazskoïe Slovo, op. cit.*, 22 October 1918; R. Hovannisian, I, *op. cit.*, p. 85; E. Ishkhanian, *op. cit.*, p. 91.
51. A. Chelebian, *op. cit.*, pp. 523 and 525.
52. *Central Historical Archives of the Armenian SSR*, fonds 200, inv. 1, d. 244, f. 38–44.
53. G. Hovhannissian, *op. cit.*, p. 152; A. Mikaelian, *op. cit.*, May 1923, p. 162; A. Astvatsaturian, op. *op. cit.*, September 1957, p. 50.
54. H. Abrahamian, 'The Struggle', *op. cit.*, 16 November 1988; K. Hovhannissian,

op. cit.; Z. Messerlian, *op. cit.*, pp. 132–3; S. Vratsian, *op. cit.*, p. 281.

55. R. Hovannisian, I, *op. cit.*, p. 85.
56. V. Sevian, *op. cit.*, 18 March 1988.
57. C. Ellis, *The Transcaspian Episode (1918-1919)* (London, 1963), p. 21.
58. *Hérodote*, nos 54–5, Paris, 1989, p. 172.
59. *Central Historical Archives of the Armenian SSR*, fonds 199, inv. 1, d. 23, f. 25–26; R. Hovannisian, I, *op. cit.*, pp. 31–2.
60. *Central Historical Archives of the Armenian SSR*, fonds 200, inv. 1, d. 244, f. 38–44; *Hérodote*, *op. cit.*, p. 174; A. Khatisian, *op. cit.*, p. 152.
61. R. Hovannisian, I, *op. cit.*, p. 61; G. Abramian, 'The Politics of English Occupation Forces with Regard to Artsakh, November 1918–August 1919', *Lraber*, Yerevan, no. 7, 1989, p. 13.
62. Sarur, 'The Annexation of Karabagh by Azerbaijan', *Hairenik*, Boston, August 1929, p. 139; *Mshak*, *op. cit.*, 20 November 1918; R. Hovannisian, I, *op. cit.*, p. 62; *Central Historical Archives of the Armenian SSR*, fonds 200, inv. 1, d. 50, f. 104–7.
63. G. Abramian, *op. cit.*, p. 13.
64. A. Chelebian, *op. cit.*, pp. 525–6; G. Gharibjanian, *op. cit.*
65. A. Mikaelian, *op. cit.*, May 1923, p. 162.
66. H. Abrahamian 'General Antranig', *op. cit.*, 28 February 1990 and 14 March 1990; R. Hovannisian, I, *op. cit.*, p. 88; S. Vratsian, *op. cit.*, p. 282.
67. H. Abrahamian, 'General Antranig', *op. cit.*, 14 March 1990; Sarur, *op. cit.*, p. 128; E. Ishkhanian, *op. cit.*, December 1933, pp. 111, 122.
68. A. Chelebian, *op. cit.*, pp. 529–530; R. Hovannisian, I, *op. cit.*, pp. 88–9; A. Mikaelian, *op. cit.*, May 1923, p. 162; G. Gharibjanian, *op. cit.*
69. A. Chelebian, *op. cit.*, pp. 530–1; R. Hovannisian, I, *op. cit.*, p. 89; G. Gharibjanian, *op. cit.*; H. Abrahamian, 'General Antranig', *op. cit.*, 14 March 1990.
70. G. Abramian, *op. cit.*, p. 13.
71. Sarur, *op. cit.*, p. 129.
72. A. Mikaelian, *op. cit.*, May 1923, p. 163; G. Gharibjanian, *op. cit.*
73. *Central Historical Archives of the Armenian SSR*, fonds 370, inv. 1, d. 39, f. 7 (appendix I).
74. S. Vratsian, *op. cit.*, p. 282; R. Hovannisian, I, *op. cit.*, p. 89; R. Hovannisian, 'The Armeno', *op. cit.*, pp. 3–39; A. Mikaelian, *op. cit.*, May 1923, p. 163; A. Astvatsaturian, *op. cit.*, September 1957, p. 50; H. Abrahamian, 'The Struggle', *op. cit.*, 16 November 1988; H. Abrahamian, 'General Antanig', *op. cit.*, 14 March 1990; G. Abramian, *op. cit.*, p. 14.
75. Sarur, *op. cit.*, p. 130; A. Astvatzadurian, *op. cit.*, September 1957, p. 60.
76. E. Ishkhanian, *op. cit.*, December 1933, p. 117.
77. Sarur, *op. cit.*, p. 131; E. Ishkhanian, *op. cit.*, December 1933, p. 118.
78. Sarur, *op. cit.*, p. 132.
79. *Ibid.*
80. *Central Historical Archives of the Armenian SSR*, fonds 200, inv. 1, d. 50, f. 104–7; S. Vratsian, *op. cit.*, p. 283; Sarur, *op. cit.*, p. 136; A. Astvatsaturian, *op. cit.*, September 1957, p. 50; A. Arslanian, 'England and the Problem of Mountainous Karabagh', *Haratch*, Paris, 8 February 1984; A. Khatisian, *op. cit.*, p. 153; A. Ter Minassian, *La Republique d'Arménie* (Paris, 1989), p. 133.
81. *Kavkazskoïe Slovo*, *op. cit.*, 1 July 1919.
82. *Ibid.*, 21 March 1919; R. Hovannisian, I, *op. cit.*, p. 162.
83. L. Khurshudian, *op. cit.*; A. Astvatzadurian, *op. cit.*, September 1957, p. 51.

84. *Central Historical Archives of the Armenian SSR*, fonds 57, inv. 2, d. 807, f. 1–2; A. Chelebian, *op. cit.*, p. 533; *Kavkazskoïe Slovo*, *op. cit.*, 17 February 1919.
85. L. Khurshudian, *op. cit.*; *Kavkazskoïe Slovo*, *op. cit.*, 1 July 1919; A. Astvatsaturian, *op. cit.*, September 1957, p. 51.
86. Sarur, *op. cit.*, p. 133; G. Libaridian, *op. cit.*, p. 11.
87. *Mshak*, *op. cit.*, 21 March 1919 (cf. Appendix II).
88. *Central Historical Archives of the Armenian SSR*, fonds 200, inv. 1, d. 243, f. 31–32; R. Hovannisian, I, *op. cit.*, p. 168.
89. G. Abramian, *op. cit.*, p. 17.
90. Sarur, *op. cit.*, p. 134.
91. E. Ishkhanian, *op. cit.*, November 1933, p. 123.
92. *Ibid.*, November 1933, p. 121.
93. H. Abrahamian, 'The Struggle', *op. cit.*, 23 November 1988; H. Abrahamian, 'General Antranig', *op. cit.*, 14 March 1990.
94. A. Chelebian, *op. cit.*, pp. 532 ff.
95. *Ibid.*, p. 549; R. Hovannisian, I, *op. cit.*, p. 191; G. Gharibjanian, *op. cit.*
96. *Central Historical Archives of the Armenian SSR*, fonds 370, inv. 1, d. 39, f. 7 (s.v. Appendix I); G. Gharibjanian, *op. cit.*
97. R. Hovannisian, *op. cit.*, I, p. 190; H. Abrahamian, 'General Andranik', *op. cit.*, 14 March 1990.
98. R. Hovannisian, I, *op. cit.*, p. 192.
99. H. Abrahamian, 'The Struggle', *op. cit.*, 6 November 1988; A. Harutiunian, *Turkish Intervention in Transcaucasia in 1918* (Yerevan, 1984), pp. 328 ff.; Avo, *Nzhdeh* (Beirut, 1968), pp. 78–9.
100. H. Abrahamian, 'The Struggle', *op. cit.*, 23 November 1988; *Central Historical Archives of the Armenian SSR*, fonds 200, inv. 1, d. 243, f. 107–8.
101. R. Hovannisian, I, *op. cit.*, p. 171; Sarur, *op. cit.*, p. 136; A. Astvatsaturian, *op. cit.*, September 1957, p. 52.
102. S. Vratsian, *op. cit.*, p. 285; Sarur, *op. cit.*, p. 136; A. Astvatsaturian, *op. cit.*, p. 52; *Central Historical Archives of the Armenian SSR*, fonds 200, d. 612, f. 128.
103. L. Khurshudian, *op. cit.*; R. Hovannisian, I, *op. cit.*, p. 172; G. Libaridian, *op. cit.*, p. 17.
104. *Central Historical Archives of the Armenian SSR*, f. 201, inv. 1, d. 42, f. 17 and fonds 190/507, inv. 1, d. 252, f. 81 *ff.*; *Kavkazskoïe Slovo*, *op. cit.*, 21 April 1919; S. Vratsian, *op. cit.*, pp. 284–5.
105. *Archives of the Republic of Armenia*, d. 9/9 in R. Hovannisian, I, *op. cit.*, p. 170; S. Vratsian, *op. cit.*, p. 284.
106. A. Astvatsaturian, *op. cit.*, August 1957, p. 55.
107. *Central Historical Archives of the Armenian SSR*, fonds 190/507, inv. 1, d. 252, f. 171–3; G. Abramian, *op. cit.*, p. 21.
108. *Central Historical Archives of the Armenian SSR*, fonds 252, inv. 1, d. 1, f. 64.
109. Sarur, *op. cit.*, p. 136.
110. *Central Historical Archives of the Armenian SSR*, fonds 190/507, inv. 1, d. 252, f. 171–3.
111. Sarur, *op. cit.*, pp. 137–8, E. Ishkhanian, *op. cit.*, December 1933, p. 124.
112. V. Sevian, *op. cit.*, 19 March 1988; *Kavkazskoie Slovo*, *op. cit.*, 1 July 1919; Sarur, *op. cit.*, p. 137; A. Astvatsaturian, *op. cit.*, October 1957, p. 45; *Central Historical Archives of the Armenian SSR*, fonds 190/507, inv. 1, d. 252, f. 174.
113. *Central Historical Archives of the Armenian SSR*, fonds 190/507, inv. 1, d. 252, f. 171–4.

114. *Ibid.*, fonds 190/507, inv. 1, d. 252, f. 171–4 and fonds 200, inv. 1, d. 309, f. 168; S. Vratsian, *op. cit.*, pp. 286–7; R. Hovannisian, I, *op. cit.*, p. 176; Sarur, *op. cit.*, p. 137; H. Abrahamian, 'The Struggle', *op. cit.*, 30 November 1988.

115. *Central Historical Archives of the Armenian SSR*, fonds 200, d. 309. f. 199 in L. Khurshudian, *op. cit.*, 23 August 1989.

116. *Central Historical Archives of the Armenian SSR*, fonds 190/507, inv. 1, d. 232, f. 138 and fonds 190/507, inv. 1, d. 552, f. 139; S. Vratsian, *op. cit.*, p. 287; Sarur, *op. cit.*, p. 138, (cf. Appendix III).

117. Sarur, *op. cit.*, p. 138.

118. S. Vratsian, *op. cit.*, p. 287; L. Khurshudian, *op. cit.*, 23 August 1990; Sarur, *op. cit.*, p. 139; E. Ishkhanian, *op. cit.*, December 1933, p. 125 (cf. Appendix III).

119. R. Hovannisian, I, *op. cit.*, pp. 177 ff.; S. Vratsian, *op. cit.*, pp. 287 ff.; A. Astvatzadurian, *op. cit.*, September 1957, p. 52.

120. *Kavkazskoïe Slovo, op. cit.*, 1 July 1919; A. Astvatzadurian, *op. cit.*, p. 53.

121. *Central Historical Archives of the Armenian SSR*, fonds 200, inv. 1, d. 50, f. 104–7 (cf. Appendix III); R. Hovannisian, I, *op. cit.*, pp. 180 ff.

122. Sarur, *op. cit.*, p. 138; E. Ishkhanian, *op. cit.*, December 1933, p. 125.

123. *Central Historical Archives of the Armenian SSR*, fonds 190/507, inv. 1, d. 252, f. 137 in L. Khurshudian, *op. cit.*, 23 August 1990.

124. *Central Historical Archives of the Armenian SSR*, fonds 190/507, inv. 1, d. 252, f. 171–3; S. Vratsian, *op. cit.*, p. 289; Sarur, *op. cit.*, p. 140.

125. *Kavkazskoïe Slovo, op. cit.*, 1 July 1919.

126. Sarur, *op. cit.*, p. 141.

127. *Ibid.*, p. 141; A. Astvatsaturian, *op. cit.*, September 1957, p. 53.

128. Sarur, *op. cit.*, p. 140; A. Astvatsaturian, *op. cit.*, September 1957, p. 53.

129. *Central Historical Archives of the Armenian SSR*, fonds 190/507, inv. 1, d. 252, f. 168.

130. Sarur, *op. cit.*, p. 143; A. Astvatsaturian, *op. cit.*, September 1957, p. 53; S. Vratsian, *op. cit.*, p. 290.

131. A. Astvatsaturian, *op. cit.*, September 1957, p. 54; S. Vratsian, *op. cit.*, p. 290.

132. R. Hovannisian, I, *op. cit.*, p. 183; S. Vratsian, *op. cit.*, p. 290.

133. Sarur, *op. cit.*, p. 142.

134. R. Hovannisian, I, *op. cit.*, pp. 184 ff.; S. Vratsian, op cit., p. 291; Sarur, *op. cit.*, p. 142.

135. R. Hovannisian, 'The Armeno', *op. cit.*, pp. 35 ff.; S. Vratsian, *op. cit.*, pp. 291 ff.; Sarur, *op. cit.*, p. 143.

136. Sarur, *op. cit.*, p. 144.

137. G. Libaridian, *op. cit.*, pp. 21–4; *Kavkazskoïe Slovo, op. cit.*, 29 August 1919; A. Mikaelian, *op. cit.*, May 1923, p. 164; A. Astvatsaturian, *op. cit.*, p. 54; S. Vratsian, *op. cit.*, pp. 291–2; R. Hovannisian, I, *op. cit.*, pp. 186–7.

138. A. Tabrizli, *Histoire du Daglig (Haut)-Garabagh à la lumière de documents historiques* (Strasbourg, 1989), p. 75; *Hérodote, op. cit.*, p. 175; C. Mutafian, 'Hérodote: Transcaucasia in the Collection: "Les Marches de la Russie"', *Haratch*, Paris, 24 February 1990.

139. *Central Historical Archives of the Armenian SSR*, fonds 200, inv. 1, d. 50, f. 104–7.

140. A. Mikaelian, *op. cit.*, June 1923, pp. 110 ff.

141. R. Hovannisian, II, *op. cit.*, p. 129; G. Abramian, *op. cit.*, p. 22.

142. G. Libaridian, *op. cit.*, p. 156.

143. A. Astvatsaturian, *op. cit.*, October 1957, p. 51; *Hérodote, op. cit.*, p. 176; R. Hovannisian, I, *op. cit.*, pp. 221 ff.

144. A. Astvatsaturian, *op. cit.*, August 1957, pp. 54–5.
145. *Archives of the French Ministry of Foreign Affairs 1918–1919, Caucasus*, vol. 4, pp. 84–8 in *Hérodote*, *op. cit.*, p. 176.
146. C. Walker, *op. cit.*, p. 278; A. Khatisian, *op. cit.*, p. 168.
147. A. Mikaelian, *op. cit.*, May 1923, pp. 160–1.
148. C. Walker, *op. cit.*, p. 278; Sarur, *op. cit.*, p. 144; H. Abrahamian, 'The Struggle', *op. cit.*, 11 October 1989.
149. A. Astvatsaturian, *op. cit.*, October 1957, pp. 49–50.
150. R. Hovannisian, II, *op. cit.*, pp. 209 ff.; H. Abrahamian, 'The Struggle', *op. cit.*, 11 October 1989; S. Vratsian, *op. cit.*, p. 341; Sarur, *op. cit.*, p. 145; E. Ishkhanian, *op. cit.*, December 1933, p. 126; A. Astvatsaturian, *op. cit.*, October 1957, p. 50.
151. *Mshak*, *op. cit.*, 22 November 1919, p. 2.
152. C. Walker, *op. cit.*, p. 287.
153. V. Sevian, *op. cit.*, 19 March 1988; L. Khurshudian, *op. cit.*, 23 August 1989.
154. A. Khatisian, *op. cit.*, p. 167.
155. *Central Historical Archives of the Armenian SSR*, fonds 200, inv. 1, d. 427 (part II), f. 240–2; A. Mikaelian, *op. cit.*, July 1923, p. 117; S. Vratsian, *op. cit.*, p. 341.
156. S. Vratsian, *op. cit.*, p. 341.
157. A. Mikaelian, *op. cit.*, July 1923, p. 117.
158. *Kommunist*, 13 April 1923 in L. Khurshudian, *op. cit.*, 23 August 1989.
159. A. Mikaelian, *op. cit.*, July 1923, p. 118.
160. Z. Messerlian, *op. cit.*, pp. 138–9; A. Mikaelian, *op. cit.*, September 1923, p. 111.
161. S. Vratsian, *op. cit.*, p. 342; A. Mikaelian, *op. cit.*, September 1923, p. 111.
162. A. Mikaelian, *op. cit.*, September 1923, p. 111.
163. G. Libaridian, *op. cit.*, p. 28.
164. *Central Historical Archives of the Armenian SSR*, fonds 200, d. 563, f. 29–35; S. Vratsian, *op. cit.*, p. 341; A. Mikaelian, *op. cit.*, September 1923, p. 114.
165. A. Mikaelian, *op. cit.*, September 1923, p. 116.
166. *Central Historical Archives of the Armenian SSR*, fonds 200, inv. 1, d. 427 (part II), f. 240–2 and fonds 198, inv. 1, d. 11, f. 4; *Mshak*, *op. cit.*, 4 April 1920; H. Abrahamian, 'The Struggle', *op. cit.*, 11 October 1989, A. Mikaelian, *op. cit.*, July 1923, p. 117.
167. S. Vratsian, *op. cit.*, p. 342; *Mshak*, *op. cit.*, 4 April 1920; H. Abrahamian, 'The Struggle', *op. cit.*, 11 October 1989.
168. H. Abrahamian, 'The Struggle', *op. cit.*, 18 October 1989; *Kommunist*, no. 229, 10 October 1921; L. Khurshudian, *op. cit.*, 23 August 1989.
169. S. Vratsian, *op. cit.*, p. 342; A. Mikaelian, *op. cit.*, October 1923, pp. 118 ff.
170. V. Sevian, *op. cit.*, 19 March 1988; A. Khatisian, *op. cit.*, p. 169; S. Vratsian, *op. cit.*, p. 342; *Grkeri Ashkhar* (*The World of Books*), Yerevan, no. 8 (251), 27 August 1989.
171. S. Vratsian, *op. cit.*, pp. 342–3.
172. L. Khurshudian, *op. cit.*; H. Abrahamian, 'The Struggle', *op. cit.*, 18 October 1989; A. Mikaelian, *op. cit.*, October 1923, p. 124.
173. S. Vratsian, *op. cit.*, p. 343.
174. A. Ter Minassian, *La République*, *op. cit.*, pp. 199 ff.
175. S. Vratsian, *op. cit.*, p. 347.
176. L. Khurshudian, *op. cit.*, 23 August 1989.
177. H. Abrahamian, 'The Struggle', *op. cit.*, 8 November 1989.
178. *Central Archives of the October Revolution of the USSR*, fonds 130, d. 4, ch. 496, f. 115.

179. *Central Historical Archives of the Armenian SSR,* fonds 130, inv. 4, d. 496, f. 142.
180. L. Khurshudian, *op. cit.,* 23 August 1989.
181. H. Abrahamian, 'The Struggle', *op. cit.,* 25 October 1989.
182. *Central Historical Archives of the Armenian SSR,* fonds 220, inv. 1, d. 581, f. 98.
183. H. Abrahamian, 'The Struggle', *op. cit.,* 25 October 1989.
184. H. Abrahamian, 'The Struggle', *op. cit.,* 8 November 1989.
185. A. Mikaelian, *op. cit.,* p. 125.
186. A. Mikaelian, *op. cit.,* p. 126.
187. H. Abrahamian, 'The Struggle', *op. cit.,* 8 November 1989.
188. A. Ter Minassian, *La République, op. cit.,* pp. 205 ff.
189. H. Abrahamian, 'The Struggle', *op. cit.,* 8 November 1989.
190. S. Kevorkian, *op. cit.,* 2 March 1979.
191. C. Walker, *op. cit.,* p. 289.
192. *Ibid.*
193. *Institute of Marxism-Leninism, Central Party Archives,* fonds 2, d. 14/516, f. 2 in V. Mikaelian and L. Khurshudian, 'Historical Questions Relative to Mountainous Karabagh', *Lraber,* Yerevan, no. 4, 1988.
194. *Ibid., Central Committee of the Communist Party of the Soviet Union,* general section, section 6, d. 44-33A, pp. 55–6 in L. Khurshudian, *op. cit.,* 23 August 1989.
195. *Ibid.,* fonds 64, d. 2, ch. 5, f. 19 in V. Mikaelian and L. Khurshudian, *op. cit.*
196. *Ibid.,* f. 2, d. 14516, p. 2v in V. Mikaelian and L. Khurshudian, *op. cit.*
197. *Central Historical Archives of the Armenian SSR,* fonds 130, inv. 4, d. 496, f. 142; H. Abrahamian, 'The Struggle', *op. cit.,* 8 November 1989.
198. *Institute of Marxism-Leninism,* fonds 64, inv. 1, d. 21, f. 62.
199. L. Khurshudian, *op. cit.,* 23 August 1989.
200. B. Ulubabian, *op. cit.,* 15 June 1988.
201. *Institute of Marxism-Leninism,* fonds 64, inv. 1, d. 10, f. 9–10.
202. *Central Historical Archives of the Armenian SSR,* fonds 200, inv. 1, d. 581, p. 262.
203. A. Poidebard, 'La Transcaucasie et la république d'Arménie dans les textes diplomatiques (1918–1921)', *Revue des Etudes Arméniennes,* Paris, no. 4, 1924, pp. 61 ff.
204. *Grakan Tert,* Yerevan, no. 24, 8 June 1990.
205. C. Walker, *op. cit.,* p. 290.
206. *Ibid.,* p. 305.
207. *Hérodote, op. cit.,* p. 185.
208. A. Khatisian, *op. cit.,* p. 269.
209. A. Poidebard, *op. cit.,* pp. 70 ff.
210. S. Afanasyan, *L'Arménie, l'Azerbaïdjan et la Géorgie (1917–1923)* (Paris, 1981), p. 148.
211. Cf. Appendix IVA.
212. *Mountainous Karabagh, op. cit.,* p. 29; S. Kevorkian, *op. cit.,* 23 February 1979.
213. G. Libaridian, *op. cit.,* p. 35.
214. *Central Historical Archives of the Armenian SSR,* f. 114, inv. 1, d. 45, f. 13.
215. *Bakinski Rabochi (Baku Worker),* Baku, 3 December 1920.
216. Cf. Appendix IVB.
217. *Institute of Marxism-Leninism,* fonds 2, inv. 1, d. 24503, *ff.* 1–2 in K. Barseghian, *The Truth Is Most Dear* (Yerevan, 1989), pp. 106–7.
218. *Institute of Marxism–Leninism,* fonds 2, inv. 1, d. 24504, f. 1 in K. Barseghian, *op. cit.,* p. 109.

219. E. Zohrabian, 'Partition of Territories at the Second Russo-Turkish Conference in Moscow, February–March 1921', *Lraber,* Yerevan, no. 2, 1989, pp. 14 ff.

220. O. Injikian, 'The Armenian Question and Soviet–Turkish Relations', *Lraber,* Yerevan, no. 6, 1988, p. 12 (in Russian); 'Political Memories of Ali Fuad Jibisuy', *Vatan (Motherland,* Turkish newspaper), 24 April 1954 in S. Kevorkian, *op. cit.,* 8 March 1979.

221. O. Injikian, *op. cit.,* pp. 3 ff.; E. Zohrabian, *op. cit.,* pp. 15–16.

222. A. Poidebard, *op. cit.,* pp. 74 and 85.

223. A. Mikaelian, *op. cit.,* June 1923, p. 114.

224. L. Mkrtichian, *op. cit.,* pp. 46–7; L. Khurshudian, *op. cit.,* 23 August 1989; H. Ghahrian, 'Tevan Stepanian: Myth and Reality', *Artsakh,* Stepanakert, July 1989, pp. 42–4.

225. *Kommunist,* Baku, 5 May, 17 May, 10 October, 19 October 1921.

226. *Institute of Marxism-Leninism,* fonds 64, inv. 1, d. 1, f. 77.

227. *Sovetakan Haiastan (Soviet Armenia),* 19 June 1921; *Bakinski Rabochi,* 22 June 1921.

228. *Institute of Marxism-Leninism,* fonds 64, inv. 2, d. 7, f. 13 in V. Mikaelian and L. Khurshudian, *op. cit;* V. Sevian, *op. cit.,* 19 March 1988.

229. *Central Historical Archives of the Armenian SSR,* fonds 128, inv. 1, d. 1420, f. 15–17; S. Kevorkian, *op. cit,* 23 February 1979.

230. S. Kevorkian, *op. cit.,* 24 February 1979.

231. *Institute of Marxism-Leninism,* f. 65, inv. 18, d. 229, f. 1–2 in S. Kevorkian, *op. cit.,* 27 February 1979; B. Ulubabian, 'Mountainous Karabagh', *Haireniki Dzain, op. cit.,* 22 June 1988.

232. *Institute of Marxism-Leninism,* fonds 64, inv. 2, d. 117, f. 41-42.

233. *Ibid.,* fonds 85, inv. 13, d. 66, f. 1.

234. *Ibid.,* fonds 17, inv. 13, d. 384, f. 66 (cf. Appendix VA).

235. *Ibid.,* fonds 85, inv. 18, d. 58, f. 18 and f. 64, inv. 1, f. 117–18 in S. Kevorkian, *op. cit.,* 27 February 1979.

236. *Institute of Marxism–Leninism,* fonds 85, inv. 18, d. 58, f. 18 in L. Khurshudian, *op. cit.,* 24 August 1989 (cf. Appendix VB).

237. C. W. Bosworth, 'Kara Bagh', *Encyclopedia of Islam* (new edition 1978), p. 573.

238. S. Kevorkian, *op. cit.,* 27–28 February 1979.

239. *Institute of Marxism-Leninism,* fonds 1, inv. 1, d. 232, f. 22–3 in V. Mikaelian and L. Khurshudian, *op. cit.*

240. S. Kevorkian, *op. cit.,* 9 March 1979.

241. V. Mikaelian and L. Khurshudian, *op. cit.*

242. Letter of 12 November 1921 in *Institute of Marxism-Leninism,* f. 3 (Stalin), inv. 1, d. 52.4, doc. 2 in S. Kevorkian, *op. cit.,* 9 March 1979.

243. *Le dur passé du Caucase* (Moscow, 1988), pp. 10 and 13.

244. *Institute of Marxism-Leninism,* fonds 1, inv. 1, d. 40, f. 29.

245. J. B. Gouliev, 'History of the Formation of the Autonomous Region of Mountainous Karabagh', in *Izvestia of the Academy of Sciences of the Azerbaijan SSR,* Baku, History, Philosophy and Law Series, no. 3, 1973 (in Russian).

246. L. Mkrtichian, *op. cit.,* pp. 48–9.

247. *The Truth About Mountainous Karabagh* (Yerevan, 1989), pp. 56–7.

248. *Bakinski Rabochi,* 9 July 1923, in J. B. Gouliev, *op. cit.*

249. G. Mirijian, 'Mountainous Karabagh', *Haratch,* 7 January 1988; G. Libaridian, *op. cit.,* p. 37; Gu. Hovhannissian, *The Installation of Soviet Power in Mountainous Karabagh* (Yerevan, 1971).

250. G. Libaridian, *op. cit.*, pp. 42–6.
251. L. Khurshudian, *op. cit.*, 24 August 1989.
252. Z. Messerlian, *op. cit.*, p. 167.
253. J. B. Gouliev, *op. cit.*
254. G. Mirijian, *op. cit.*
255. J. B. Gouliev, *op. cit.*
256. *L'Azerbaïdjan* (Moscow, 1981), p. 12.
257. *Mountainous Karabagh, op. cit.*, p. 55.
258. A. Aivazian, *op. cit.*
259. *Encyclopedia of Islam, op. cit.*, p. 190.
260. *Mountainous Karabagh, op. cit.*, p. 47.
261. *Glasnost*, no. 1, Paris, February 1989, p. 90; Z. Messerlian, *op. cit.*, p. 156.
262. *Mountainous Karabagh, op. cit.*, p. 56.
263. A. Rado, *Guide à travers l'Union Soviétique* (Berlin, 1929), p. 756; C. Mouradian, 'Le probleme du Haut-Karabagh', *Slovo*, vol. 7, 1985, p. 56.
264. A. Rado, *op. cit.*, p. 756.
265. S. Avagian, *Pages, op. cit.*, pp. 52 ff.
266. *Pravda*, 15 January 1989.
267. *Mountainous Karabagh, op. cit.*, p. 45.
268. B. Mirzoian, 'There Is Only One Truth', *Kommunist*, Yerevan, 19 July 1989.
269. V. Khojabekian and G. Asatrian, 'The Population of Mountainous Karabagh', *Haireniki Dzain*, Yerevan, 1 June 1988; C. Mouradian, 'The Problem', *op. cit.*, p. 64; *Mountainous Karabagh, op. cit.*; H. Barseghov, *The Right to Self-Determination Is the Foundation for the Democratic Solution of Interethnic Problems* (Yerevan, 1989), p. 122.
270. *Mountainous Karabagh, op. cit.*, p. 46.
271. L. Mkrtichian, *op. cit.*, pp. 58–9.
272. *Encyclopedia of Islam, op. cit.*, p. 573.
273. G. Libaridian, *op. cit.*, p. 76.
274. Anonymous, 'Karabagh Wants Re-Unification with Armenia', *Haratch*, Paris, 14 April 1988 (originally 7 January 1928).
275. L. Mkrtichian, *op. cit.*, p. 50.
276. G. Libaridian, *op. cit.*, p. 41.
277. L. Mkrtichian, *op. cit.*, pp. 51–2.
278. *Institute of Marxism-Leninism*, Armenian section, fonds 1, inv. 25, d. 41, f. 1 in K. Barseghian, *op. cit.*, p. 112; *The Truth About Mountainous Karabagh, op. cit.*, p. 60.
279. I. Aliev, *Mountainous Karabagh: History, Facts, and Events* (Baku 1989), p. 89; T. Hadjibeyli, 'La Question du Haut-Karabagh: Un Point de vue Azerbaïdjanais', special issue of *Revue du monde musulman et de la Méditerranée*, Aix-en-Provence, nos 48–49 1988/2–3, p. 288.
280. T. Hadjibeyli, *op. cit.*, p. 288.
281. G. Libaridian, *op. cit.*, pp. 42–6.
282. L. Mkrtichian, *op. cit.*, p. 53.
283. *The Truth About Mountainous Karabagh, op. cit.*, pp. 100 ff.
284. L. Karapetian, 'A New Perspective on the Autonomous Republic of Mountainous Karabagh', *Kommunist*, Yerevan, 14 July 1989.
285. Z. Messerlian, *op. cit.*, p. 170.
286. G. Libaridian, *op. cit.*, pp. 47–8.
287. *Sovetakan Karabagh*, 24 November 1973.

288. *Ibid.*, 23 March 1975.
289. Z. Messerlian, *op. cit.*, pp. 177 ff.
290. G. Libaridian, *op. cit.*, pp. 49–51.
291. S. Aivazian, 'Memorandum to First Secretary of the Communist Party of the Soviet Union, M. S. Gorbachev', *Haratch*, Paris, 4 December 1987 ff.; G. Libaridian, *op. cit.*, pp. 81–4; *Artsakh: Chronology*, Los Angeles 1989, pp. 61 ff.
292. G. Libaridian, *op. cit.*, pp. 86–8.
293. *Ibid.*, p. 68.
294. *Ibid.*, p. 69.
295. *Haratch*, Paris, 19 November 1987.
296. *Glasnost*, *op. cit.*, pp. 26–7.
297. *Ibid.*, p. 27.
298. *Ibid.*, pp. 86 ff.
299. *Ibid.*, pp. 30 and 84 ff.
300. G. Libaridian, *op. cit.*, pp. 88–9.
301. *Glasnost*, *op. cit.*, p. 42; *Artsakh: Chronology*, *op. cit.*, p. 167.
302. *Glasnost*, *op. cit.*, p. 43.
303. *Ibid.*, p. 45.
304. *Sovetakan Karabagh*, 21 February 1988; *Artsakh: Chronology*, *op. cit.*, p. 9; *Mountainous Karabagh*, *op. cit.*, p. 88 (cf. Appendix VIA).
305. G. Libaridian, *op. cit.*, pp. 97–8.
306. G. Libaridian, *op. cit.*, pp. 101–2.
307. G. Libaridian, *Le Dossier Karabagh* (French edition of *The Karabagh File*, *op. cit.*), p. 87.
308. *Glasnost*, *op. cit.*, p. 47.
309. *Ibid.*, pp. 172 ff.; *Artsakh: Chronology*, *op. cit.*, pp. 91 ff.
310. *Glasnost*, *op. cit.*, pp. 70–1.
311. *Mountainous Karabagh*, *op. cit.*, p. 89; *Glasnost*, *op. cit.*, p. 58; *Sovetakan Karabagh*, 18 March 1988.
312. *La Pensée Russe*, 18 March 1988; F. Thom, 'La violence dans l'Est européen', *Etudes polémologiques*, Paris, no. 46, February 1988, p. 96; *Glasnost*, *op. cit.*, pp. 54–5.
313. *Glasnost*, *op. cit.*, pp. 148 ff.; Libaridian, *Le Dossier Karabagh*, *op. cit.*, pp. 103 ff.
314. G. Libaridian, *Le Dossier Karabagh*, *op. cit.*, p. 106.
315. Cf. Appendix VIII.
316. G. Libaridian, *Le Dossier Karabagh*, *op. cit.*, p. 108; *Mountainous Karabagh*, *op. cit.*, pp. 74 ff.; *Artsakh: Chronology*, *op. cit.*, pp. 12 ff.
317. With one exception, all were under 45 years old.
318. *Mountainous Karabagh*, *op. cit.*, pp. 90–1; *Bakinski Rabochi*, *op. cit.*, 14 June 1988 (cf. Appendix IX).
319. *Mountainous Karabagh*, *op. cit.*, pp. 92–3; *Kommunist*, 16 June 1988; *Grakan Tert*, 17 June 1988; *Artsakh: Chronology*, *op. cit.*, pp. 18–9.
320. *Artsakh: Chronology*, *op. cit.*, p. 193.
321. *Ibid.*, pp. 20–21; *Sovetakan Karabagh*, 24 June 1988.
322. *Artsakh: Chronology*, *op. cit.*, pp. 199 ff.
323. *Mountainous Karabagh: Historical Handbook*, Athens 1988, pp. 84 ff. (English edition); *Sovetakan Karabagh*, 13 July 1988.
324. *Artsakh: Chronology*, *op. cit.*, p. 205.
325. *Sovetakan Hayastan*, 20 July 1988; *Artsakh: Chronology*, *op. cit.*, pp. 23–4; *Mountainous Karabagh*, *op. cit.*, pp. 87 ff. (English edition).

326. *Artsakh: Chronology, op. cit.*, pp. 27–8 and 217; L. Khurshudian, *op. cit.*, 24 September 1988.
327. *Notre malheur à tous, Armenie* (Moscow, 1988), p. 10.

SELECT BIBLIOGRAPHY

Abrahamian, H. 'General Antranig and the Artsakh Armenians', *Haireniki Dzain*, Yerevan, 28 February 1990–14 March 1990 (in Armenian).
Abrahamian, H. 'The Struggle for Survival in Mountainous Karabagh, 1917–1923', *Haireniki Dzain*, Yerevan, 2 November 1988 *et seq.* (in Armenian).
Abramian, G. 'The Politics of English Occupation Forces with Regard to Artsakh (November 1918–August 1919)', *Lraber*, Yerevan, no. 7, 1989 (in Russian).
Afanasyan, S. *L'Arménie, l'Azerbaïdjan et la Géorgie (1917–1923)*. Paris, 1981 (in French).
Aivazian, A. *The Monuments of Nakhichevan*. Yerevan, 1987 (in Armenian).
Aivazian, S. 'Memorandum to First Secretary of the Communist Party of the Soviet Union, M. S. Gorbachev', *Haratch*, Paris, 4 December 1987 *et seq.* (in Armenian).
Aliev, I. *Mountainous Karabagh: History, Facts, and Events*. Baku, 1989 (in Russian).
Alishan, Gh. 'Geography of Armenia and Artsakh', *Bazmovep*, Venice, 1988, 1989 (in Armenian).
Anonymous. 'Karabagh Wants Re-Unification with Armenia', *Haratch*, Paris, 14 April 1988 (originally 7 January 1928; in Armenian).
Anonymous. 'On the Special Governmental Committee in Mountainous Karabagh', *Haratch*, Paris, 11 March 1989 (in Armenian).
Arslanian, A. 'Britain and the Armeno-Azerbaijani Struggle for Mountainous Karabagh, 1918–1919', *Middle Eastern Studies*, no. 1, 1980.
Arslanian, A. 'England and the Problem of Mountainous Karabagh', *Haratch*, Paris, 8 February 1984 (in Armenian).
Artsakh: Chronology. Los Angeles, 1989 (in Armenian).
Asdvatsaturian, A. 'Azerbaijan and Armenia on the Eve of and During Independence', *Hairenik*, Boston, August–October 1957 (in Armenian).
Avagian, S. *History of the Press in Karabagh, 1828–1920.* Yerevan, 1989 (in Armenian).
Avaguian, S. *Pages from the Cultural Life of Mountainous Karabagh.* Yerevan, 1982 (in Armenian).
Avo. *Nzhdeh.* Beirut, 1968 (in Armenian).
L'Azerbaïdjan. Moscow, Novosti Publications, 1981 (in French).
Baedeker, K. *La Russie.* 3rd edition, Leipzig, 1902 (in French).
Bakinski Rabochii (Baku Worker). Baku (in Russian).
Baldwin, O. *Six Prisons and Two Revolutions.* London, 1924.
Barkhudariants. *Artsakh.* Baku, 1895 (in Armenian).
Barseghian, K. *The Truth is More Precious....* Yerevan, 1989 (in Russian).
Barseghov, H. *The Right to Self-Determination Is the Foundation for the Democratic Solution of Interethnic Problems.* Yerevan, 1989 (in Russian; Armenian translation, Yerevan, 1990).
Bennigsen, A. 'Islam soviétique: le détonateur caucasien', *Arabies*, Paris, July 1988 (in French).
Caratini, R. *Dictionnaire des nationalités et des minorités en URSS.* Paris, 1990 (in French).
Carrere d'Encause, H. *La gloire des nations ou la fin de l'Empire soviétique.* Paris, 1990 (in French).
Chantre, Mme. *A travers l'Arménie russe.* Paris, 1893 (in French).
Chelebian, A. *General Antranig and the Armenian Revolutionary Movement.* 2nd edition, Beirut, 1986 (in Armenian).
'Documents on the History of Mountainous Karabagh', *Armenian Archive Messenger*, Yerevan, vol. 1, no. 83, 1989 (in Russian).
Le dur passé du Caucase. Moscow, Novosti Publications, 1988 (in French).
Ellis, C. *The Transcaspian Episode (1918–1919).* London, 1963.
Encyclopedia of Islam. New edition. Leiden, 1978, 1979, 1983.

Ghahrian, H. 'Tevan Stepanian: Myth and Reality', *Artsakh*, Stepanakert, July 1989 (in Armenian).

Gharibjanian, G. 'Antranig in Zangezur and Artsakh', *Sovetakan Haiastan*, Yerevan, December 1988 (in Armenian).

Ghazian, A. 'Shushi', *Haireniki Dzain*, Yerevan, 6 November 1988.

Glasnost, no. 1, Paris, February 1989 (French translation of *Glasnost* no. 17, May 1988, in Russian).

Gouliev, J. B. 'History of the Formation of the Autonomous Region of Mountainous Karabagh', in *Izvestia of the Academy of Sciences of the Azerbaijan SSR*; History, Philosophy, and Law Series, no. 3, Baku, 1973 (in Russian).

Hadjibeyli, T. 'La Question du Haut-Karabagh: Un point de vue Azerbaïdjanais', in *Le Monde musulman à l'épreuve de la frontière*, special issue of *Revue du monde musulman et de la Méditerranée*, Aix-en-Provence, nos 48–49, 1988/2–3 (in French).

Harutiunian, A. *Turkish Intervention in Transcaucasia in 1918*. Yerevan, 1984 (in Armenian).

Harutiunian, Ch. *A Brief Chronology of the History of the Armenian People, 1801–1917*. Yerevan, 1955 (in Armenian).

Harutiunian, V. B. *A Chronology of Events in Mountainous Karabagh, Part I, February 1988–January 1989*. Yerevan, 1990 (in Russian).

Henry, J. D. *Baku: An Eventful History*. London, 1905.

Hérodote, Paris, no. 54–55, 1989 (in French).

Hovannisian, R. 'The Armeno-Azerbaijani Conflict over Mountainous Karabagh, 1918–1919', *The Armenian Review*, Boston, Summer, 1971.

Hovannisian, R. *The Republic of Armenia*. 2 vols. Los Angeles, 1971, 1982.

Hovhannissian, G. 'The Battle of Msmena', *Banber*, Yerevan, March 1968 (in Armenian).

Hovhannissian, Gu. *The Installation of Soviet Power in Mountainous Karabagh*. Yerevan, 1971 (in Armenian).

Hovhannissian, K. 'One of the Heroic Battles in Mountainous Karabagh', *Haratch*, Paris, 27 April 1988 (in Armenian).

Injikian, O. 'The Armenian Question and Soviet–Turkish Relations', *Lraber*, Yerevan, no. 6, 1988 (in Russian).

Ishkhanian, E. 'Events in Karabagh: Details and Comments', *Hairenik*, Boston, November–December 1933 (in Armenian).

Karapetian, B. *And About It*. Yerevan, 1990 (in Armenian).

Karapetian, B. *Dialogue One Century Ago*. Yerevan, 1990 (in Armenian).

Karapetian, L. 'The Autonomous Republic of Mountainous Karabagh and the Birth of a New Way of Thinking', *Kommunist*, Yerevan, 14 July 1989 (in Russian).

Kavkazskoïe Slovo (Voice of the Caucasus), Tiflis (in Russian).

Kazemzadeh, F. *The Struggle for Transcaucasia (1917–1921)*. New York, 1951.

Kevorkian, S. 'Concerning the Problem of the Creation of the Autonomous Region of Mountainous Karabagh', *Baikar*, Boston, February–March 1979 (in Armenian).

Khatisian, A. *The Birth and Development of the Armenian Republic*. Athens, 1930 (in Armenian; French translation, Athens, 1989).

Khojabekian, V. *Artsakh in Its Time of Ordeal*. Yerevan, 1991 (in Armenian).

Khojabekian, V. and B. Asatrian. 'The Population of Mountainous Karabagh', *Haireniki Dzain*, Yerevan, 1 June 1988 (in Armenian).

Khurshudian, L. 'The Only Criterion in the Science of History Is Truth', *Erekoyan Yerevan*, Yerevan, 23 August 1989 *et seq.* (in Armenian).

Leo. *Border Disputes: Lori–Akhalkalak–Karabagh*. 2nd edition, Athens, 1990 (in Armenian).

Libaridian, G. *The Karabagh File*. Cambridge, MA, Paris, Toronto, The Zoryan Institute, 1988. French edition, *Le Dossier Karabagh*, Paris, 1988.

Matossian, M. *The Impact of Soviet Policies on Armenia*. Leiden, 1962.

Melkumian, S. *Mountainous Karabagh*. Yerevan, 1990 (in Armenian).

Messerlian, Z. *On the Armenian Question*. Beirut, 1978 (in Armenian).

Mikaelian, A. 'The Latest Events in Karabagh', *Hairenik*, Boston, May–October 1923 (in Armenian).

Miridjian, G. 'The Destruction of Armenian Monuments', *Haratch*, Paris, 9 September 1983 (in Armenian).

Miridjian, G. 'Mountainous Karabagh', *Haratch*, Paris, 6 January 1988 *et seq.* (in Armenian).

Mirzoian, B. 'There Is Only One Truth', *Kommunist*, Yerevan, 19 July 1989 (in Russian).

Mkrtichian, L. *Artsakh-Karabagh: Its Past and Present*. Athens, 1988 (in Armenian). English translation, Athens, 1990.

Mountainous Karabagh: Documents and Materials. Yerevan, 1990 (in Russian).

Mouradian, C. 'Conflits nationaux en Transcaucasie', *L'autre Europe*, vol. 10, 1986 (in French).

Mouradian, C. *De Staline à Gorbatchev: Histoire d'une république soviétique: l'Arménie*. Paris, 1990 (in French).

Mouradian, C. 'Le problème du Haut-Karabagh', *Slovo*, vol. 7, 1985 (in French).

Mourier, J. *Guide au Caucase*. Paris, 1894.

Muradian, P. 'Armenians on Trial by Azerbaijani Scholars', *Grakan Tert*, Yerevan, 1 September 1989 (in Armenian).

Mutafian, C. 'Hérodote: Transcaucasia in the Collection "Les marches de la Russie"', *Haratch*, Paris, 24 February 1990 (in Armenian).

Nassibian, A. *Britain and the Armenian Question (1915–1923)*. London, 1984.

New Thinking on the Armenian Question. Yerevan, 1989 (in Russian).

Notre malheur à tous, Arménie. Novosti Publications, Moscow, 1988 (in French).

Panzer gegen Perestroika – Dokumentation zum Konflikttin und um 'Arzach' ('Karabach'). Bremen, 1989 (in German).

La Pensée Russe. 18 March 1988 (in French).

Poidebard, A. 'La Transcaucasie et la république d'Arménie dans les textes diplomatiques (1918–1920)', *Revue des Etudes Arméniennes*, 3, 1923, pp. 63–79; 4, 1924, pp. 31–98 (in French).

Rado, A. *Guide à travers l'Union soviétique*. Berlin, 1929 (in French).

La République arménienne et ses voisines: Questions territoriales. Paris, Delegation of the Armenian Republic, 1919 (in French).

Rost, Y. *Armenian Tragedy*. London, 1990.

Sarkisyanz, M. *A Modern History of Transcaucasian Armenia*. Leiden, 1975.

Sarur. 'The Annexation of Karabagh by Azerbaijan', *Hairenik*, Boston, August 1929 (in Armenian).

Sevian, V. 'On Mountain Paths in the Homeland', *Haratch*, Paris, 17 March 1988 *et seq.* (in Armenian).

Shahmuration, S. *The Sumgait Tragedy*. New Rochelle, NY, 1990.

Swietochowski, T. *Russian Azerbaijan, 1905–1920: The Shaping of National Identity in a Muslim Community*. Cambridge, 1985.

Tabrizli, A. *Histoire du Daglig (Haut)-Garabagh à la lumière de documents historiques*. Strasbourg, 1989 (in French).

Tarpinian, A. *Remembrances of the Armenian Liberation Movement, 1890–1940*. Paris, 1947 (in Armenian).

Tashjian, J. 'The Problem of Karabagh', *The Armenian Review*, Boston, no. 1, 1968.

Tavtian, R. 'Shushi Remembered', *Haratch*, Paris, 2 April 1988 (in Armenian).

Les Temps Modernes. Arménie-diaspora. Paris, Summer 1988 (in French).

Ter Minassian, A. 'Particularités de la révolution de 1905 en Transcaucasie' in *1905: La première révolution russe*. Paris, 1986 (in French).

Ter Minassian, A. *La République d'Arménie*. Paris, 1989 (in French).

Ternon, Y. 'Les éléments historiques de la revendication arménienne sur le Haut-Karabagh', *Haratch*, Paris, 24 March 1988 (in French).

Thom, F. 'La violence dans l'Est europeén', *Etudes polémologiques*, no. 46, February 1988, Paris (in French).

The Truth About Mountainous Karabagh. Yerevan, 1989 (in Russian).

Ulubabian, B. 'Mountainous Karabagh: An Historical-Geographic Survey', *Haireniki Dzain*, Yerevan, 8 June 1988 *et seq.* (in Armenian).

Valesian, L. and Y. Muradian. 'Results and Problems Concerning Economic Development in Nagorny-Karabagh', *Lraber*, Yerevan, no. 5, 1988 (in Russian).

Varandian, M. *History of the Armenian Revolutionary Federation*. Paris, vol. I, 1932 (in Armenian).

Vereshagin, B. 'Voyage dans les provinces du Caucase. Seconde partie: la Transcaucasie', in *Le*

Tour du Monde, no. 19, 1869 (in French).

Verluise, P. *Arménie: La Fracture*. Paris, 1989 (in French).

Villari, L. *Fire and Sword in the Caucasus*. London, 1906.

Vratsian, S. *The Republic of Armenia*. Paris, 1928 (in Armenian).

Walker, C. *Armenia: The Survival of a Nation*. London, 1980 (2nd edition, 1990).

Yerasimos, S. 'A propos du Karabagh et des troubles ethniques d'Arménie et d'Azerbaïdjian', *Hérodote*, Paris, January–March 1988 (in French).

Zarevand. *United and Independent Turania*. Leiden, 1971 (Armenian original, Boston, 1926).

Zohrabian, E. 'Partition of Territories at the Second Russo–Turkish Conference in Moscow, February–March 1921', *Lraber*, Yerevan, no. 2, 1989 (in Russian).

CONCLUSION

Patrick Donabedian and Claude Mutafian

Artsakh's destiny has been cruel and complex: an Armenian land since ancient times, ravaged by invasions, becoming Karabagh under Turkic–Mongol occupation, and then progressively reduced in size to its elevated region of Mountainous Karabagh. There is also the illustrious history of a people with an ancient culture who have resisted against wind and tide to preserve their identity, waiting for the hour when Armenia would revive. Would their hopes, disappointed in the wake of the Russian conquest of the Caucasus, be realized a century later after the 1917 revolution and the Sovietization of the region? That was not part of the Bolshevik Revolution's agenda and its export to the Moslem East, nor of pan-Turkism which flirted with Bolshevism.

On 5 July 1921, Karabagh provided our first demonstration of the arbitrary and violent character of the Stalinist system. With regard to the Armenian protests, did not the future dictator Stalin declare that from then on 'Nationalism must be eradicated with a red hot iron'? Since 1988, the same Karabagh has been what the late Andrei Sakharov described as 'the test of *perestroika*': a just solution to its problem would have been the first and best proof of Moscow's will to resolve national questions equitably. None of Moscow's actions indicated that such a will existed.

On the contrary, from the manner in which Moscow managed this question, Karabagh revealed that the demons of imperialism were alive and well at the Kremlin. In effect, if there were doubts concerning the degree of manipulation by Moscow, it was, on the other hand, clear that nothing had been done to calm spirits and promote dialogue. A problem of decolonization, a political problem posed by an oppressed population asserting its right to self-determination, has been misrepresented as inter-ethnic conflict, a mere seemingly archaic struggle over a piece of land. This altercation was familiar and useful to the central government authorities, since it allowed for decision making on the usual grounds of expediency rather than justice rooted in demographics and historical claims, and it promised (this time falsely) to strengthen the hand of the central authorities by allowing them to play the old game of divide and conquer. The result is tragic – confrontations resembling civil war, massive population exodus, and the distress of a people with its back against the wall, subject to years of economic blockade and, after Armenian and Azerbaijani secession from the Union and independence in the fall of 1991, to shelling and invasion.

Yet the determination of the Karabagh Armenians remains steadfast. Without obtaining the reunification of Mountainous Karabagh with Armenia, popular pressure wrested from Moscow a development plan and a special management committee, the Volsky Commission (1989). It was a poor compromise when one realizes that Azerbaijan continued to hold all the reins of power – in particular, power to dispose as it wished of the funds allocated to the 'Autonomous Region'. In the absence of a genuine decision, a union offering at least real self-management, the situation remained explosive. The centre then opted for stronger methods: in December 1989 Soviet armed forces occupied Mountainous Karabagh and tried to impose a new administrative authority, no longer federal but Azerbaijani. As for the local councils, accused of fomenting dissidence, they were dissolved. Without really satisfying Baku, whose rulers were aware of the impossibility of maintaining guardianship over the Armenian region, this decision aroused the anger of the indigenous Armenians who constitute (how many more times?) 80 per cent of the population.

In a state of 'civil insubordination' with regard to Baku, and exposed to harassment and arbitrary violence from an increasingly brutal army, this population tried to preserve or restore its own structures of management. Thus it constituted (as it had after 1917) a Mountainous Karabagh National Council. After adopting a resolution with the Armenian Supreme Soviet for the unification of the two territories to make up a new Republic of Armenia, the Council organized local elections for the Armenian parliament. Mountainous Karabagh is henceforth represented in Yerevan. In a parallel development, Armenian deputies and intellectuals, from both Mountainous Karabagh and the Armenian Republic, struggled for the official re-establishment of local administrative structures and awaited the confederation recommended by Sakharov in his time, in which all national formations will enjoy equal rights and no longer will some be dependent upon others.

Born at the outset of 1988, the Karabagh Movement upset all the givens, not only in Armenia, but to a certain degree throughout the entire Soviet Union. It marked the re-emergence of civil society. The 20 February 1988 vote by which the parliament of Mountainous Karabagh declared its sovereignty was truly revolutionary. Within the remote borders of the autonomous oblast, the vote suddenly took on real significance, and democratic political life asserted itself in the USSR for the first time since the 1920s. The December 1988 earthquake added a tragic dimension to the situation. But neither the earthquake nor the repression stopped the members of the Karabagh Committee, arrested after the catastrophe and released in the spring of 1989, from continuing to mobilize opinion. The Committee was behind the creation of the Armenian National Movement in Yerevan in June of 1989. In turn, this movement won the parliamentary elections, for the first time democratic, in the spring of 1990. Yesterday's dissident intellectuals are now at the head of the Republic of Armenia (henceforth a name without the qualifiers 'Socialist' and 'Soviet').

This democratic victory in Armenia was one of the achievements of the struggle which began in February of 1988, and it is consistent with the avant-garde role which has always been played by Karabagh. But this will only permit the resolution of ethnic problems tied to relations with neighbouring republics if these republics designate leaders aware of their responsibilities and ready to renounce colonial attitudes of the past in favour of respect for cultures and national aspirations. Unfortunately, for the present, the results of the elections in Azerbaijan of September–October 1990 show an unexpected and significant reinforcement of the old Communist oligarchy and the mafia. One must hope that these will yield to an open dialogue, the only way to understanding between two peoples destined to live together.

Appendices

Appendix I

LETTER OF THE COMMANDER IN CHIEF IN ZANGEZUR (ANDRANIK) TO THE COMMANDER OF ALLIED TROOPS IN BAKU CONCERNING THE IMMEDIATE BAN ON AZERBAIJANI TROOP CONCENTRATIONS IN KARABAGH AND ZANGEZUR (MARCH 1919)

My advance on Shushi last year, 1918, was halted on the order of Major-General Thomson. I was informed of the end of the Great War and of the victory of the Allied forces with whom I am proud to be a companion in arms. I was promised that measures would be taken to prevent all possibility of troop movements, aggressive actions, and harassment on the part of the Moslems. I followed the order, and I returned to Zangezur, giving my word to spare no effort and to take all essential measures in order to restore peace and calm and to give proof of the kindest attitude *vis-à-vis* all peoples without distinction to nationality in all the territory under my military command.

Unfortunately, I have been informed today of Moslem troop movements, concentrations of military units, and the transfer of war materials from one place to another in Karabagh and Zangezur.

Considering all of this as a turning point in the arrangements which have been undertaken to this day, which are certainly unfavourable to Armenians, and, also, as a challenge thrown out by the Moslems to the Armenians of Zangezur and Karabagh and to myself, I do humbly ask, for the well being of the population, that you take measures in order to stabilize the situation as it had been before mid-November, that is to say to give an order to pull out military units from Khankend and other localities in order to calm passions and not to bring forth reaction on the part of the Armenians.

I consider it my responsibility to inform you that Armenians in Karabagh and in the vast region of Zangezur and the districts of Ghapan, Sissian, and Meghri, home to over 400,000 Armenians, cannot in any case recognize any right of Azerbaijan over their territories.

Major-General Andranik, Commander in Chief of Armenian Forces in Zangezur

Central Historical State Archives of the Armenian SSR
Fonds 370, inv. 1, d. 39, f. 7 (in Armenian)

Appendix II
DECLARATION OF H. BAHATRIAN, KARABAGH ARMENIAN NATIONAL COUNCIL
REPRESENTATIVE, ON THE SITUATION IN KARABAGH (21 MARCH 1919)

The British mission has been interfering in relations between Karabagh and
Azerbaijan, and it has submitted to the Armenian National Council the general
outline of its mandatory decision which defines the relationship of Karabagh
vis-à-vis Azerbaijan. The National Council rejected it. By means of an intermediary, a former Russian officer now the English Lieutenant Maslennikov,
the mission has made every effort to sow discord between the National Council
and the Armenian military command. A separate letter and text for signature
was sent to the latter, proposing that it accept the same plan. The Armenian
military command has rejected this and returned the document at the same
time that it has affirmed its total agreement with the National Council which
it considers as the legitimate expression of the political thought of the country.
Lieutenant Maslennikov has rejected this step and demanded the signature.
Once again in vain.

The attempt by the British military to establish the authority of the
Azerbaijani governor-general thus received no cooperation. In general the
mission ignores the National Council of Karabagh, no doubt because of the
influence of Lieutenant Maslennikov, who was, at first, an officer of the local
division and, also, apparently, employed as an agent for Azerbaijan on the
Karabagh problem.

Taking all of this into consideration, the National Council of Karabagh sent
its representatives, Vahan, Bishop of the Diocese of Karabagh, and Bahatrian,
a member of the Council, to see General Thomson in Baku. They presented
General Thomson with a note on the situation in Karabagh and on the demands
of the National Council, which expressed the intentions of Karabagh's
Armenians.

The most basic of these demands is the removal of Azerbaijani authority. It
is necessary, therefore, either to

1 Provisionally re-attach Karabagh to the Republic of Armenia pending the
  decision of the Paris Peace Conference;

2 Restore the situation in Karabagh existing prior to the entry of the Turks into
  the region;

3 Name an English governor-general in regions inhabited by Armenians while
  preserving local authority (Armenian);

4 Name an English governor-general for the whole of Karabagh while confirming its autonomy.

General Thomson was informed, without a doubt, by the British mission concerning the activities of the National Council. He gave the delegates an evasive answer, and obviously is willing to go on with his own above-mentioned agenda as far as Karabagh and Azerbaijan are concerned.

... Azerbaijan is in the midst of preparing its armed forces, troops, and cannon, which it is sending to Aghdam; in short, it is preparing a military expedition.

Mshak, Tiflis, no. 82

Appendix III

AN APPEAL FROM THE ARMENIAN NATIONAL COUNCIL OF KARABAGH TO COLONEL HASKELL, HIGH COMMISSIONER IN ARMENIA, TO UNDERTAKE MEASURES TO LIBERATE KARABAGH FROM AZERBAIJANI AUTHORITIES AND TROOPS WHO HAVE ORGANIZED POGROMS AND MASSACRES OF ARMENIANS (TIFLIS, 18 AUGUST 1919)

From the moment of the arrival of British forces in Transcaucasia, the Turks and their allies among the Azerbaijanis were forced to evacuate the places that they had occupied in Mountainous Karabagh, the city of Shushi, and the ancient frontier fortress of Askeran. The Armenian population breathed a sigh of relief, thinking that the hour of its liberation was at hand.

Believing that the presence of British authorities and troops in Transcaucasia was the best guarantee of their personal security and the inviolability of their homes and property, the Armenians in Karabagh and Zangezur carried out all demands issued by the British command. General Andranik left the boundaries of Karabagh and Zangezur with his detachment, and the local forces rejoined their original units and then were demobilized. But the just and legitimate hopes of Karabagh Armenians were not satisfied. The British command demanded the surrender of Armenian Karabagh to Azerbaijan and her straw man, Khosrov bey Sultanov, well-known Turkish agent and Armenophobe, arguing the necessity of opening lines of communication and assuring that food supplies would reach the local population.

All appeals to the British command made by recognized Armenian organizations in Mountainous Karabagh – the National Council, the delegates to the Congresses, the associations of Armenians in Karabagh and Zangezur, and the representatives of cultural institutions – in the form of reports, news bulletins, petitions, and statements on the inadmissibility of the establishment of Turkish–Azerbaijani power in the region and the necessity to install a provisional Allied administration while awaiting a definitive solution to the problem from the Paris Peace Conference, all these appeals have been in vain. Poorly informed on the current state of affairs in Karabagh, failing to understand the nature of relations between peoples of Transcaucasia, and plied with tendentious information by the Azerbaijani authorities, the British command has committed a fatal error against the Armenians by not paying attention to the above-mentioned appeals and by authorizing the Azerbaijani government to concentrate major troop forces in Askeran, Khankend, Shushi, and Zabukh. The Azerbaijani government, executing the Turkish pogrom for the conquest of Transcaucasia, immediately took advantage of these favourable circumstances to introduce troops into the region, as well as Turkish emissaries, to organize massacres there.

The repeated warnings from the above-mentioned organizations were rejected and in vain. Such an attitude by the British government does not correspond to the Allied principle of the inadmissibility of the force of arms to resolve disputed territorial questions ... instead of bringing peace or restoring legal order to the region, it opens the way to bloodshed and massacres.

Thus in early June, Sultanov, governor-general of Karabagh, disregarded the British mission and troops in Shushi and organized an attack on the Armenian section of the city as well as the neighbouring villages of Ghaibali-kend, Kerkjan, and others. The massacre claimed many victims, several hundred innocent women, children, and elderly.

The British High Command assured the Armenian government and the angry public representatives that measures would be taken to guarantee personal safety and property and to dismiss Dr Sultanov who was responsible for the massacres. Instead, one month later, to the surprise of all, English troops left Karabagh, Dr Sultanov resumed his prior post, and, on 10 August, the British mission was recalled from Shushi. Thus the Armenian population of Karabagh, without a defence, found itself totally at the mercy of the bloody instincts of the Azerbaijani authorities and Turkish emissaries and troops. We are on the verge of a new massacre, inevitable, and still more terrifying, in Karabagh. The representatives of the American aid mission have also left Karabagh, depriving the most desperate portions of the population of the aid they had received until then and condemning them to die of hunger.

The President of the Armenian National Council of Karabagh, Hrant Bagaturov (Bahatrian)

The President of the Karabagh and Zangezur Friendship Committee, Ar. Babajanian

Representatives of the same Friendship Committee: L. Gulian, Y. Khununts, and M. Karabekian

Central Historical Archives of the Armenian SSR Fonds 200, inv. 1, d. 50, f. 104–107 (in English)

Appendix IVA

Declaration of the Revolutionary Committee of Azerbaijan, Signed by Narimanov, President of the Committee, and Huseinov, People's Commissar of Foreign Affairs (30 November 1920)

The government of Workers and Peasants of Azerbaijan, having heard the news of the proclamation in Armenia in the name of the insurgent peasantry of the Soviet Socialist Republic, salutes the victory of the fraternal Armenian people. From this day forward, the former borders between Armenia and Azerbaijan are suspended. Mountainous Karabagh, Zangezur, and Nakhichevan are recognized as integral parts of the Socialist Republic of Armenia. Long live the fraternity and union of workers and peasants of Soviet Armenia and Azerbaijan.

Kommunist, Yerevan, 7 December 1920 (in Armenian)

Appendix IVB

Declaration of Narimanov at the Baku Soviet (1 December 1920)

Soviet Azerbaijan, joining the working and fraternal people of Armenia in their struggle against Dashnak power which made and continues to make the blood of thousands of our Communist comrades in Armenia and in Zangezur flow, declares that henceforth no territorial conflict will cause bloodshed between these two age-old neighbourly peoples, Armenian and Moslem. Zangezur and Nakhichevan are an integral part of Soviet Armenia. The full right to self-determination is accorded the people of Karabagh.

Documents on the Victory of Soviet Power in Armenia, doc. 293, p. 437, Yerevan, 1957 (in Russian).
Kommunist, Baku, 2 December 1920 (in Russian)

Appendix VA

Propositions Put to a Vote by the Caucasian Bureau (of the Communist Party) on the Status of Karabagh (Tiflis, 4 July 1921)

1 Leave Karabagh within Azerbaijan.
   For: Narimanov, Makharadze, Nazaretian
   Against: Orjonikidze, Miasnikian, Kirov, Figatner

2 Organize a referendum in all of Karabagh with the participation of the entire population, Moslem as well as Christian.
   For: Narimanov and Makharadze

3 Unify the Mountainous portion of Karabagh with Armenia.
  For: Orjonikidze, Miasnikian, Figatner, Kirov

4 Organize a referendum limited to Mountainous Karabagh, that is to say only among the Armenian population.
  For: Orjonikidze, Miasnikian, Figatner, Kirov, and Nazaretian

Final decision: Unify Mountainous Karabagh with Soviet Armenia, organize a referendum limited to Mountainous Karabagh.

Institute for Marxism-Leninism, Central Committee Archives Fonds 17, inv. 13, d. 384, f. 66 (in Russian)

Appendix VB
DECISION OF THE CAUCASIAN BUREAU (OF THE COMMUNIST PARTY) ON THE STATUS OF KARABAGH (TIFLIS, 5 JULY 1921)

Comrades Orjonikidze and Nazaretian proposed that the decision on Karabagh taken at the previous plenum be re-examined. It was decided, taking into consideration the need for national peace between Moslems and Armenians and taking into consideration the economic link between Mountainous and Lower Karabagh and their ongoing ties with Azerbaijan:

1 To leave Mountainous Karabagh within the borders of the Azerbaijani SSR while granting a large degree of regional autonomy. The centre is to be the city of Shushi which will constitute part of the Autonomous Region.

2 To confer upon the Central Committee of Azerbaijan the decision on the borders of the Autonomous Region, to be submitted to the Central Committee of the Communist Party of Russia.

3 To confer upon the presidency of the Caucasian Bureau of the Central Committee the responsibility of discussing with the Central Committee of Armenia and the Central Committee of Azerbaijan the candidates for the Special Commissioner for Mountainous Karabagh.

4 The degree of autonomy for Mountainous Karabagh should be decided by the Central Committee of Azerbaijan and submitted for ratification by the Caucasian Bureau of the Central Committee.

Institute for Marxism-Leninism, Central Committee Archives, Fonds 85, inv. 18, d. 58, f. 18 (in Russian)

Appendix VIA

SPECIAL SESSION OF THE 20TH MEETING OF THE DEPUTIES OF THE SOVIET OF THE AUTONOMOUS REGION OF MOUNTAINOUS KARABAGH. TEXT OF THE RESOLUTION BY THE PARLIAMENT OF THE AUTONOMOUS REGION OF MOUNTAINOUS KARABAGH REQUESTING INCORPORATION INTO SOVIET ARMENIA (20 FEBRUARY 1988)

After having heard and examined the contributions of the deputies of the Soviet of the Autonomous Region of Mountainous Karabagh 'On the demand for mediation of the Supreme Soviets of the Azerbaijani SSR and Armenian SSR for the transfer of the Autonomous Region of Mountainous Karabagh from the Azerbaijani SSR to the Armenian SSR', the 20th Special Session of the Regional Soviet of People's Deputies of Mountainous Karabagh decides:

In conformity with the wishes of the workers of the Autonomous Region of Mountainous Karabagh, to ask that the Supreme Soviets of the Azerbaijani and Armenian SSRs show the highest level of understanding concerning the aspirations of the Armenian people of Mountainous Karabagh and settle the question of the transfer of the Autonomous Region of Mountainous Karabagh from the Azerbaijani SSR to the Armenian SSR; and to ask, at the same time, that the Supreme Soviet of the USSR arbitrate in order that the question of the transfer of the Autonomous Region of Mountainous Karabagh from the Azerbaijani SSR to the Armenian SSR be settled in a positive manner.

Soviet Karabagh, 21 February 1988 (in Armenian)
(*Glasnost*, no. 1, p. 57)

Appendix VIB

DECISION OF THE PLENUM OF THE REGIONAL COMMITTEE OF MOUNTAINOUS KARABAGH OF THE AZERBAIJANI COMMUNIST PARTY CONCERNING THE DEMAND OF THE PROLETARIAT AND COMMUNISTS OF THE REGION TO REATTACH THE AUTONOMOUS REGION OF MOUNTAINOUS KARABAGH TO THE ARMENIAN SSR (17 MARCH 1988)

The Plenum of the Regional Committee of Mountainous Karabagh of the Azerbaijani Communist Party decides:

Expressing the wish of the Armenian population of the Region and the will of the majority of communists of Mountainous Karabagh, we request the Political Bureau of the Central Committee of the Communist Party of the USSR to examine and positively solve the problem of reattaching the Autonomous Region of Mountainous Karabagh to the Armenian SSR, thus correcting the error committed during the 1920s in determining the territorial status of Karabagh.

Soviet Karabagh, 18 March 1988 (in Armenian)
(*Glasnost*, no. 1, p. 58)

Appendix VII

LETTER FROM ANDREI SAKHAROV ADDRESSED TO THE SECRETARY GENERAL OF THE CENTRAL COMMITTEE OF THE COMMUNIST PARTY OF THE SOVIET UNION, M. S. GORBACHEV (21 MARCH 1988) (EXCERPTS)

Dear Mikhail Sergeievich:

In this letter I would like to call to your attention the two most pressing national problems of this moment: the return of the Tatars to the Crimea and the reunification of Mountainous Karabagh with Armenia. In both cases, it is a matter of correcting injustices committed against the peoples of our country.

...We can imagine that the unification of Mountainous Karabagh with Azerbaijan stems from the initiative of Stalin, who was motivated by internal and external political considerations. The annexation was carried out contrary to the wishes of the population of Karabagh and contrary to prior declarations by Stalin and the leadership of Azerbaijan. Throughout the following decades, it has constituted a perpetual source of tension between nationalities. A multitude of facts attest to the national discrimination suffered by the Armenians, to the *diktat* which has been imposed on them, and to the undermining of their culture up till the very present.

Perestroika has given hope to the Armenian population of Karabagh, that their problem would find a constitutional solution. On 20 February, at the session of the Regional Soviet of Workers' Deputies, a resolution was adopted to ask the Supreme Soviets of Azerbaijan, Armenia, and the USSR to attach the aforementioned region to the Republic of Armenia. Analogous resolutions had been adopted earlier by four of the five district soviets of workers' deputies. The resolutions by the regional and district soviets were supported in Mountainous Karabagh as well as in Armenia by peaceful demonstrations by many thousands of people. This was undeniably the expression of new means of democratic action made possible by *perestroika*.

However, later developments did not follow a favourable course. Instead of taking a request emanating from an organ of Soviet power and considering it in a normal and constitutional manner, the authorities have engaged in manoeuvres and arrangements which have been directed, in the last analysis, against the Armenians. During this period, the press and television broadcast materials which presented events in a distorted and one-sided manner. The legitimate demands of the Armenian people were presented as extremist, letting it be understood in advance, as it were, that the response would be negative. One must admit, unfortunately, that this is not the first time that *glasnost* has been left out of play in a deteriorating situation where openness is particularly necessary....

The problems of the Crimean Tatars and that of Mountainous Karabagh referred to in this letter are valuable as a test of *perestroika*, of its capacity to overcome resistance and the weight of the past. We cannot wait additional decades to find a just and definitive solution to these questions and allow permanent zones of tension to exist within the country.

With my most profound and sincere respect.

Glasnost, no. 1, p. 5 (in Russian)

Appendix VIII

RESOLUTION OF THE PRESIDIUM OF THE SUPREME SOVIET OF THE USSR REJECTING THE REUNIFICATION OF MOUNTAINOUS KARABAGH WITH ARMENIA (23 MARCH 1988)

On 23 March 1988 the Presidium of the Supreme Soviet of the USSR examined the situation in Mountainous Karabagh, in the Azerbaijani SSR, and in the Armenian SSR. Based on Article 81 of the Constitution of the USSR, the Presidium of the Supreme Soviet of the USSR:

1 Stresses that the situation in the Azerbaijani SSR and the Armenian SSR within the framework of events in Mountainous Karabagh undermines the peoples of these republics and, in general, the continuous reinforcement of friendship between peoples of the USSR as a united federated multinational state.

Considers it inadmissible to try to resolve complex national and territorial problems by exercising pressure on the organs of state power in a climate marked by heightened emotions and passions. The activation of all sorts of illegal organizations advocating the redrawing of state borders and administrative frontiers fixed by the Constitution of the USSR could have unforeseeable consequences.

Resolutely condemns criminal acts by certain groups and persons which have claimed victims. Takes into consideration the fact of administrative legal proceedings and penalties initiated against guilty parties.

2 Guided by the resolutions of the 27th Party Congress, the Plenary Sessions of the Central Committee of the Communist Party of the Soviet Union which followed, and an appeal by Mikhail Gorbachev, Secretary General of the Central Committee of the Communist Party of the Soviet Union to the workers and peoples of Azerbaijan and Armenia, it is the task of the Soviets of People's Deputies of the Azerbaijani SSR and the Armenian SSR to dramatically improve their mass political and educational work among the people in the spirit of the inviolability of Leninist principles concerning the politics of nationalities and the friendship and cohesion of brotherly peoples of the USSR. They should analyse in a detailed fashion all aspects of the

reasons for the exacerbation of inter-ethnic relations and eliminate them promptly, energetically oppose all manifestations of nationalism and extremism, create a calm and constructive atmosphere in work enterprises and learning institutions while mobilizing the efforts of workers of all nations and ethnic groups inhabiting these republics to carry out the revolutionary transformations under way in our society.

3 The Presidium of the Supreme Soviet of the Azerbaijani SSR and the Presidium of the Supreme Soviet of the Armenian SSR are instructed to devise necessary measures for strengthening socialist legality and public order, in order to protect the legitimate interests of the citizens of all nationalities, and to initiate vigorous legal procedures against those whose actions destabilize the situation by undermining the friendship and cooperation of fraternal Soviet peoples.

4 It is the task of the Council of Ministers of the USSR to adopt measures to resolve the urgent problems of economic, social, and cultural development facing the Autonomous Region of Mountainous Karabagh.

5 The Minister of State and the Minister of the Interior of the USSR are instructed to take all measures required to assure public order and to protect the legitimate interests of the population of the Azerbaijani and Armenian SSRs.

TASS, 23 March 1988, reprinted in *Actualités Soviétiques*, no. 776, 30 March 1988
Le Dossier Karabagh, p. 106 (French edition only)

Appendix IX
RESOLUTION OF THE PRESIDIUM OF THE SUPREME SOVIET OF THE AZERBAIJANI SSR CONCERNING THE APPEAL MADE BY THE DEPUTIES OF THE PEOPLE'S SOVIET OF THE AUTONOMOUS REGION OF MOUNTAINOUS KARABAGH TO TRANSFER THE REGION FROM THE AZERBAIJANI SSR TO THE ARMENIAN SSR (13 JUNE 1988)

The Presidium of the Supreme Soviet of the Azerbaijani SSR observes that in accordance with the constitutions of the USSR and the Azerbaijani SSR the legal status of the Autonomous Region of Mountainous Karabagh is defined by 'The Law on the Autonomous Region of Mountainous Karabagh', adopted by the Supreme Soviet of the Azerbaijani SSR after its recommendation by the Regional Soviet of People's Deputies.

This statute allows for the satisfaction of the economic, social, and spiritual needs of representatives of all nations and ethnic groups in the Autonomous Region of Mountainous Karabagh. But at the same time, the situation in Mountainous Karabagh and the problems which preoccupy the workers there reveal serious errors committed up until recently by the administration of the region. In particular, the national characteristics of the people have not entirely been taken into account.

The resolution adopted on 24 March 1988 by the Central Committee of the Communist Party of the Soviet Union and the Council of Ministers of the USSR, 'On Measures for the Accelerated Socio-economic Development of the Autonomous Region of Mountainous Karabagh in the Azerbaijani SSR during the Years 1988–1995' and the actions undertaken by the Central Committee of the Communist Party of Azerbaijan and the Council of Ministers of the republic create favourable conditions for the accelerated development of productive forces in the Autonomous Region of Mountainous Karabagh and for the resolution of problems concerning the areas of living conditions, housing, and culture.

Having examined all aspects of the request presented by the deputies of the Soviet of People's Deputies of the Autonomous Region of Mountainous Karabagh asking that the Autonomous Region of Mountainous Karabagh be transferred from the Azerbaijani SSR to the Armenian SSR, the Presidium of the Supreme Soviet of the Azerbaijan SSR considers it unacceptable given its opposition to the interests of the Azerbaijani and Armenian population of the Region and its opposition to the objectives of strengthening friendship between all the peoples of our country and the objectives of *perestroika*.

The Presidium of the Supreme Soviet expresses its strong assurances that in response to the declaration of Comrade M. S. Gorbachev, Secretary General of the Central Committee of the Communist Party of the USSR, the Azerbaijani and Armenian people will work hard to preserve and consolidate the friendship and brotherhood which exists between them. They will contribute positively to the revolutionary regeneration of socialist society.

President of the Presidium of the Supreme Soviet of the Azerbaijani SSR, S. Tatliev
Secretary of the Presidium of the Supreme Soviet of the Azerbaijani SSR, R. Kazieva

Bakinski Rabochii (*Baku Worker*), 14 June 1988 (in Russian)

Appendix X

SPEECH BY HENRIK POGHOSIAN, FIRST SECRETARY OF THE REGIONAL COMMITTEE OF MOUNTAINOUS KARABAGH, COMMUNIST PARTY OF AZERBAIJAN, BEFORE THE PRESIDIUM OF THE SUPREME SOVIET OF THE USSR (18 JULY 1988) (EXCERPTS)

For those who are informed, there is no doubt whatsoever that Mountainous Karabagh has always been inhabited by Armenians and constitutes a part of their homeland.

Given the above, how is it that Mountainous Karabagh finds itself in the Azerbaijani SSR? Unfortunately, Azerbaijani leaders of that time took advantage of Stalin's support and of the extremely complex situation which prevailed in Azerbaijan and all of Russia, and they were successful in including the territory, whose population was more than 94 per cent Armenian, in the Azerbaijan SSR.

For the Armenian population of the Autonomous Region, these sixty-five years of supposed 'autonomy' have been years of oppression. In general, all important positions in the leadership of the Autonomous Region were preserved for the emissaries of Baku. In scientific works and school and university handbooks published in Azerbaijan, perfectly well-known and indisputable historical facts are interpreted in a simplistic manner and even sometimes distorted. In the Republic (of Azerbaijan), the issue of the origins of the indigenous people has become a truly pathological question. Research on this question is often accompanied by a tendency to backdate and expand the role of the Azerbaijani people at the expense of the neighbouring people.

For several decades, funds allocated by higher-level budgetary proceedings (federal Soviet) each year to the Autonomous Region have consisted of an annual average of ninety-one million roubles, whereas the actual budget of the Autonomous Region is forty-two million, or 46 per cent of allocations. This is to say that we have never been beneficiaries of gifts and that we have never been a burden. *Per capita*, the Autonomous Region has produced 67 kg of meat as opposed to 27 for the Republic as a whole and 320 kg of milk as opposed to 155. We have not benefited from subsidies; on the contrary, we have furnished essential products to the Republic.

We have followed the 17 June (1988) session of the Azerbaijani Supreme Soviet with great interest. The major idea expressed there was 'The Azerbaijani border is a convention, we do not force anyone to stay, those who do not wish to live among us have only to go elsewhere.' Others were more precise: 'They have only to disappear.'

Fine. But they forget that we were included in Azerbaijan as an autonomous entity, with our lands. They forget Article 11 of the Constitution which specifies that everywhere in the Soviet Union land is the exclusive property of the state and, collectively, of the Soviet people. In this case, why do the Azerbaijani people have the right of veto over the resolution of our question? How can we allow one people in a socialist state to decide the destiny of another people?

Certain legal specialists try to escape from the problem by invoking appropriate articles from the Constitution. I do not find the argument convincing that it is impossible to resolve the question of Mountainous Karabagh in a constitutional manner. Some try to use it to torpedo the real problem. They try to advance an alleged contradiction between the demands of the Armenians in Mountainous Karabagh and the opinions of numerous Armenian populations in other regions of the Republic. We reject these attempts. Our opponents also object that Mountainous Karabagh cannot be unified with

Armenia because there is no common border. But they forget that the Autonomous Region is seven times closer to the Armenian border than Nakhichevan is to the Azerbaijani SSR.

I would like you to understand me well: the Armenian population of Mountainous Karabagh cannot be satisfied with material goods at the expense of its national, cultural, and spiritual development.

As experience has shown, an unjust solution to the problem of Mountainous Karabagh inevitably leads the Armenian population to leave its ancestral lands. The destiny of Armenians in the Autonomous Republic of Nakhichevan is both proof and condemnation.

It is no longer a secret that a serious break has been created in the good relations between Armenians and Azerbaijanis. It will take time to bandage the wound; despite our efforts, it will require years for the wounds to heal, for the bitterness and offences of both sides to be forgotten, for Sumgait to be forgotten.

The representatives of these two communities are obliged to have innumerable daily contacts. Today these contacts are impossible, and, being realistic, they cannot be renewed so soon. It is beyond the means of administration to control everyone's behaviour and to encourage expressions of understanding and the spirit of compromise. In the existing situation, the only just solution is the separation of Mountainous Karabagh from Azerbaijan. I see no other alternative.

I have tried to present to you succinctly, without embellishment, today's situation and the causes which engender it. I do not know if I have succeeded. In any case, I have tried to follow scrupulously the principle proclaimed by M.S. Gorbachev during the 19th Party Congress: 'Better the truth whatever it may be than a half-truth one wishes to hear.'

On the matter of economic links between Mountainous and Lower Karabagh: there is no economic link between Mountainous and Lower Karabagh. There is a very clear dependence, an economic dependence, of Mountainous Karabagh with regard to the whole of Azerbaijan.

To this very day the Autonomous Region does not have a flour mill, nor an animal feed factory, nor a facility to produce reinforced concrete, nor the structures for the construction of individual homes.

Our annual production capacity in construction is twenty million roubles. We have been given four hundred million roubles. Four hundred million roubles for seven years. In seven years, by virtue of twenty million per year, we can only utilize one hundred and forty million. Who will use the rest in our place since we lack the productive capability?

Kommunist, Yerevan, 20 July 1988 (in Russian)

Appendix XI
THE MEDIATION MISSION OF ANDREI SAKHAROV AS INTERPRETED BY ZIYA BUNIYATOV, ACADEMY OF SCIENCES OF AZERBAIJAN (15 APRIL 1989) (EXCERPTS)

About two months ago we had a visit to Baku by the famous Alikhanian-Bonner, who was moreover not alone, but accompanied by her husband, the academician Andrei Sakharov, as well as three 'informals', as they call themselves, two members of the Institute of Ethnography of the Academy of Sciences of the USSR, Batkin and the hysterical Starovoitova, and the laboratory assistant Zubov, barred from the Institute of Oriental Studies of the Academy of Sciences for parasitism....

The large number of interviews flowing from Sakharov to the outside world since Gorky by means of his intermediary Alikhanian-Bonner, in spite of their malicious intent and subversiveness, have aroused and moulded opinion. Of course! Such a martyr! This is a Nobel Prize winner who was not allowed to receive his award on his own soil and whom one wishes to expel from his country!

But already at Gorky a brutal change took place in Sakharov's thinking. The serious scholar was transformed into a commonplace researcher whom one kept up with as an idler and source of gossip. Goodbye to science. Sakharov metamorphosed into a defender of peace and *perestroika* at the same time that he denigrated everything in our country and sowed inter-ethnic hatred. Through his companion in arms, Alikhanian-Bonner, he passed to the outside his notes full of ignominies and vulgarities directed against all that is Soviet. He says not to interfere in the internal affairs of the Soviet government. In whose name does he speak? If he had dared murmur such things in earlier times....

Thus Sakharov arrived in Baku, holding an olive branch of peace, to order us to, no more no less, return Karabagh to the Armenians. Evidently this Sakharov expedition was planned by the Dashnak-Aganbegyanists by means of Alikhanian-Bonner, and in order that the team be more imposing, they added to the old shark his confederates Batkin, Zubov, and Starovoitova....

The goals and objectives of the magazine *Homeland* [*Rodina*] lead us to believe that this sheet is an organ of the Sakharov–Bonner clique. In the first two issues they have published an hysterical editorial by Starovoitova on the Autonomous Republic of Nakhichevan who argues that it must be separated from the Azerbaijan SSR and joined with the Armenian SSR by means of a plebiscite organized among the Armenians. Karabagh is not enough for them! It is certainly true that the appetite grows while eating!

Elm (*Science*), a weekly official publication of the Presidium of the Academy of Sciences of the Azerbaijani SSR, Baku, no. 15, 171 (in Russian).

Appendix XII
ANALYSIS BY ZIYA BUNIYATOV, AZERBAIJANI ACADEMICIAN, CONCERNING THE EVENTS
IN KARABAGH AND SUMGAIT (13 MAY 1989) (EXCERPTS)

In 1921 Soviet power gave the Armenians the sovereignty they had lost in the fourth century, and in the 68 years since then they have had all that citizens in the other fourteen republics have had. All the difficulties and joys experienced by the peoples of the USSR have been their experience, and, in addition, they have done quite well and spread out and settled in all the other Soviet republics, which cannot be said of the citizens of the other fourteen republics.

...Now we come to the year 1948. By means of an ingenious plan, thousands of Armenians from abroad began to immigrate to the Armenian SSR. In fact, the majority of these immigrants were no more than old Dashnaks in the mould of Hairikian, Manucharian, or the daughter of Parunak, a member of the Central Committee of the Dashnaktsutiun....

Armenian ambitions reached their climax when the Armenian international mafia succeeded in claiming a key post for Levon Karapet Paljian,[1] a personal friend of Marshall Ion Antonescu. By means of international Armenian tycoons and the sermons of Paljian, bellicose Dashnak propaganda increased from year to year.

Then there was a profusion of senseless publications. A confidant of Karapet Paljian, Paruir Kazarian, who met a sad end,[2] was the first to vilify the Azerbaijani people. He was followed by B. Zohrabian, S. Khanzadian, and B. Ulubabian who was raised on Azerbaijani soil and nourished by her bread....

They resurrected the carrion of the 'krunk',[3] the one-legged creature which began to agitate its featherless mates. Local 'revolutionary' louts began to travel abroad to visit foreign Armenian colonies where the Dashnak functionaries filled the crane of all these Abels with the idea of the chosen people. Thanks to subsidies from foreign millionaires, they unleashed a barrage of anti-Azerbaijani propaganda in the Western press and during all sorts of meetings which used to feed high-level personages such as Aghanbegyan.

The Armenian commercial mafia abroad, and also in our country, has known how to get its people appointed to high-level positions in our country. They only wait for the propitious moment, as always, for a revolutionary situation to initiate vigorous action against the Azerbaijanis. Then they will risk everything for everything. *Perestroika* and *glasnost* initiated in our country offered them favourable conditions to go on the offensive and realize the chimerical goals that they had to surrender in the fourth century.

In February 1988, the 'Karabagh Committee', which had been established abroad and brought to Yerevan, began its famous campaign for the unification of the Autonomous Region of Mountainous Karabagh with Armenia. As an activist recently declared, 'It is astonishing. I recently went to Karabagh clandestinely and I realized that everyone there looked like me!'

A small digression. In 1978, ten years ago, in the village of Leninavan (formerly Maraghashen), a marble obelisk was solemnly erected in memory of the 150th anniversary of the transfer to Karabagh (following the Treaty of Turkmenchai in 1828) of the first two hundred Armenian families from Maragha (southern Azerbaijan).[4] That is to say that the oldest Armenian cemetery stone in Maraghashen is no more than 160 years old.[5] How can they say that Karabagh belongs to Armenia?

...The Sumgait tragedy was carefully prepared by the Armenian nationalists. Several hours before it began, Armenian photographers and TV journalists secretly entered the city where they waited in readiness. The first crime was committed by a certain Grigorian who pretended to be Azerbaijani and who killed five Armenians in Sumgait. As for what follows, it is no more than a technical question because there was now no way of stopping the enormous crowd....

Elm (Science), a weekly official publication of the Presidium of the Academy of Sciences of the Azerbaijani SSR, Baku, no. 19, p. 175 (in Russian)

Translator's Notes:
1 The author is referring to the Catholicos, the Supreme Patriarch of All Armenians, H. H. Vazgen I, a native of Romania, but with no ties whatsoever to the dictator Ion Antonescu.
2 Paruir Sevak (whose real name was Ghazarian), a famous poet who died in an automobile accident.
3 'Krunk' means 'crane', an emblematic bird very popular in Armenian tradition. It is also the name of the Committee for the Rights of Karabagh Armenians.
4 In Baku it is maintained that Armenians did not arrive in Karabagh until the nineteenth century.
5 See the text on Armenian burial stones and architectural monuments, especially note 219 in Chapter 3.

Appendix XIII
INTERVIEW WITH ELENA BONNER, WIDOW OF ANDREI SAKHAROV, IN *LE FIGARO* (26 JULY 1990) (EXCERPTS)

Karabagh was, it seems, the first to believe in the slogan 'All power to the Soviets', and by the resolution of its Soviet followed the path chosen by her people – the 75 per cent of the people living in the territory – which is to say reunification with Armenia. Armenia supported this movement which was the expression of *perestroika* and only opposed the type of Stalinist power which decides where each people should settle and live. Not having understood that, the government has defended the Stalinist constitution above all, even above its own existence. Nowhere else in the country and at no other time was there such a level of support for *perestroika* and its leader as there was in Armenia and Karabagh.

Let us recall the main slogan of those days, 'Yes to Gorbachev'. But fear of all mass, popular, spontaneous movements is characteristic of our government. It is afraid. That gave unsupervised forces the opportunity to organize Sumgait.

... In December 1988 a group from Moscow accompanied Sakharov to the Caucasus. There they met with the First Secretary [of the Communist Party of Azerbaijan], Vezirov. Like an actor, he gave us a lecture on Armenian–Azerbaijani friendship. Andrei Sakharov was hard pressed to interrupt this rumbling voice of a trained orator. We explained why we had come. No reaction. Once again he started up on friendship. 'We are fraternal peoples.' Then I said that even among brothers there are disputes, but in the midst of tragedy they forget the past. For example, the earthquake – that was a tragedy! 'You are upset that the world has not noticed your kindness. Return Karabagh to the Armenians since, over there, there isn't even a single piece of land on which to settle. Then the entire world will come to its knees and thank your people.' You should have seen his face when he cut in, 'Land is not given. It has to be conquered. With blood.' And he repeated it with great satisfaction, 'With blood!' That ended our talk with the authorities in Baku. Vezirov promised blood. There you have it.

... Two world wars, the civil war, the Armenian genocide of 1915, the genocide of the Jews, Cambodia, our Gulag. Isn't that sufficient? All these young Azerbaijanis, Armenians, and Russians who have tinted the pink rocks of the Caucasus with their blood? Isn't it enough for the president of the largest country in the world – a sixth of the planet? And if he listened?... But he will not listen, not any more than he listened to the words of Andrei Sakharov in the Supreme Soviet: 'For Azerbaijan, Karabagh is a question of prestige; for Armenia, it is a question of life and death....'

Appendix XIV
INTERVIEW WITH GALINA STAROVOITOVA, DEPUTY IN THE SUPREME SOVIET OF THE USSR, IN *HARATCH* (19 SEPTEMBER 1990) (EXCERPTS)

...There are numerous problems linked to the modifications of borders.... But it seems to me that the problem of Artsakh should not be placed in this category. It is not, in fact, a territorial question.... In reality, it is a question of self-determination by one part of a people. It is a matter of the defence of the political, cultural, and religious rights of an ancient people.

I believe it is necessary to outline three criteria which can be employed to decide to whom a region belongs.

1 The historic background of a given region: here it is undeniable that this region is Armenian. There exist, to be sure, several falsifiers of history (such as Ziya Buniyatov) who sow doubts on Karabagh's past. This allows the passions of the Azerbaijani people to be churned.

2 The actual demographic profile of the region: this profile does not always correspond with the historic background as we can see today in the case of Nakhichevan, or the Abkhazians who do not constitute more than 17 per cent of the population on their historic lands. Fortunately, and despite the policies of all these years, Armenians still continue to constitute 80 per cent of the population of Artsakh.

3) The will of the people: the population must say with whom it wishes to be unified. Its will must be expressed in a constitutional manner, be it through the ballot box or by means of a decision by the legal authorities in the territory concerned. Since 1988, the people of Artsakh have expressed their will five times by means of decisions by the Soviet of the Autonomous Region.

I would like to stress that these three criteria rarely coincide, but this is precisely the case for Artsakh. That is why, if one considers the problem from a democratic and humanitarian point of view, there can be no doubt as to the legitimacy of the demand.

... In February 1988, the population of Artsakh expressed its desire to be unified with Armenia. It was not necessary to explain to me the nature of the problem. I recognized the legitimacy of this demand immediately, and I have expressed my solidarity at every opportunity.

I am sometimes criticized for taking the side of one people against another. Sometimes, I am also the object of threats by the Azerbaijanis. Azerbaijani newspapers smear me by saying that I am in the pay of the Dashnaks.... I do not respond to this level of criticism....

I hope that the development of democracy in Azerbaijan will raise it to a level where the Azerbaijani people will understand that errors have been made, which have taken them on an ill-chosen path.

To defend the cultural interests of an ancient people can only honour those who chose this path. But I believe that in the case of Artsakh, it is a matter of the defence of democracy in general....

Haratch, Paris, 20 September 1990 (in Armenian)

INDEX